You're Welcome:
Guide to investment opportunities in Canada

投資加拿大指南

Written and edited by
Richard I. Mann

Gateway Books

Toronto, Canada
A division of 590432 Ontario Inc.

Copyright 1988.

First Published 1987
by Gateway Books
A division of 590432 Ontario Inc.k
493 Durie Street,
Toronto, Ontario, Canada M6S 3G8.
P.O. Box 144, Station 'M',
Toronto, Ontario, Canada M6S 4T2

2nd printing, 1988.

ISBN   0-921333-12-9

Typeset in Canada by:
J.P.S. Graphic Services Limited,
307 Evans Avenue
Toronto, Ontario, Canada M8Z 1K2
Tel: 416/252-3329

Printed and bound in Singapore by:
Khai Wah Litho Pte Ltd.,
16 Kallang Place, No. 07-02,
Singapore 1233.
Tel: 2968644 (5 lines).
Cable and telegram "PRINTING".
Telex RS50302.

Chinese translation except Chapter 12:
Aloysius Lui,
Al Lui Associates,
Management Consultants,
35 Millgate Crescent,
Willowdale, Ontario, Canada M2K 1L5
Tel: 416/223-0962

By the same author

Canada Our Land Chinese immigrants in Canada today.
Toronto Chinatown guide; with Johnny Koo
Publisher: **TradeAsia magazine**
Toronto Waterfront guide
Canadians in Indonesia

加國環境人嚮往
投資創業樂無窮

Acknowledgements

Like **'Canada Our Land'** this book, **'You're Welcome: Guide to investment opportunities in Canada'** aims to improve mutual understanding and business contact between Canada and the peoples of the Far East, particularly those of Chinese origin who continue to be among the world's great traders and emigrators.

The far sightedness of a number of leading Canadian corporations and governments has made this book possible including: the Federal Government of Canada, Royal LePage Limited, The Royal Bank of Canada, Burns Fry Investment Management Limited, Price Waterhouse and Clarkson Gordon Woods Gordon.

And the understanding and empathy of a number of Canadian Chinese professionals and entrepreneurs from across Canada has once again contributed that unique element of experience without which this book would be so much less useful.

'You're Welcome' is a somewhat unusual publication in that it contains advertising and advertorial and there is no doubt that in supporting this project the overwhelming majority of companies and governments made a special effort to register their commitment and to tailor their messages to the needs of individuals and corporations joining the new but growing trans-Pacific investment stream to our country.

I would like to offer a sincere thanks to all our editorial contributors, sponsors and advertisers without which the shelves in the bookshops of Asia would have remained totally empty of even a single volume highlighting the substantial opportunities for investment and for a new life in a safe, growing, young country that Canada offers.

Contents

Advertorial and advertising contents

11

Hongkong Bank Speaks Your Language

Hongkong Bank of Canada (HKBC), with its heritage firmly rooted in its Asian beginnings, with its strong capitalization and its commitment to service, is in a unique position to help Asian customers achieve their financial goals in Canada.

It's more than just the fact that HKBC staff speak the languages of Asia. It's more to do with an understanding that Asian banking and business styles are different from those in North America. It's an awareness of the nuances of culture, of trust, of appropriateness.

HKBC is Canada's ninth largest bank with 55 offices and 1,500 employees across Canada providing full personal and commercial banking services.

HKBC, as a wholly owned subsidiary of The Hongkong and Shandhai Banking Corporation, benefits from its parent's more than 100 years experience in international banking. And its customers share those benefits.

"We believe we can serve our Asian customers better than our competitors because of our excellent connections with Asia — the result of our parent company's heritage in that market," said Louis Loong, HKBC's vice president of Asian Markets. "Because of that heritage, we have a good branch presence in Asia. It also means HKBC is well-positioned to act as a bridge between North America and Asia."

HKBC opened its first retail branches in 1983 in Toronto and Vancouver, in recognition of the importance of its business with Asian immigrants and investors. The Asian Markets division now includes two Private Banking units in Vancouver, British Columbia, and Toronto, Ontario, as well as six branches in Vancouver, Toronto, Montreal, Calgary and Edmonton, Alberta serving the Asian community. More new branches are planned.

Most Asian customers are very familiar with Hongkong Bank long before they reach Canada and find it is comforting to do business with an organization they know, with people who speak a common language and who are sensitive to changing financial needs.

HKBC staff are in a position to interpret Canadian culture and business practices to Asian customers in a way which is comfortable.

David Tam, assistant vice president and manager of HKBC's busy branch on Dundas Street in Toronto's Chinatown, explained that the Bank is used to meeting the high expectations of its customers in terms of efficiency and turnaround time. Of the Bank's four offices in the Toronto area, three serve the growing Asian community.

"We promise fast decisions world-wide," said Ian Marshall, assistant vice president and manager of the Toronto Commercial Banking Centre.

"For example, letters of credit usually take only 30 hours on average to turn around. Our reputation is personal, friendly customer service. The bank really tries to make service the difference in all aspects of our business."

According to Marshall, the bank can handle the specific needs of a number of groups of Asian customers, including:

- young people from Hong Kong who were educated in Canada, returned to Hong Kong, and now are coming back to live in Canada;
- the experienced business person who starts quietly in real estate and amoves on to other investments and business ventures;
- the Asian families who have lives in Canada for many years;
- the person who wants to stay in Hong Kong for now but begins to invest in Canada, a group which is growing steadily.

David S. Lee, assistant vice president and manager of HKBC's Vancouver Chinatown branch, agreed one of the main advantages the bank has over other financial institutions is the staff's ability to speak Asian languages and to understand Asian cultures. His branch's clientele is nearly 100 per cent Asian.

One of the most popular services HKBC offers, he said, is its retail mortgage plan, designed for new immigrants and non-residents. "Under this program, the customers don't need a Canadian source of income. Clients need a reasonable downpayment and a bank reference that confirms their ability to carry financing."

As is customary in Asia, the bank acts as a referral centre, providing customers with names of professionals in fields from accounting to architecture.

Eddie Wang, manager of Private Banking in Vancouver, said full banking services are available to high net-worth individuals who want one-stop banking and personal attention to all aspects of their financial affairs. These services include:

- personalized deposit services with attractive interest rates. Deposits can be made in a variety of currencies including Canadian dollars, Swiss Francs, Deutsche Marks, French Francs, Pounds Sterling, Hong Kong Dollars, Japanese Yen and U.S. Dollars. All deposits are fully and unconditionally guaranteed by The Hongkong and Shanghai Banking Corporation;
- loan services such as real estate financing, offshore guarantees, overdraft facilities, foreign currency loans;
- international services such as documentary credit facilities, international trade financing, foreign exchange handling, collections and remittances, information on foreign trade practices, letters of introduction, and cross-border and cross-currency financing;
- referrals to other professionals.

An extensive Canada Business Profile provides a wealth of information including geography, history, trade statistics, investment policies and incentives, banking and government. This guide is one of a series of foreign business profiles published by The Hongkong and Shanghai Banking Corporation. Business profiles and more information are available in any Hongkong Bank of Canada office or by contacting Vincent Lee, Managing Director, British Columbia Financial Corp. (HK) Limited in Hong Kong, telephone 5-266677.

匯豐與您，同聲同氣

加拿大匯豐銀行源起亞洲，根基穩固。資本雄厚及服務態度認眞。正處獨一無二地位協助亞洲客戶在加拿大發展其財務計劃。

這不只是因爲匯豐職員與亞洲客戶講同一語言。更因爲他們瞭解亞洲銀行業務及商業作風與北美洲不盡相同。彼此有不同的文化，信任程度及價值觀念。

加拿大匯豐銀行乃加拿大第九大銀行。橫跨加拿大有五十五間分行，超過一千五百位職員提供私人或商業機構各類銀行服務。

加拿大匯豐銀行乃香港上海匯豐銀行全資附屬機構。總括百多年國際銀行經驗，使加拿大匯豐銀行大有裨益。亦使其客戶從中受惠。

加拿大匯豐銀行亞洲市場部副總裁龍漢標說：「我們相信，匯豐之能夠比對手提供更優良服務，是因爲匯豐與亞洲市場有最密切的聯繫。」他又說：「秉承這優良傳統，我們在亞洲有良好的分行網。而加拿大匯豐銀行担當的角色是一座橫架亞洲與北美洲的橋樑。」

加拿大匯豐銀行鑑於亞洲移民及投資者之重要，早在1983年便在多倫多及溫哥華開設零售業務分行。現在亞洲市場部包括兩個私人銀行服務中心；一個在溫哥華，另一個在多倫多。另外有六間分行，分別提供各項服務給在溫哥華，多倫多及滿地河的亞洲人士。短期內將會開設卡技利及愛民頓分行。另有計劃開設更多分行。

多數亞洲客戶在抵達加拿大前早已認識匯豐銀行。他們與一間相熟銀行做生意感到安心。同時，他們亦明白匯豐銀行職員能講同一語言及對他們的財政需求能作出適當應對。

匯豐職員能對亞洲客戶解釋加拿大文化及商業習慣，顧客可以放心投資。

加拿大匯豐銀行多倫多華埠登打士街分行經理及助理副總裁譚偉雄解釋說匯豐一向以服務快捷，交收迅速來迎合客戶的要求。在多倫多的四間分行，其中有三間是爲發展中的亞洲人社區而設。

多倫多商業銀行中心經理及助理副總裁 Ian Marshall 說：「快速的決定是我們全球性的承諾。」他接着說：「例如，申請信用卡通常只需三十小時。我們的服務是以適合客戶個人需求及友善態度見稱，銀行試圖使各項服務突出有別。」

根據 Marshall 所說，匯豐銀行能處理下列各類亞洲客戶的指定要求：

＊曾在加拿大留學的香港青年人，回港後再返加定居。

＊有經驗商界人士，以前從事地產生意，現轉投其他投資及商業活動。

＊在加拿大居住多年的亞洲家庭。

＊身在香港而開始在加拿大投資的人士，這類人有增加中的趨勢。

　　加拿大匯豐銀行溫哥華華埠分行經理及助理副總裁李景琺同意匯豐其中一優勝之處乃其職員皆可用同一語言及瞭解亞洲文化。他的分行客戶幾乎百分之百是亞洲人士。

　　他說：「零售按揭計劃是爲新移民及非居民而設，現時是最受歡迎服務之一。這計劃無需貸款人在加拿大有固定收入，只需有足夠的首期付款及一封由原居地銀行發出的背景介紹書証明其還款之能力便可。」

　　匯豐亦提供客戶加幣信用卡，方便客戶毋需用原居地貨幣結數。同時，一如在亞洲，銀行會爲客戶介紹適當的專業人士，如會計師，建築師等等。

　　溫哥華私人銀行經理王彤世指出，匯豐的全面性銀行服務可使擁有大量資產人士不必四處費神便可得到專業人士處理他們財務事宜。此等服務包括：

　　＊高息存款，存款可以以加幣，瑞士法郎，馬克，法郎，英鎊，港元，日幣及美元作單位。所有加幣存款由加拿大存款保險局受保至最高額。定期存款完全及無條件由香港上海匯豐銀行担保。

　　＊放款服務，例如物業按揭，離岸担保書，透支，外幣放款等。

　　＊國際業務，例如信用証，國際貿易貸款外匯處理，匯款交收，國際貿易資料介紹書，跨國及多元貨幣貸款。

　　＊介紹各類專業服務。「加拿大商業資料一覽」提供加拿大各樣有關地理、歷史、貿易數字，投資政策銀行及政府的資料。

　　此系列刊物由香港上海匯豐銀行出版。可向匯豐在加拿大各分行或世界各地匯豐分行索閱。亦可聯絡在香港的加拿大哥倫比亞財務（香港）有限公司董事總經理李君豪，電話5‧266677。

Introduction

The purpose of this publication is to offer potential Asian emigrants to Canada a province by province description of the basic facts about opportunities for investing in manufacturing, real estate or stocks and bonds.

Canada's free market economy is the world's seventh largest with a GNP of over C$400 billion and an annual growth rate of more than 4 per cent.

Our authoritative contributors — the Canadian Federal Government Department of Regional Industrial Expansion, Royal Le Page, the Royal Bank of Canada, Price Waterhouse, Burns Fry Investment Management Limited and Clarkson Gordon Woods Gordon — have provided the latest, up-to-date information.

Canadian Chinese immigrants living in New Brunswick, Nova Scotia, Quebec, Ontario, Manitoba, Alberta and British Columbia have helped bring the basic facts to life by recounting their personal experiences in doing business in Canada.

Potential emigrants to Canada anywhere in Asia will find this book an invaluable asset but with Hong Kong's resumption by the Government of the People's Republic of China only a decade away it seems certain that more Hong Kong Chinese residents will seek to take advantage of Canada's relatively open door policy toward immigration.

For historical, political, cultural, ethnic and religious reasons southeast Asia remains an area fraught with frustrations and difficulties for certain citizens of certain countries or territories.

These frustrations coupled to Canada's open door policy and free and open society will continue to mean that emigrants will make new homes in Canada not only from Hong Kong but from Taiwan, Singapore, Brunei, Malaysia, the Philippines and Indonesia.

In the last quarter of the 1980s total foreign investment in Canada has reached almost C$8 billion per annum and 40% of this originated in the Far East, an amalgam of mainly family investment from most of the countries in the region and big corporate investment from Japan with a little from Hong Kong.

Although the majority of Hong Kong's people seem to have made up their minds that for the time being they are better off where they are — assuming China's relatively liberal policies are ongoing — Canada can look forward to a continuing steady stream of immigrants who value the long term security and prospects the country offers.

Unofficial estimates are that 70 per cent of Chinese immigrants to Canada settle eventually in Ontario, principally Toronto and its surrounding towns and cities, with the lion's share of the remaining 30 per cent heading for Vancouver despite Quebec's highly favourable special incentives to business immigrants and the vastly improved political and economic climate.

Official figures say that 48 per cent of Chinese immigrants go to Ontario, 40 per cent to Quebec and 12 per cent to Vancouver.

Our interviews in this book make clear that some Canadian Chinese feel that the current dollar requirement for business immigration is too high for many potential immigrants since, when translated into Hong Kong dollar equivalents, each investor must have between around 1.5 and 3 million Hong Kong dollars to qualify.

The Federal Government of Canada welcomes those who wish to come to Canada and who possess the capital and the knowledge to make a meaningful contribution to the nation.

Applications from potential business immigrants will be rigorously examined to see in what way a business proposal fits Canada's needs and whether the proposer already has the kind and duration of experience most likely to result in success.

Because of the need to diversify and expand their economies provincial, regional and municipal governments are often much more obviously aggressive in their approach to business immigration than at the federal level and this, too, is reflected in the advertorials contained throughout this publication.

Interviewees, on the other hand, often say either that they wish they were based in Ontario or are planning to move there in order to be at the centre of Canada's largest market not only in Ontario but in adjacent Quebec with the two provinces forming the base of an all important triangle the apex of which is centred on New York.

Toronto is, of course, a hotly competitive market and virtually all Canadian Chinese business people interviewed say that it is less competitive to be based in Canada's so-called smaller centres and that the costs of doing business are nearly always less. Many also note that the often smaller scale of investments in these areas is particularly suitable for the smaller investor's pocket.

For understandable and obvious reasons much of the glitz and glamour of the Canadian economy is centred on Ontario, home to more than 80 per cent of Canadian corporations but entrepreneurs from Asia are responsible for a lengthening list of successful enterprises in every other province ranging from high tech, through garments to fisheries and sea food.

Because of the dominance of Toronto and Ontario in the Canadian economy it seems clear that other cities and provinces will have to fight much harder to get a share of Asian immigrant investor's dollars.

As our interviews make clear a major part of this fight will involve providing much more information about towns and cities outside Vancouver, Toronto and Montreal.

In this book the Department of Regional Industrial Expansion highlights six areas in which manufacturing investment would be particularly welcome; these are: non-electrical machinery, the automotive industry, telecommunications, electronics, advanced ceramics and biotechnology.

Some specific areas include microelectronics manufacture, process control machinery manufacture, food and fish processing equipment

18

manufacture, aquaculture, residential and office furniture manufacture, jewellery making, sporting goods manufacture, toys and leisure products manufacture and garments and footwear.

Investment is also being sought in automotive parts and vehicle assembly, aerospace, resource extraction and processing, food and agricultural products, transportation or tourism projects or industries.

While the impact of Asian immigrants is being felt in manufacturing and also service industries, including import-export, many Chinese investors are attracted to real estate in which so many have been involved in one way or another in Hong Kong. Their interest is markably strong in all types of commercial real estate and in certain areas such as Vancouver or Scarborough their purchases of residential real estate are contributing to market buoyancy.

Approximately 600,000 Canadians of Chinese origin live in Canada and if present trends in immigration and the domestic birth rate continue by the year 2000 their numbers should be around one million or around four per cent of the population. Numbers in Toronto could be up from the present 260,000 to half a million or around 12 per cent of the city's probable population based on current total immigration trends and settlement patterns.

For readers who may wish to find out more about what life in Canada is like — as opposed to business prospects — they are referred to the companion volume of this publication, **'Canada Our Land'** available now from most leading book shops in Hong Kong and southeast Asia.

'Canada Our Land' is a first time collection of interviews with Canadian Chinese professionals in most provinces of Canada in which they talk candidly about their lives in their new home.

> **Richard I. Mann,**
> **Toronto, Canada**

19

Getting a Head Start on your Move to Canada

A successful move is a sure way to get a head start on your new life in Canada. **Asian Express Packing Co. Ltd.** of Hong Kong and **Tippet Richardson International** of Canada have moved over 2500 families and businesses between Hong Kong and Canada in this past year alone. With years of experience, the Asian Express and Tippet Richardson moving team have set a high standard for packing and forwarding, and our quality packing and friendly service has made us the most reliable and reputable moving team amongst all our customers.

Moving takes organized planning and careful timing. Once you have decided on having a new home in Canada, preparations should begin right away. The Asian Express and Tippet Richardson team provide a complete Door-to-Door origin and destination service. This means that with offices across Canada and Hong Kong, we will be able to assist you with your move to Canada every step of the way.

To begin, call our Asian Express office in Hong Kong at **3-7214158** and one of our estimators will be at your door. They will go through all the details of your move, and assist in developing the best moving schedule for you and your moving needs. Depending on the city of destination in Canada, a complete Door-to-Door moving schedule is assessed.

Origin Services (Hong Kong)

Packing. Our packing supervisor will be present at your residence during the move. We will pack all the items you require such as dishes, linens, clothings, books, utensils etc. For the items that you would like to pack yourself, we will provide you with all the necessary materials you need such as hanging wardrobes for your clothes and cartons for your personal files.

Custom-made. For your more fragile items ranging from mirrors and marble to your glass cabinets and piano, custom-made crates are made to ensure full protection of your items during shipment.

Wrapping. From your smallest glassware to your largest furniture peice, all items will be carefully wrapped and padded with the highest quality packing materials.

Inventory. Each item and box are carefully marked and numbered in our inventory so that you will know exactly where your belongings are.

Loading. After all your items are packed, they will be loaded into our waterproofed wooden liftvans, thereafter, a steamship container for shipment.

21

Documentation. Our experienced staff will provide full information and assistance in completing the necessary export and import Customs formalities and requirements for your shipment before you leave for Canada.

Destination Service (Canada)

Unloading. Once the container reaches Canada, our Tippet Richardson offices will handle and unload your shipment into our bonded warehouse for customs clearance and/or inspection.

Customs Clearance. A Chinese-speaking staff will contact and assist you in customs clearance formalities and procedure.

Delivery. Once your shipment is cleared and released by Customs, delivery will be arranged to your new home.

Unpacking. All your items will be delivered and unpacked into your residence; arranged according to your specifications; and all packing debris removed.

You can now relax and begin to enjoy your new home in Canada!

Moving Guide

To get a head start on your new life in Canada, the following is a guide to assist you in planning your move:

1 MONTH BEFORE MOVING DAY

• **Study** the city and area you will be moving to. The climate and lifestyle are the essential details that will help you decide what to bring with you. Ask your Asian Express representative about our library of information and maps of the various Canadian cities we have available.

• **Collect** all your personal documents such as medical and dental from your family physician and dentist, they can also recommend a medical and dental office in the city and area you'll be living in.

• **Update** all the necessary visa and immigration requirements such as photos etc. Your Asian Express representative can inform you about the details.

Clean-up Checklist

• make an **INVENTORY** of all the goods to be packed

• start to **USE UP** opened packages of goods, foods and frozen foods

• keep in mind to **DEFROST** your fridge and freezer and be sure to allow them to be aired for at least 48 hours.

• decide all the items to be **DRYCLEANED** or **WASHED** such as the curtains, carpets and the clothes that you want to ship.

• **NOTIFY** your utilities and local delivery services in your neighbourhood such as the newspaper, milkman, hydro and electricity, water and telephone company. Inform your personal banker to ensure a safe and secure transfer of accounts.

• **RETURN** borrowed items such as your library books, and retrieve the items you have loaned out.

- prepare a set of **CHANGE OF ADDRESSES** notices to your local post office, insurance, subscription, credit card companies as well as your friends and relatives.
- **CONFIRM** your packing dates with Asian Express; make an appointment with one of our representatives to go over the details of your shipment and arrange your INSURANCE coverage.
- for the items you wish to **PURCHASE** before you leave such as furniture, electrical equipment or piano, be sure to inform Asian Express and we can arrange to have these items delivered directly to our warehouse for packing with your shipment.
- gather all your **VALUABLES** so that you will know exactly where they will be placed during your move.
- **THROW OUT** and/or **DO NOT PACK** flammable, dangerous and hazardous materials. This includes aerosal cans, items containing bleach or ammonia, and bottled or gaseous items. Also remember to throw out old medicine bottles.

PACKING DAY

- **A WEEK BEFORE** your packing day, arrange to have a babysitter to avoid inconvenience on your day of packing.
- **GATHER** all your valuable **PERSONAL EFFECTS** such as your jewellery and important papers so that you will know exactly where they are.
- **SET ASIDE** the addresses, telephone numbers, plane tickets and items that you will take with you in a separate area so that they are easily accessible when you need them; be sure you have enough Canadian currency to pay for food and transportation costs when you arrive in Canada.
- once you have finished packing your suitcases and confirmed your flight arrangements and necessary documentation you can now **RELAX** and let Asian Express and Tippet Richardson take care of the rest!!!!

A happy move is a successful move, and we at Asian Express and Tippet Richardson, take great care in your moving needs because we make sure you get a good head start in your new life in Canada!!!!

亞洲捷運與您——邁向新生活

　　好的開始是成功的一半；若閣下決定移居加拿大，亞洲捷運包裝有限公司及同聯線的鐵柏李察遜國際公司必定盡力爲閣下效勞，務求爲閣下在新的環境中帶來一個舒適和美好的開始。在往年短短十二個月內，本公司榮幸地協助超過二千五百多個家庭及商戶移往加國。積聚多年之包裝搬運經驗，再加上一貫安全快捷而妥當之寄運水準及忠誠之服務態度，在顧客眼中的亞洲捷運及鐵柏李察遜是絕對可靠和有信譽的。

　　移民外地也是一門學問。有組織地去計劃及有準確的時間判斷在這門學問中佔有一定的重要性。當閣下作出了移居加國的決定後便應着手準便一切事項。選擇一間安全快捷而服務忠誠的搬運公司的確可以爲閣下省卻很多不必要的煩惱。亞洲捷運和鐵柏李察遜聯線樂意爲閣下代勞，閣下只需致電本公司（九龍電話：（三）七二一四一五八），我們經驗豐富之估價員便在約定的時間到達府上作出估價及提供一切有關移民寄運之資料，爲閣下作出適當之安排。本公司經驗豐富之包裝員工將會在預約之日期及時間在閣下香港的住所把待寄的物品分門別類地包裝妥當，繼而寄運至加拿大之新居所內。在整個裝箱寄運的過程中，本公司將盡力安排及負責每一個步驟，保証免卻閣下操勞而更可全心全意地投入一個新地域過着美好的新生活。

本地包裝服務——

　　包裝妥當——本公司將會把閣下之日常家庭用品如廚房用具，衣物，書本，器具，瓷器或古董等分門別類地包裝妥當。至於某些私人物品若閣下欲親自將之包裝，本公司將會供應適當材料。

　　特別裝箱——易碎的物件如鏡子，雲石櫃枱，鋼琴等將會被分別包裝在本公司特製的木箱內以保安全。

　　大型傢俬——從小件的玻璃器皿至大件的傢俬物件都會以最現代化的包裝材料小心封妥。

　　貨物清單——所有物件當包裝妥當將會清楚地記錄在裝箱單上（清單）以便日後閣下到達加境時報關之用。

　　運輸服務——當包裝工作完成之後，閣下之物件將會被裝運在大型之貨櫃箱內及後運送上新式之貨櫃船。

　　文件處理——在閣下離港抵加之前，本公司職員會全力協助閣下完成所有報關程序。

抵埗服務——

落貨——當閣下之貨櫃抵達加境之後，我們在彼邦的聯營公司鐵柏李察遜將會安排貨物暫存貨倉，以備日後清關或轉運至閣下之新居所內。

運輸——我們在彼邦之華籍職員將會聯絡及協助閣下完成所有清關手續，待貨物清關後便安排貨物運抵府上。

拆裝——我們將會把貨物運送至新居內及安全拆裝，更按照閣下之指示安放傢俱，令閣下安心享受遷入加拿大新居後的樂趣。

移民指南——

下列所提供之數點可令閣下更有系統地安排包裝寄運之行程：
起行前一個月——
＊在移居某城市之前先熟悉該處之地理環境、天氣概況及生活習慣。亞洲捷運之職員樂意提供給閣下詳盡資料以瞭解當地情況。
＊把閣下的私人文件，如健康履歷等處理妥當。
＊本公司職員將會爲閣下處理一切出口報關及文件手續。

清理雜物安排——

＊列出一張雜物清單。
＊處理或棄置未用完之罐頭及食物。
＊包裝之前先把雪櫃和冰箱溶雪及清潔妥當。
＊把衣物、窗簾和地毡清理乾淨。
＊歸還所有圖書館書籍及借閱之文件。
＊將新地址告予銀行、郵政局、保險公司和信用卡戶口等以方便日後郵遞轉接。
＊與本公司職員聯絡確定包裝寄運日期，如有任何疑問，例如購買船運保險等事宜，請盡早向本公司查詢。
＊如閣下欲購買傢俬、電器用品或鋼琴等之大型貨物，請通知本公司以便利日後一同寄運。
＊聚集所有貴重物品以防遺失。
＊切勿寄運任何易燃或危險物品。

包裝日——

    ＊先把家中小孩安置妥當以策不便。
    ＊聚集所有貴重物品及切記物件放置之處。
    ＊把重要的私人文件如簽証、身份証明文件及機票等收置妥當。
    ＊請準備足夠加幣以便不時之需。
    在新領域中過美好的新生活，亞洲捷運樂意協助您邁向第一步。

CHAPTER 1

Opportunities in manufacturing

Compiled from material supplied by the Department of Regional Industrial Expansion, Government of Canada

Investing in

Prince Edward Island

Prince Edward Island is a province of rolling landscapes, fertile rust-red soil, and warm, sandy beaches. Most of its population of 127,100 is engaged, in one way or another, in agriculture, fishing or tourism. A growing number are engaged in advanced-technology pursuits such as marine research, life sciences, and high-technology manufacturing. Most of the province's residents feel that they live on a little piece of Canadian paradise.

The province's active agriculture, fishing and tourism sectors offer opportunities for businesses which can help these industries to continue to grow and prosper. They also lend a charm to the province as a peaceful, pleasant and stimulating place to live and do business.

Side-by-side with some of the most productive potato farmers and lobster fishermen in the world are technology-specialized companies which manufacture and export to more than 100 countries such products as chemicals for use in diagnostic medicine, high-resolution image recorders, aluminium holloware and the world's first hypodermic syringe for self-administered injection of insulin without needles. Prince Edward Islanders take amused satisfaction from learning their province is now recognized for both the potatoes it grows and the pots they are cooked in.

On Prince Edward Island, one is never more than 10 minutes from a farm or 30 minutes from the sea. This proximity to animal and marine life and to cultivated fields provides a natural laboratory for the biological sciences — an area of research and development important to a hungry world. Island companies and institutions are gaining international reputations for research and development in the biological sciences. A major opportunity is emerging for manufacturers and service industries related to fish and animal health.

With the opening in 1986 of the *Atlantic Veterinary College* at the University of Prince Edward Island, the bio-science industry will have available advanced facilities for innovation and development in agriculture and aquaculture. Other advanced-technology industries may be attracted by the well-educated labour force, new and sophisticated R&D facilities, and supportive government programs which smooth the way for new investments and business start-ups. The province is particularly attractive to *"foot-loose"* industries which can take advantage of the island's superior quality of life.

☐ Prince Edward Island's three major traditional industries — agriculture, tourism and fishing — will continue to offer significant opportunities for new investments:

In **agriculture,** excellent growing conditions combined with an established research and support infrastructure offer exciting opportunities for the successful production of specialty crops and for processors and packagers geared to high-value product lines and markets.

In the **tourism** sector there is significant attraction-development potential, especially in the emerging resort destination areas.

Prince Edward Island's inshore **fishery** has been very successful at selling lobster and shellfish to both the fresh and institutional market. However, further opportunities for value-added processing exist.

☐ At the same time, new and emerging **advanced-technology** industries which take advantage of the island's natural setting and attractive quality of life will present opportunities in several areas:

Recently, several small **bio-science** companies have established in Prince Edward Island. The opening in 1986 of the Atlantic Veterinary College will give added impetus to investors wishing to establish new state-of-the-art facilities.

Existing facilities in the **computer-enhanced image processing, medical devices, diagnostic chemicals** and **fish vaccines** sectors and the anticipated establishment of companies in such areas as **defence** and **veterinary science** could be augmented by others in component manufacture, service and transportation.

Existing **consumer-oriented producers** of high fashion eyewear, video productions, gourmet foods such as crab, Malpeque oysters, cheese, etc., and top quality cookware, indicate that the range of successful initiatives possible in P.E.I. are only limited by the imagination.

Investing in
Newfoundland

Although the vast majority of the province's population is located on the island of Newfoundland, modern air and sea connections provide convenient daily access to the prime Canadian and US markets — especially the highly-urbanized regions of central & Atlantic Canada, and the northeastern US. In fact, the province's strategic location along major transportation routes between continental North America and Europe make it an ideal site for export-oriented businesses. On its own, the $6 billion Newfoundland economy offers a base of demand for a wide range of goods and services.

Both long-established and newly-discovered offshore resources remain to be fully exploited. The fisheries, which have been the mainstay of the province's economy for centuries, are continually evolving to respond to new technologies, new markets and new product demands. More recently, major oil and gas finds along Newfoundland and Labrador's continental shelf have paved the way for the province to become a major petroleum producer.

Newfoundland continues to be a major generator of hydroelectric power. The potential availability of a virtually limitless supply of cheap electricity makes the province an excellent location for a wide range of energy-intensive industries — especially those that take advantage of Newfoundland's vast mineral and forest resources.

The province boasts a sizeable labour force which is well-educated, experienced and highly-productive. Participation rates are high and wages competitively low.

Business operating in Newfoundland enjoy ready and direct access to a comprehensive range of financial & business advisory services which are delivered through a mature network of international, national and local banks and other financial and business consulting institutions active in the province. In addition, several world-class research & development facilities provide specialized support to industry. This includes state-of-the-art research facilities and programs catering to the offshore marine sector and to firms involved in resource extraction and processing operations.

Government and industry work closely together to promote and support new investments and business initiatives which help Newfoundland pursue its economic and business development objectives. New enterprises and innovative technologies are welcome, and government assistance programs help smooth the way for investment.

The province offers a rich range of opportunities for new investments and business initiatives, including attractive prospects for joint-ventures.

The **fisheries industry:**

Continued expansion of the export market for **underutilized species** such as turbot, flounder, redfish and catfish.

More innovative harvesting methods and more aggressive marketing techniques for **herring, mackerel, salmon, trout, scallops, lobster and crab,** especially in European and North American markets.

Penetration of Asian and Far East markets for Newfoundland and Labrador **delicacies such as capelin, squid, shrimp and eel.**

Development and marketing of **fish by-products** such as medicinal cod liver oil, halibut liver oil and manufactured fish meal as animal food supplements.

Introduction of new synthetic and compound fish product variations, such as the successful surimi products produced in Newfoundland from a cod and crab base, and sold internationally.

Modernization of **harvesting vessels and technology,** and upgrading of **fish processing facilities** to improve yields and productivity, while promoting continuity of supply and viability of year-round operations in all sectors of the industry.

The **pulp & paper and other forestry industries:**

Enhancement of **pollution controls** and **modernization and**

upgrading of facilities.

Expansion of **silvicultural operations,** including stand improvement, reforestation and harvesting procedures to maximize sustainable yields.

Exploitation of underutilized **high-density spruce and fir stands** in the Labrador region.

Diversification to expand production of **quality hardwoods** for artisans and wood craftsmen producing furniture, hardwood cabinets and other manufactured products.

The **tourism industry** markets include:

Naturalists and photographers interested in the province's tide pool periwinkles, humpback whales, unique fens and marshlands, boreal forests and sea coasts.

Sports enthusiasts attracted by trophy big-game moose and caribou hunting and some of the best Atlantic salmon angling in eastern North America.

Family vacationers, hikers and backpackers lured by the province's diverse natural landscape, intriguing prehistory and dynamic cultural life as well as the two national parks, several provincial parks, and numerous other historic parks and sites.

Newfoundland's **offshore oil and gas industry** will continue to offer a wide range of investment opportunities, in areas ranging from research and development to the design, construction, supply and servicing of specialized exploration, extraction and processing facilities.

Potential expansion of **hydroelectric power generation** will continue to make the province an attractive place for locating **energy-intensive processing and manufacturing operations.**

Other small to medium-scale and diversified **manufacturing and high-technology** businesses can take advantage of convenient and modern "incubator malls" which augment the numerous industrial parks in the province.

Investing in

New Brunswick

In addition to its own domestic market of C$8.1 billion, New Brunswick offers direct road and rail access to the prime markets of Ontario, Québec, Atlantic Canada and the northeastern United States.

The province's strong resource extraction and processing industries are balanced by modern, diversified and rapidly growing manufacturing and service sectors.

New Brunswick's labour force is well-educated and remarkably stable, with a good supply in all professional and support occupations.

The province is officially bilingual (English and French) and more than one-quarter of the population speaks both languages. This places New Brunswick in the enviable position of being able to cater to both anglophone and francophone markets in Canada and around the world.

With a large and well-established export trade, New Brunswick offers ready penetration of prime U.S. and overseas markets — and not just for the province's rich supply of raw materials and energy. Fully three-quarters of the province's exports are processed and manufactured goods.

In addition to supplies of virtually all major industrial raw materials from the rest of Canada, New Brunswick has an impressive natural. resource base of its own. Energy is cheap and plentiful. The province welcomes investments which increase the value-added from resource processing of its key mineral, forestry, agricultural and fisheries resources. Major reserves of peat and potash remain to be fully exploited.

The province maintains efficient road and rail connections to the rest of Canada and the United States. At the same time, it boasts large and sophisticated seaport facilities, which provide ready access to markets in Europe, Asia, South & Central America and the American seaboard.

The province has adopted a vigorous and enthusiastic approach to attracting new businesses. Investments for the modernization and expansion of the existing industrial base are very welcome. Comprehensive financial services, superior R&D facilities and supportive government assistance programs provide a healthy climate for investment.

New Brunswick's resource-based industries have traditionally been the backbone of the province's economy, and some opportunities remain for investment in the resource sectors. In all sectors, there are opportunities to extend the province's value-added processing of material prior to shipment outside of New Brunswick. Some major examples include:

Development of a **chemical industry** for the production of fertilizer, saltcake, hydrochloric acid and calcium chloride

Establishment of a **zinc reduction plant** and modernization of a **lead smelter**

Modernization, adaptation of new technologies, expansion, and market diversification in the **forestry and fish processing sectors**

The non-resource based industries offer even more significant opportunities for growth. A major thrust of industrial development policy in the province is to strengthen, expand and diversify the industrial base, while stressing technological advancement and innovative product and process development.

Some examples of opportunities in the non-resource based sectors include:

Machinery and metal fabrication industries, including marine hardware as well as mining, fishing, forestry and construction-related machinery & equipment.

Shipbuilding and repair industries, including support for the Canadian Patrol Frigate Program and offshore oil and gas activities as well as related spin-offs (e.g. Arctic-class vessels, LNG carriers and semi-submersible drilling platforms).

Industrial services, including advanced engineering, prototype design and development services; technically-advanced equipment repair and maintenance; and other innovation-related services.

31

Investing in
Nova Scotia

With a population of almost 900,000 people, Nova Scotia is the largest of Canada's four Atlantic provinces. Halifax, the province's capital city, is the largest urban centre in Atlantic Canada.

Gross provincial expenditures in the province totalled more than $10 billion in 1984 — personal expenditures on consumer goods and services alone approached $8 billion — making Nova Scotia a significant market in its own right. In addition, the province's modern and efficient road, air, marine and rail transportation systems provide Nova Scotia-based firms with direct access to major urban centres in Canada, the United States, and overseas countries.

Halifax Harbour operates two of the busiest container terminals in the world, and helped Nova Scotia to export more than $1-1/2 billion in finished and unfinished goods to numerous countries.

Manufacturing industries in the province had total shipments in excess of $4.8 billion in 1985, and play a key role in Nova Scotia's economy. The province's tourist industry has also been experiencing significant growth in recent years; many opportunities are available for further expansion in both of these key industry sectors.

A high priority is placed on ensuring that Nova Scotia-based firms have access to state-of-the-art technology. In addition to world-class universities and research centres, the province has undertaken specific measures to ensure that advanced technology firms locating in Nova Scotia have access to fully-serviced industrial land.

The province is currently experiencing a growth in the number of firms using advanced technology in their production and research activities. These include firms using ocean science technology, defence-related firms, and numerous other manufacturing establishments.

The province's system of universities, vocational schools, and technical institutes, ensures that firms located in Nova Scotia have direct access to a large supply of well-educated workers. Labour-management relations have been very good in recent years; workers are motivated, and wages are competitive.

In addition to being virtually self-sufficient in electrical power, the province boasts an abundant supply of other natural resources, including large stocks of fish and a strong agriculture sector. Further expansion of resource-based industries is encouraged.

Nova Scotia welcomes and encourages new investment in its traditional and newly emerging industry sectors. The complete range of financial services, an advanced industrial infrastructure, and government incentive programs are already in place to assist individuals and businesses wishing to invest in the province.

Ocean science technology and ocean related industries have been identified as among the most promising investment opportunities in the province. The Nova Scotia fishery is in a period of transition as factory freezer trawlers and new processes are being adopted to strengthen the international competitiveness of the industry. In addition to a rejuvenated ocean fishery, **aquaculture** is also projected to assume increasing importance as one of the major growth sectors in the future.

Ocean industry development in Nova Scotia is also driven by spin-offs from **offshore oil and gas projects.** Exploration efforts have resulted in discoveries of hydrocarbons. Gas production from offshore is currently in the planning stage. The project is anticipated to have a capital cost of approximately three billion dollars including a major subsea pipeline and several offshore production platforms.

Another area of major emphasis in Nova Scotia's ocean industry sector is **research and development.** The province has sophisticated scientific and educational organizations with a concentration on ocean related applications and is at the forefront of advanced technology in this area.

The **development and growth of advanced technologies** in Nova Scotia is another area where new investment is being encouraged. Symbolic of this are two multi-year agreements totalling $64 million which were recently signed by the federal and provincial governments to provide Nova Scotian industry with the most advanced technological tools available — from CAD/CAM and flexible manufacturing systems training to a supercomputer. Steps have been taken to accelerate the commercial application of new technologies within the province's small and medium size businesses and to ensure that there is a skilled workforce available to operate them effectively.

As home of Canada's Maritime Command, Nova Scotia benefits from the **economic spin-offs derived from military and defence spending.** The Department of National Defence employs more than 21,000 people in Nova Scotia and has an annual operating budget in the hundreds of millions of dollars. This results in an economic impact on the provincial economy of an estimated $1.8 billion annually. More development is expected in the next five to ten years as the Government of Canada undertakes major procurement programs for projects such as Low Level Air Defence (LLAD), Microwave Landing Systems (MLS), Tactical Command, Control and Communication Systems (TCCCS) and the Radar Modernization Program (RAMP).

As "Canada's Ocean Playground" Nova Scotia benefits from a booming **tourist industry.** Each year the province hosts more than one million visitors who come to enjoy the refreshing maritime climate, spectacular coastal scenery and easy-going way of life. The recent opening of the **World Trade & Convention Centre** has drawn attention to Halifax as a most attractive location for convention business.

Nova Scotia's **coal industry** is also an attractive area for investment. Two new coal mine developments, the promise of commercial feasibility of the carbogel coal based fuel process, and the development of coal export markets indicate a strong future for coal. Exploration for new minerals is at an all-time high.

The **forestry sector** is also an area where future expansion is likely. Production from Nova Scotia's 10 million acre forest area supports five mills producing pulp, paper, hardboard and other related wood products. Christmas tree production is a growing part of the forest industry with sales now valued at more than $10 million annually.

Investing in

Québec

With a large and affluent population, Québec constitutes a major market for consumer and industrial goods & services. The province's superb location in relation to the markets of North America, Europe and Asia, places Québec among the most strategic regions in the world to do business. Superior and well-maintained air, road, rail and sea facilities provide Québec with ready, direct and efficient access to the prime urban and industrial centres in Canada, the United States and other major industrial nations around the world.

Québec's cosmopolitan and well-educated peoples are not only active and sophisticated consumers, but productive and industrious workers. Although the vast majority of the population speaks French, most Québeckers in urban areas are bilingual. This places Québec in the enviable position of being able to cater equally well to anglophone and francophone markets in Canada and around the world.

Québec has a dynamic and diverse industrial and tourism base. The province's resource-based sector is balanced by a sophisticated and rapidly-evolving manufacturing industry which is often at the forefront of technological advancement and change. Many of Québec's established industries have recently initiated major expansions and modernizations. Investment opportunities abound for continued expansion, innovations and new start-ups.

The province's well-established export trade does a large volume of business with scores of countries around the world. Close to 50 countries, representing all five continents, each imported $25 million or more worth of goods from Québec in 1984. One-third of these countries imported $100 million or more.

Commerce, industry and tourism in the province are supported by a comprehensive network of specialized services and facilities. Research and development expenditures in Québec have recently topped the $1 billion mark per year, and the province boasts superior R&D facilities in virtually every industrial and commercial sector. World-class banking and other financial institutions provide a comprehensive range of investment and busines advisory support.

Major investments in Québec industry over the next several years will focus on efforts to adopt new production technologies, and to introduce other innovations which will keep Québec in the forefront of industrial production and productivity.

Major expansions, new start-ups, and significant innovation projects will be sought in industrial sectors where Québec already has an established base and reputation: transportation equipment, electronic goods, defence equipment and supplies, laser optics, pharmaceuticals, biotechnology, plastics & other new materials, foods, computer software, and automotive parts manufacture.

Taking advantage of Québec's abundant supplies of cheap electrical energy, the province will also be seeking new investments in energy-intensive industries such as the electrochemical and electrometallurgical sectors.

There are significant major investment opportunities in several sectors of the Québec economy:

In Québec's rapidly-expanding **transportation and defence industries,** major opportunities exist for involvement in design and construction of systems and sub-systems for airplanes and for specialized military and space equipment.

In the **electronics industry** there are three major sub-sectors with attractive investment opportunities:

Production process equipment, including control systems and devices, robotics, lasers (including industrial and medical applications) and computer-aided design/computer-aided manufacturing (CAD/CAM).

Telecommunications, including mobile cellular telephones, teletex and videotex.

Other specialized electronic equipment, including office equipment, video discs, aviation equipment and avionics.

In the **machinery sector** there is a demand for new and specialized equipment for use in processing operations (especially in the pulp & paper and food sectors), as well as new industrial fields such as biotechnology.

The **computer software and related industries** are growing to support the rapidly-expanding information-based industrial and commercial sectors of Canada's and the world's economies.

The **electrometallurgical and electrochemical industries** will see new developments, in particular in the following product areas: hydrogen, magnesium, electro-processing, plasma and industrial ceramics.

The **biotechnology and related industries** (including foods and pharmaceuticals) have a need for new investments in areas such as food processing technologies, production of artificial sweeteners from potatoes, frozen vegetable production, and manufacture of biological pesticides, diagnostic products and medical electronic equipment & supplies.

The **mineral extraction and processing industries** present opportunities for new development in such areas as cokefaction of peat for energy, manufacture of activated carbon, enhancement of gold ore processing using new solution agents, and production of iron alloys.

Investing in

Ontario

The province of Ontario plays a key role in the North American economy, and is an integral part of North America's industrial heartland. Ontario is

Canada's largest producer of manufactured goods, and supplies Canada, the U.S., and overseas markets with a wide spectrum of products ranging from automobiles and related parts & accessories, to electronics, telecommunications equipment, processed food, and beverages. The province's broad and diversified industrial base makes it particularly suitable for joint ventures, licensing arrangements, and other forms of industrial cooperation.

With a population of more than 9 million people, and the highest per capita income of any Canadian province, Ontario represents a major market for consumer and industrial goods and services. An additional 120 million American consumers are accessible within one day's trucking, placing Ontario at the centre of the world's single-largest consumer market. The province's strategic location also provides direct marine access to European and Asian markets via the Great Lakes/St. Lawrence Seaway system.

The full range of financial services is available. Location in Ontario provides ready access to Canada's world-class chartered banks, numerous foreign banks, and the Toronto Stock Exchange — the largest stock exchange in Canada, and 9th largest in the world.

Ontario's economy continues to grow and diversify. Thousands of new manufacturing, service, retail and resource-based businesses start-up each year. Existing firms continue to modernize and expand, as Ontario stays at the forefront of technological innovation and trends in business and consumer demand.

Ample supplies of natural resources and energy are available domestically at competitive prices. The province's sophisticated transportation and telecommunications networks ensure that Ontario-based businesses are in touch with the world.

The province's labour force is highly motivated, and skilled. Labour-management relations are excellent. The government-supported educational system ensures that Ontario's work force ranks among the best educated in the world.

The province is committed to being at the forefront of technological innovation. The Government of Ontario has put in place a program to encourage technology research in colleges, universities and the private sector. The transfer of technology to private industry is of the highest priority.

Given Ontario's dynamic and highly-diversified economy, there are investment opportunities in virtually every industrial sector. Government programs help foreign businesses with new start-ups, joint ventures, licensing arrangements and other business and investment initiatives in Ontario.

The province of Ontario offers a stable, diversified, and growing business environment for new capital investment. The province's proven strength in a wide range of manufacturing industries, abundant supply of natural resources and energy, highly-trained labour force and positive labour-management climate, provide a superb location for the start-up of new businesses, or the expansion and modernization of existing commercial operations. In addition, the province's strategic location in North America provides direct access to Canadian, U.S. and overseas markets.

Investments which make the most of the province's inherent strengths, promote economic activity in all regions of the province and/or encourage the development and transfer of new technology, are especially welcome.

The **high-technology sector** presents major growth and investment opportunities. The provincial government recently announced the creation of a $1 billion, 10-year fund to encourage technology research in colleges, universities and the private sector. Many of Ontario's high-technology companies are already enjoying tremendous success, and are producing a wide range of products from telecommunications equipment to sophisticated instrumentation and robotics. Significant concentrations of high technology industries are in Toronto, Ottawa/Kanata, Markham, Kitchener/Waterloo, and Mississauga.

The **microelectronics and telecommunications industries** in particular provide considerable investment opportunity for the supply of high-technology products ranging from specialty software to the high-volume manufacture of custom and semi-custom products. The introduction of microelectronics into the manufacturing process (e.g. CAD/CAM, robotics, numeric process control, etc.), as well as into manufactured end-products used by consumers, business and industry, is necessary to remain competitive in international markets. Similarly, the transition from analog to digital systems in the telecommunications field reflects the changing needs in the market place that have led to new investment opportunities in Ontario's telecommunications industry.

Ontario's **manufacturing industries** continue to be a major source of new investment opportunities. In 1984, one-fifth (21%) of total new investment in plants, equipment and machinery in the province went to manufacturing industries.

Recent high levels of investment in the following specific industries in the manufacturing sector have signalled major growth and success:

Transportation Equipment Industries, which received approximately one-sixth (16%) of total new investment in manufacturing industries in 1984. Recent major acquisitions and expansions reflect the confidence industry has in this sector and signal new growth opportunities for the future.

Food and Beverage Industries, which have experienced exceptional growth over the past two years, particularly in the form of new investment in plant modernization and expansions. In 1984, this sector received approximately one-eighth (12%) of total new investment in the manufacturing industries.

The **Chemical and Chemical Products Industries** have also been experiencing rapid growth — accounting for one-ninth (11%) of total new investments in the manufacturing sector.

Small businesses are a rapidly-emerging force in Ontario's overall economic success. Most of the 95,000 new businesses started in Ontario in 1985 were small or medium-sized — demonstrating that opportunities for success are virtually limitless.

The size, diversity, and rapid growth of Ontario's **tourism** industry provides potential investors with an extremely wide range of new investment opportunities. The province's natural tourist attractions range from beautiful scenic landscapes and wilderness, to major sporting events, family vacation parks, and arts & cultural attractions in urban centres. Opportunities exist to provide tourism products and services that capitalize on the province's existing strengths, and/or develop new attractions.

While much of Ontario's industry is concentrated in the south, investment opportunities exist to build on the strengths of Ontario's northern and eastern regions. **Northern Ontario** offers extensive forest and mineral resources, an important tourism sector boasting hunting, fishing and fly-in services, a scenic and lengthy freshwater shoreline, a hard working and enthusiastic labour force, and special government assistance programs to encourage secondary industry.

Eastern Ontario is strategically located in the transportation corridor linking Canada's two largest industrial and financial centres — Toronto and Montréal — with the industrialized and populous Great Lakes States in the U.S. As home of the nation's capital, the region possesses an extensive public administration and defence base, as well as a bustling high-technology community with a skilled labour force, and some of the province's finest recreational resources.

Opportunities exist in all regions and sectors of the province.

Investing in

Manitoba

In addition to an abundant supply of natural resources and inexpensive energy, the province's strong and diversified economy benefits from an impressive and growing manufacturing sector. Manitoba's economy produced over $13 billion in gross domestic product in 1983, including $1.6 billion in the manufacturing sector alone.

Manitoba can accommodate firms ranging in size from small commercial enterprises to large multinationals. A provincial population of over 1 million people gives Manitoba-based firms direct access to a sizeable consumer and industrial market. An additional 80 million Canadian and U.S. consumers within a 1,600 km (1,000 mile) radius of Winnipeg provides limitless scope for new business opportunities.

The province's efficient road, rail, air, and marine transportation systems link Manitoba firms with major national and international transportation networks. In 1984, the province exported finished and unfinished goods to over one-hundred countries, including products valued at almost $1.3 billion to the United States.

Manitoba boasts a skilled and dependable labour force. Wage rates are competitive and the province enjoys exceptional labour-management relations. In addition, industry benefits from the steady supply of university and college-trained graduates produced every year by Manitoba's educational system.

The province is fully integrated with Canada's worldclass banking and finance sector. Manitoba's advanced telecommunications system allows firms to stay in touch with the world. Industry can also draw on the province's vast infrastructure of research and development support agencies and facilities.

Investment opportunities are currently available in areas ranging from agriculture and food processing to transportation equipment and electronics. The province welcomes new investments to finance new start-ups, expansions or modernizations.

The priorities for investment promotion in Manitoba include a diversified range of industrial sectors which represent key components of the province's economy. These sectors include transportation equipment, aerospace, machinery, electrical and electronic products, food and beverage industries, as well as metal fabricating and paper and allied products industries. Priority is also on opportunities which can capitalize on Manitoba's economic strengths, especially low-cost energy, rich natural resource endowments, and a skilled, well-trained labour force that is stable and affordable.

Opportunities will result from specific initiatives such as the $50 million agreement between the Government of Canada and the province of Manitoba to establish Winnipeg as a national centre of expertise for the technological development and manufacture of **advanced urban buses and other related industrial products.** Known as the **Canada-Manitoba Subsidiary Agreement on Urban Bus Industrial Development,** this agreement means that the province can financially assist technological development with programs focused on research and development, as well as prototype development and demonstration.

In addition, under the **Western Transportation Industrial Development Program,** emphasis is placed on the establishment and expansion of facilities in the **food processing** and **railway supply sectors.** This program provides assistance to new and existing industries in setting-up or expanding operations in these two key industrial sectors.

Investing in

Saskatchewan

Saskatchewan's internal domestic market of more than C$17 billion offers a wide range of business and investment opportunities — especially in industries which cater to the province's strong primary resource sectors. At the same time, the province's major urban centres are located on major air, road and rail routes connecting the prime industrial and commercial markets in the heart of North America. Millions of consumers are located within one or two day's trucking of Saskatchewan.

The province's strong agriculture, mining and energy sectors are complemented by growing manufacturing and service sectors. In recent years, many new advanced-technology firms have started up in Saskatchewan, taking advantage of the province's technological skills and specialized facilities.

Saskatchewan's labour force is experienced, productive and well-educated. Industrial wages are highly competitive.

The province's population is ethnically diverse, with strong roots in the United Kingdom, northwest and eastern Europe, and parts of Asia. Saskatchewan welcomes investments and business immigrants from around the world.

With impressive worldwide sales of grain, oilseeds, potash and other raw and processed resources, Saskatchewan is a major exporter with established trade links in the U.S.A., Europe, Asia and Pacific Rim countries. The province's domestic market for manufactured products in the agriculture, mining, forestry and energy sectors provides a spring-board for specialized export firms active in these sectors.

Saskatchewan has ready access to virtually all major industrial raw materials from the rest of Canada. It also has an impressive natural resource base of its own. Renewable agriculture and forestry resources are complemented by rich endowments of potash, uranium, oil, coal, natural gas, and other metallic and non-metallic minerals. Structural materials are in good supply, and energy is cheap and plentiful. The province welcomes investments which will further tap the province's renewable and non-renewable resources, including initiatives which will improve productivity and/or increase the value-added from resource processing activities.

The province's efficient road and rail networks connect Saskatchewan to the rest of Canada and the United States. Although the province is landlocked, it is in fact a major marine exporter. Well-established road and rail facilities provide direct access to major west coast ports and the Saint Lawrence Seaway system in the east.

Saskatchewan has consistently maintained a welcome stance toward new businesses and investments. Modern financial services, state-of-the-art R&D facilities and a wide range of government assistance programs create a healthy climate for investment.

The **agriculture sector** in Saskatchewan will continue to be a dominant force in the economic future of the province. Continued expansion of agricultural operations in the province coupled with continuous evolution in the industry to introduce innovative technologies, develop and market new products, and improve productivity will present opportunities for investment and joint-venturing in a wide range of areas, including:

Meat packing, processing and marketing:

Continued diversification in the raising and processing of new **field crops** (field peas and beans, lentils, buckwheat, faba beans, mustard and canary seed, safflower, sunflower, corn and wild rice) plus other crops made feasible by new irrigation programs:

Continued expansion and diversification of the short-line **agricultural implement industry.**

The emergence of the **mining sector** as a major growth industry in

Saskatchewan has opened up several significant areas for new investments:

The **potash and uranium industries** will maintain a dominant share of the world's market:

Other minerals, including recently discovered deposits of gold, copper, zinc, limestone and gypsum remain to be fully exploited:

The **supply and service industries** directly supporting the **mining sector** will continue to offer attractive opportunities for new business ventures.

In the **forestry sector,** there are large volumes of poplar (hardwood) which are uncommitted. Opportunities exist for production of housing and building materials and for applications in the manufacture of hardwood furniture.

Saskatchewan will be undertaking new major investments in **public and industrial infrastructure,** including continued modernization of telecommunications facilities, hydroelectric power installations and petroleum extraction and processing infrastructure. At the same time, the province will also be seeking to attract additional **high-technology firms** which will help to further diversify the province's economy. Advanced-technology firms involved in the design and manufacture of products such as microelectronics instrumentation and process control equipment, as well as telecommunications equipment and supplies are particularly welcome.

Investing in

Alberta

With a population in excess of 2 million people, and gross provincial expenditures totalling $60 billion in 1984, Alberta constitutes a major market for consumer and industrial goods and services. Lead primarily by the oil and gas industry, the provincial economy has enjoyed unprecedented growth over much of the past decade.

Alberta's economy is becoming more diversified. A major transition away from a reliance on the province's traditionally strong natural resource-based industries is emerging, as tourism, health care industries, food processing, and advanced technology industries gain in importance.

The province's labour force is well-educated and highly-motivated. Wages are competitive, and labour-management relations are excellent. Alberta's system of world-class universities and colleges ensures that industry has access to a steady supply of highly-trained workers.

Alberta has an impressive record as an exporting province. The province is working to increase exports to the United States and growing Pacific Rim markets, as well as European countries. The province's modern transportation systems enable the efficient transport of goods and people throughout the province, and provide direct links to major national and international, rail, road, marine and air routes.

The province is endowed with rich and plentiful natural resources. Exploration and development activities in the oil and gas, and mining

41

sectors, will continue to play a major role in Alberta's economic future. In addition, the province's strong agricultural sector will provide substantial economic growth as Alberta-based firms continue to play an increasing role in the processing of food and beverage products.

The province's banking and finance sector, infrastructure for research and development, and telecommunications systems, ensure that businesses located in Alberta receive the services, support and assistance required to compete worldwide.

New investments that contribute to the diversification of the province's industrial base by building on existing strengths are strongly encouraged.

Major new investments in Alberta industry will focus on the development of new production processes and technologies required by traditional industry, as well as the establishment of new advanced industries that will enable the province to diversify its manufacturing base.

In addition to encouraging new investment to enable the expansion of Alberta's traditionally strong industries, such as **oil and gas exploration & development,** and **agricultural production,** the province is committed to the continued growth of new and emerging industries that will facilitate the diversification of Alberta's industrial base, and promote the use of production processes based on advanced technologies. Several major industrial sectors, already given a high priority by the federal and provincial governments, offer significant investment opportunities.

A full spectrum of **advanced technology industries** are being given a high priority by the federal and provincial governments. These industries will benefit from the steady stream of highly trained graduates produced by Alberta's colleges and universities, as well as from the various government, university and industry sponsored research institutes and centres of excellence. Areas being afforded particularly high attention include: electronics, telecommunications, computer systems and laser applications.

Alberta's **food processing** industry, which benefits from an impressive supply of provincially-produced agricultural products, is full of opportunities for new start-ups and expansions of businesses engaged in areas such as: frozen entrees, specialty processed meats and other specialty foods, baked goods, snack foods and condiments.

Tourism remains one of Alberta's most important industries, and expansion of this sector is being encouraged by the provincial government. Alberta's scenic landscape and attractive urban centres provide almost limitless opportunities for tourism-related enterprises throughout the province.

Alberta's **health care products sector** is becoming one of the fastest growing industry sectors in the province. With one of the highest per capita expenditures on health care in the world, Alberta provides a major base of demand for firms involved in the production of pharmaceuticals and other health care products. Firms engaged in R&D activities can tap into Alberta's highly advanced medical resource community for expertise and equipment necessary for success in this challenging field.

Good opportunities exist for firms engaged in the **petrochemical, chemical and plastics industries.** Businesses can take advantage of an established infrastructure to support research and development, as well as production and distribution of end products. An ample supply of feed stock and raw materials is available at competitive prices.

Oil and gas equipment and service industries stand to benefit from the economic spin-offs of major exploration and development projects planned in Alberta for the near future. Industries located in Alberta are also likely to benefit from spin-offs originating from major projects in neighbouring provinces. For example, the $3.5 billion heavy oil upgrader planned for Saskatchewan by Husky Resources is likely to produce numerous spin-offs for Alberta-based firms.

Investment opportunities also exist in the province for the production of **fabricated metal products.** Demand from the petroleum industry is high, and Alberta possesses an abundant supply of minerals required as raw materials.

Investing in

British Columbia

The provincial economy produces over $40 billion in goods and services annually. This high level of output, combined with a population approaching 3 million people, results in an economy that possesses limitless commercial and industrial investment opportunities.

British Columbia's geographic location on Canada's Pacific coast provides businesses located in the province with ready access to the growing markets in Pacific Rim countries, the densely-populated market of the western United States, as well as many European countries.

The province's labour force is well-trained. Wage rates are very competitive and below the national average in many industry sectors. British Columbia's system of universities and community colleges provides industry with a steady supply of well-educated graduates ready to enter the labour force.

The province's economy is undergoing rapid change as the traditional resource industries meet the challenge of a competitive international environment. The development of new technologies necessary to this process augments the growing strength of new manufacturing capabilities in areas as diverse as electronics, ocean industries, and biotechnology. In addition, tourism is the fastest growing industry sector in the province, based on an enormous array of natural scenery and attractions, as well as a strategic location adjacent to rapidly growing Pacific Rim tourism markets.

This wide range of investment opportunities is all the more desirable in a province with abundant and relatively cheap energy resources, a transportation system second to none, and a well established research and development infrastructure.

The province possesses investment opportunities in a wide range of industry sectors, including: ocean and marine-based industries, tourism, telecommunications, and aerospace.

Investments in emerging sectors, as well as in the province's traditionally strong sectors, are equally welcome.

British Columbia's expanding workforce of skilled and educated people, its abundant and moderately priced energy resources, and a strong research and development infrastructure make the province an ideal location for investment. Expansion, new start-ups and the commercial development of innovative technologies will be sought in all industries to further the province's competitive edge in industrial production and productivity. Investment opportunities exist in many sectors of the economy:

The highly skilled labour force and developed infrastructure are incentives for a wide variety of investment in the **telecommunications and electronics industry.** Specifically, opportunities exist in the development and manufacturing of all communications equipment.

In the **ocean industries** investment opportunities exist in all aspects of ocean technology including underwater electronics, cameras, suits, telephones, offshore resource exploration equipment and search and rescue equipment.

In the **fisheries sector** the extensive coastline and favourable environment offer unique opportunities for the development of aquaculture and the production of materials to support this industry.

In the **resource machinery sector** there is a demand for new production techniques, and the development of new equipment.

The **medical supply industry** will continue to expand to keep pace with advancements in medicine. The development of innovations in medical equipment and techniques is a significant area for investors. Developments in **biotechnology** offer important opportunities in both the medical field and in the production of advanced food technology to supply growing export markets.

The **advanced materials sector** offers unlimited opportunities to meet the needs of the province's resource and manufacturing industries including developments in:

advanced metallic materials
advanced ceramics
advanced polymers
advanced composites
surface treatment and modification

The **tourist industry** is expected to grow rapidly building on the province's natural environment and attractive urban centres. Significant opportunities exist in the development of resort facilities.

The **aerospace industry** offers significant opportunities in the development of new and innovative products and new technology for repair and overhaul.

In the **automotive sector,** opportunities exist for the manufacture of parts to supply manufacturing and assembly operations within and outside of Canada.

Investing in
Northwest Territories

Northwest Territories (NWT) is still in a relatively early stage of development, and its extensive renewable and non-renewable resources remain largely untapped. There is plenty of room for new investors and business operators with a strong entrepreneurial spirit and innovative ideas. Start-ups, joint-ventures and business expansions are possible in all areas of economic activity.

More than half the population is of native ancestry, with traditional values and a knowledge of the land which dates back thousands of years. NWT is particularly attractive to entrepreneurs who enjoy small-community life and who seek direct access to the unique northern wilderness.

The population has almost tripled in the last three decades. A reliable system of air transportation now connects most northern communities, and provides vital links to major urban centres in Canada, the United States and Greenland. Improved road facilities link Yellowknife, Hay River and other communities in the southern Mackenzie area directly to Alberta and British Columbia. Communities in the Mackenzie Delta enjoy road access to southern Canada via the Alaska highway system.

The mining and tourism industries have grown significantly in recent years to complement other resource-based activities such as fishing and trapping. Many traditional pursuits now cater to expanding world markets for specialty products such as native arts and crafts, Arctic Ocean and northern freshwater fish, wild furs, and northern game.

Businesses operating or seeking to establish in the Territories can take advantage of NWT's energetic and reliable labour force, as well as its increasingly sophisticated industrial and commercial infrastructure. In addition, northern businesses can access the range of financial and technical services available from the rest of Canada.

The governments of Canada and Northwest Territories strongly support new business ventures and investments in the north, and work closely with entrepreneurs and investors to help them start-up, expand or improve their businesses in the Territories.

Northwest Territories offers **tremendous potential for investment in many sectors.** The diverse resource base provides opportunities not only in resource exploration and extraction industries but also in the related processing and service sectors.

Investments which expand economic and employment opportunities for northern residents and/or reduce NWT's dependence on goods and services imported at great cost from outside the north are particularly welcome. This includes initiatives which take advantage of previously untapped potential as well as business improvements and/or new ventures which increase the local value-added of existing enterprises.

The **mining industry** provides virtually unlimited scope for investment. Of particular interest are new opportunities for exploration and development of unique rare-earth minerals which have high-technology applications. Exploration work is encouraged, and no regulatory control is exercised, other than standard environmental protection safeguards.

The **oil and gas industry** will continue to seek new investments to assist in exploration and development activities. Major opportunities include provision of supplies and support services, improvement of environmental protection equipment and techniques, innovative exploration and drilling technologies, and expanded local refining capacity.

The **renewable resources** of NWT offer opportunities for harvesting and marketing of furs and exotic food products. Development potential exists in fur farming and indigenous livestock ranching (e.g. caribou, muskox, etc.) to satisfy growing interest in world markets.

The **tourism** and **outfitting sectors** are recognized as industries with significant growth potential. Major markets include naturalists, sports enthusiasts, camping and outdoor enthusiasts, and field researchers and scientists. There is a need for capital investments in transportation equipment, accommodation facilities and other amenities, as well as the conservation and/or development of natural, historic and cultural sites and attractions. There is also a need for investment in the development and marketing of packaged tours, and the expansion and improvement of all support services (e.g. supply of food and equipment, provision of visitor and tourist services, etc.).

The **retail trade and service sectors** offer possibilities for new businesses and expansions to meet the needs of government agencies, communities and the oil and gas industry. Preferential policies for purchasing and contracting are in place for resident NWT firms supplying goods and services to government and to the mining and oil & gas industries.

Joint-venturing with native economic development corporations and native businesses is strongly encouraged, and offers many attractions:

Involvement of peoples accustomed to the northern environment, and knowledgeable of local business conditions:

Access to native-controlled capital resources:

Special incentives and other support for recruitment and training of local workers.

Investing in

Yukon

The Territory's abundant supplies of precious metals, and promising supplies of emerging rare-earth minerals, combined with recent major oil and gas discoveries, mean that natural resource development will continue to play a major role in Yukon's long-term economic future.

Yukon's rich cultural history and magnificent scenic wilderness combine to make the Territory one of Canada's most exciting tourist attractions.

In addition, opportunities in Yukon's growing renewable resource sector, especially in agriculture and forestry, are expected to increase as development of this major sector of the territorial economy continues to improve.

The efficient transportation system operating in Yukon is based on a network of major highways which enable the economic shipment of goods throughout the Territory as well as to southern Canada, Alaska, and NWT. The system also includes a reliable air transportation network which links a number of Yukon communities, and connects Yukon to urban centres in southern Canada. In addition to the large number of visitors to Yukon from all parts of Canada and the U.S., an increasing number of people are travelling to Yukon from European countries.

A high proportion of the labour force is well-trained, and has earned a university or college degree or diploma. The local labour force provides employers with a reliable source of highly-motivated workers who are knowledgeable of Yukon's natural environment and cultural heritage.

The Territory's abundant supplies of precious metals, and promising supplies of emerging rare-earth minerals, combined with recent major oil and gas discoveries, mean that natural resource development will continue to play a major role in Yukon's long-term economic future. In addition, opportunities in Yukon's growing renewable resource sector are expected to increase as development of this major sector of the territorial economy continues to improve.

The Governments of Yukon and Canada attach a very high importance to the attraction of new business investment in Yukon. Government programs are in place to assist investors wishing to establish new businesses, or to expand and improve existing enterprises. Investments in the Territory's mineral-based industries, as well as in newly-emerging business opportunities, are strongly encouraged.

Yukon's wealth of mineral resources, superb natural environment, and rich cultural history will serve as the primary source of economic expansion in the Territory over the short and medium term. Investments which can build on these inherent strengths, and which at the same time take advantage of Yukon's stable and well-trained labour force, will have the greatest chance for success. The Government of Canada, and the Yukon Government are working together to ensure that potential investors are provided the support and assistance required to start-up, expand and/or modernize Yukon businesses.

Yukon's **mineral reserves** continue to provide significant investment opportunities. Especially promising supplies of rare earth minerals are likely to increase in importance as industrial and commercial products using innovative, advanced materials become more popular. In addition, numerous deposits of metals such as gold, silver, zinc, and lead have been discovered, but have not yet been developed. With modern, more efficient extraction techniques, placer gravel deposits distributed in a large number of Yukon river valleys provide as good a potential for the successful extraction of gold as they have for the last one-hundred years.

The growing **tourism sector** is already demonstrating significant potential for economic growth and success. Local firms are emerging to provide a wide range of goods and services to the growing number of tourists visiting Yukon from other parts of Canada, the U.S., and overseas countries. New business initiatives range from the restoration of the town of Dawson City to its original beauty and heritage, as part of the Klondike National Historic Site, the the development of recreational vehicle parks throughout Yukon, and the expansion of commercial tourist attractions in Carcross.

The five-year Canada-Yukon **Tourism Subsidiary Agreement,** signed in May 1985, provides a $10 million fund to help the private sector capitalize on the wide range of opportunities available.

Renewable resources continue to play a key role in the Yukon economy, and will play an even greater role as a result of the **Renewable Resources Sub-Agreement** signed by the federal and Yukon governments in 1985. Under this agreement, $4.2 million will be made available by the two governments over a four year period to encourage the growth of Yukon's renewable resource sector by assisting private businesses in the start-up of new initiatives, or the improvement of existing operations. Particularly promising opportunities for the expansion of business operations based on renewable resources include **agriculture** and **forestry.** Opportunities also exist for establishing modern sawmills in southeast Yukon, perhaps in joint-venture with local native development corporations.

Native and local arts and crafts firms possess considerable scope for new investment. Assistance in the identification and development of new markets provides the greatest opportunity. Many local firms have already demonstrated their ability to successfully serve Canadian, U.S. and overseas markets. However, numerous firms still require expansion of marketing and distribution networks in order to significantly increase their scale of operations. In addition, many firms could become even more profitable with improvements to their production processes.

Preferential purchasing policies are in place to assist Yukon-based companies. Firms willing to assist in the training of local personnel are especially welcome.

Priority sector opportunities

Investing in
Canada's Biotechnology Industry

Canada constitutes a major market for biotechnological products and services in a wide range of areas. Canada is also a major exporter, making the country an ideal location for firms seeking access to the prime U.S., European and Asian markets.

Canada's traditional strengths in the natural resources sector will provide substantial opportunities for long-term returns on investment in biotechnology catering to agriculture, forestry and mineral production. With a sizeable manufacturing base, high per capita incomes, and increasing concern over environmental protection and resource conservation in Canada, there also are major opportunities for biotechnology developments in fields such as health care, waste treatment, synthetic materials production and industrial processes.

Canada has a comprehensive network of university, government and industry research facilities already in place. All three sectors recognize the importance of cooperation in order to develop successful commercial products and services.

☐Following are sectors where commercial applications of biotechnology are most promising and immediate. Significant opportunities also exist in other fields. These opportunities are made even more promising given Canada's ready access to U.S., European and Asian markets.

Agri-food industry (especially agricultural products, animal veterinary products, enzymes, additives, sweetners and new protein products)

metal extraction and recovery

waste treatment process system development and consulting services (especially processing of food, animal, and pulp & paper wastes)

pharmaceutical and biological industries (niches of particular interest include monoclonal antibodies, diagnostic kits, vaccines and anti-toxins, veterinary medicines, blood products and cancer treatment pharmaceuticals)

specialty chemicals and **energy production** (especially processes involving the conversion of cellulosic biomass)

☐Since Canada's biotechnology industry is still in an early stage of growth, investment opportunities exist for the development of the **commercial infrastructure required to test, market and distribute new products and processes.**

Investing in
Canada's Machinery Industry

Canada's domestic machinery market of C$17.5 billion provides a solid base of demand for machinery products and related materials and services.

Location in Canada gives direct access to lucrative U.S. markets, where Canadian firms are major suppliers.

Canada's machinery industry is strongly export-oriented; Canada offers a pipeline to major European, Pacific Rim and other overseas markets.

Canada's machinery industry is highly diversified — both in terms of the range of goods produced and the size and location of firms. Start-ups are easy, and welcome in all regions.

Firms which can help Canada further penetrate U.S. and overseas markets and/or reduce Canada's levels of foreign imports will be especially welcome.

The industry is strong and buoyant; earnings and profits remained significant even throughout the world-wide recession. Shipments, exports, profits and new capital investments are all growing rapidly.

Canada's healthy and diverse machinery sector provides great scope for investment. Some of the areas where growth potential is particularly high include:

☐**Machinery and equipment for the electronics industries (North American market: $1,200 million)**
  e.g.
  equipment for semi-conductor production
  automated component-handling devices
  assembly equipment

☐**Equipment and processes for pulp & paper production (North American market: $2,300 million)**
  e.g.
  processes to increase pulp yields and reduce chemical consumption
  equipment for production of fine papers

☐**Environmental equipment (North American market: $2,500-3,000 million)**
  e.g.
  sewage & waste water treatment equipment
  air pollution control equipment
  solid waste control devices

☐**Specialized machine tools and material handling equipment (North American market: $1,000 million)**

☐**Food processing equipment (North American market: $3,700 million)**
  e.g.
  fruit & vegetable canning equipment
  freezing & packaging systems

Investing in
Canada's Automotive Industry

The total value of shipments of Canadian manufactured vehicles and parts reached an all-time high in 1985.

Under the Canada-U.S. *Auto Pact,* Canadian firms producing new automobiles, trucks, buses and original equipment parts, with 50% North American content, can export duty-free to the United States. (Approximately 97% of Canadian automotive exports to the U.S. fall under the *Auto Pact.*)

The Canadian industry is comprised of a number of internationally-competitive vehicle assemblers as well as numerous parts and accessory manufacturers.

Recent levels of new capital expenditures, and innovative production processes will produce a wide range of economic spin-offs and investment opportunities.

Firms which can help Canada further penetrate North American and overseas markets are especially welcome.

Canada's strong and growing automotive industry provides a wide range of investment and joint-venture opportunities in traditional, emerging and innovative areas, e.g.:

Substantial economic spin-offs are likely to occur from **new major assembly start-ups and modernizations.**

The movement toward **plastic and ceramic parts** and accessories will create new areas of demand.

Computerized **electronic control systems** for suspension, braking and other functions constitute a major growth market.

Many opportunities exist to produce domestically a wide range of **products currently imported** into Canada.

Changes in the purchasing patterns of assemblers are also creating opportunities for the production and marketing of complete or integrated **automotive systems,** such as:

  seating systems
  braking systems
  dashboard display and control systems

The demand for new and improved **production process control techniques** such as bar coding, just-in-time delivery, and statistical process control will present new and major challenges in the original equipment parts sector.

Investing in
Canada's Telecommunications Equipment Industry

Canada's domestic market for telecommunications equipment and related components offers a base of demand for a wide range of products and related services. The total Canadian domestic market and total Canadian shipments of telecommunications equipment and components both reached all-time high levels in 1985.

Canada is a major exporter of telecommunications equipment and components. Since 1981, one-half to three-quarters of more of Canadian production has been destined for export markets. Location in Canada gives ready access to U.S., European and Asian markets.

Canada has consistently been at the forefront of technological and industrial innovations in the telecommunications field, and Canadian-based firms invest heavily in research and development as well as capital expansions and improvements.

Foreign investments, joint ventures and licencing arrangements are all welcome.

☐ Canadian experience in providing telecommunications services to sparsely populated areas in remote locations makes Canada a perfect location for investors wishing to develop, manufacture and market telecommunications **products and services for export to developing countries.**

☐ The early commitment of the Canadian telecommunications industry to digital technology puts it in a good position to install and exploit the benefits of **Integrated Services Digital Networks** which will become the backbone of modern communications networks in the 1990s. Canadian trials are beginning in 1986; substantial spin-offs are likely to occur.

☐ Specific areas that combine Canada's competitive advantages with prospects for strong market growth, include:

data communications (including local and wide area private data networks) and **data switching** (North American market projected to triple by 1990)

fibre optic communications systems, for long-distance, high-speed voice, data and video transmission as well as local distribution (North American market forecast to quadruple by 1990)

mobile personal communications, including paging, mobile telephone and, in the future, satelite-based systems.

☐ Investments that promote **advanced engineering and sophisticated production techniques** and that respond to the **needs of leading telecommunications markets** in Canada and around the world are especially welcome.

Investing in
Canada's Electronics Industry

Canada's strong domestic market for advanced technology products and the success of Canadian-based firms in penetrating foreign markets have resulted in an industry that can support firms of all sizes. Large multinationals, medium and small Canadian businesses, and subsidiaries of foreign firms all currently operate in Canada. New investors can gain from this large pool of expertise present in the Canadian industry.

Firms located in Canada also have access to the steady supply of well-trained graduates from Canadian universities and colleges. As well, university and government research centres assist industry in the search for new technology.

The Government of Canada, provincial governments and municipalities provide assistance to individuals and companies wishing to invest in Canada. In addition, Canada's tax system encourages investment and no restrictions are placed on the transfer of profits out of the country.

The Canadian electronics industry is competitive in world markets. In 1985, exports reached $5.1 billion — an all-time high. Firms located in Canada can benefit from established trade links with countries located around the world.

The **consumer electronics** sector continues as a major source of demand for electronics products. Among the wealthiest people in the world, Canadians are already large consumers of new, innovative products. Consumer demand is expected to increase for new-technology products such as large-screen stereo televisions, video cassette recorders and compact disc players. **Automotive electronics,** especially car radios and electronic subsystems and components, will also be in high demand.

In the **microelectronics industry,** the demand by Canadian telecommunications suppliers and the generous government funding provided to Canadian reserach centres and universities provide an attractive base for new investment.

Opportunities in the **instrumentation and process control** sector involve serving Canada's numerous resource-based industries, especially firms in the pulp and paper, forestry, and mining industries. In addition, many of Canada's manufacturing industries require advanced electronic instrumentation, as does the health care sector.

Investing in
Canada's Advanced Ceramics Industry

Canadian industry recognizes the growing importance of advanced ceramic materials in the development of new and innovative products and the improvement of Canada's traditional industries and processes.

Canada boasts a long scientific tradition in advanced ceramics, with a strong international focus. University as well as federal and provincial government laboratories are actively involved in the search for commercially-viable applications of advanced ceramics. Canadian industry is undertaking research in private sector laboratories. All sectors cooperate in the sharing of ideas and facilities.

Established and successful Canadian firms in a wide variety of industry sectors are actively seeking partners to join with them in the discovery, development and marketing of innovative products employing advanced ceramics.

☐ The market for advanced **structural** ceramics is expected to be strong. Technology transfer is the preferred method of getting into the market, followed by new product development. Future success depends upon innovative approaches to create new markets by developing new applications. Some future opportunities for new products include:

non-engine applications, e.g.
  chemical pumps
  steel fabrication parts
  machinery parts and cutting tools
  consumer products
engine applications

☐ Opportunities also exist for the processing of advanced **ceramic powders.** The following powders present the greatest opportunities:

silicon carbide powders
silicon nitride powders
zirconia powders
boron nitride powders

CHAPTER 2

Canada-U.S. Free Trade: The Outlook for Trade and Investment

Extracted with permission from newsletters published by Clarkson Gordon/Woods Gordon, members of Arthur Young International

Canada and the U.S. signed a Free Trade Agreement on January 3, 1988. The Agreement is designed to reduce trade barriers between the two countries, and expand the cross-border flow of goods, services and investment. If ratified by the legislatures of both countries, implementation will begin on January 1, 1989.

Implications for Canada-U.S. Trade

The Free Trade Agreement eliminates all tariffs on Canada-U.S. trade by 1999, some immediately, some over five or ten years. Other trade barriers will be reduced, by prohibiting import or export restrictions, harmonizing product standards, liberalizing government procurement, and easing restraints on imports of services. Existing trade law governing countervailing and antidumping duties remains in effect, but appeals of trade disputes to a binational panel will be possible, and new trade laws will be negotiated over the next 7 years. The Agreement provides both countries with limited protection against the imposition of new trade barriers.

These provisions will make that portion of Canada's merchandise exports to the U.S. which have been subject to duties — about 20% of the total — more price competitive in U.S. markets. Liberalizing bids for government procurement will give Canadian access to some $4 billion in U.S. purchases. Harmonizing product standards could reduce the costs and time required for many Canadian manufacturers to qualify their products for sale in the U.S.

At the same time, the Free Trade Agreement will reduce tariffs for U.S. exports into Canada, give American multinationals an opportunity to rationalize their North American operations, and will make Canadian markets much more competitive, forcing, domestic producers to seek ways to differentiate on quality and service, and produce cost-effectively.

The Agreement has specific implications for a number of sectors, including the automotive industry, agriculture, wine and distilled spirits, energy, telecommunications, computer services, and textiles, among others.

Overall, the Free Trade Agreement is expected to expand Canada-U.S. trade, which at $130 billion is already the largest trading relationship in the world.

Implications for Investment

The Free Trade Agreement commits both countries to give investors from either country "national treatment", which means that investors will be allowed to establish new businesses in the other country, and operate them under the same rules as apply to domestic firms. While Canada retains the right to review the acquisition of firms in Canada by U.S. investors, higher thresholds for review have been agreed to. These initiatives in the Free Trade Agreement are consistent with the more "open for business" approach that Canada has taken toward foreign investment in recent years.

In general, the Free Trade Agreement will make it easier for companies investing in Canada to obtain access to markets in the United States, and vice versa.

Implications for Exporters to Canada and the U.S.

Firms which export products to Canada or the U.S. which are further processed before being sold in North American markets will need to become familiar with the "rules of origin" in the Free Trade Agreement. These rules of origin will be used to determine whether goods manufactured from imported materials will qualify for duty reductions based on the Agreement.

The rules of origin are based on the new Harmonized System (HS) of tariff classification, which Canada, and other international traders have developed and adopted. Generally speaking, goods imported into Canada or the U.S. from third countries under one tariff commodity classification must be processed sufficiently so that they fit under another commodity classification in the HS to be eligible for duty reductions under the Free Trade Agreement.

The Agreement indicates the specific tariff classification changes required for various articles to qualify under the rules of origin. In some cases, the new rules of origin are tougher than current practices, but in other cases (such as garments, for example) the new rules are more liberal.

In addition, the Free Trade Agreement restricts the ability of Canada or the U.S. to offer duty remissions or similar programs to importers, and requires the phase-out of existing programs. It is vital that exporters to Canada and the U.S. understand the specific implications of the Free Trade Agreement for their products.

The Debate About Freer Trade

The Free Trade Agreement has been approved by the U.S. Administration and the Canadian Government. However, both the U.S. Congress and the Canadian Parliament must approve the deal in 1988 for it to be implemented. Debate continues in both countries about the wisdom of the Agreement.

In Canada, the two major Opposition parties, and three provinces, are opposed to the deal. The essence of the debate is whether the Free Trade

Agreement will lead to more jobs as Canadian exports to the U.S. expand, or fewer jobs, due to higher U.S. imports and rationalization by U.S. multinationals of their Canadian operations.

In the U.S., the debate is part of that country's more general concern about its trade performance, and whether more protectionist laws will provide a solution. If Congress passes an Omnibus Trade Bill in 1988, the Canadian Government hopes that as a result of the Free Trade Agreement, Canada will be exempted from some of its more protectionist provisions.

Stay Tuned

It is impossible to predict how these debates will be resolved, particularly since 1988 is an election year in the U.S., and there will be a federal election in Canada in 1988 or 1989. Our advice to firms doing business with either country is to monitor events closely, and ensure that they are aware of the implications of the Free Trade Agreement for their products. We believe that prudent business executives are now developing strategies based on the assumption that free trade will proceed, and are incorporating contingency plans in the event that it does not.

Our experience in analysing the Agreement on behalf of clients is that generalizations are frequently incorrect, and it is important to assess each case individually. The approach we have used in working with our clients is as follows:

1. Develop an in-depth understanding of the relevant parts of the Agreement, and of the 50 other pieces of Canadian, American, and international legislation which are affected by the Agreement.
2. Acquire a broad understanding of the overall competitive situation in the relevant markets on both sides of the border.
3. Design an appropriate strategic response to the new pressures stemming from free trade — develop a plan, research market opportunities, consider ways to improve productivity and effectiveness, and assess tax implications.

We have learned that this approach leads to creative ideas and action plans that substantially improve the competitive position in the North American marketplace.

Canada - U.S. forecasts

Extracted from the 'econoscope' by kind permission of the Royal Bank of Canada

During the first half of 1987, the U.S. economy expanded at a 3.4% annualized rate with the focus of growth being inventory investment and net exports. Final domestic demand, following several years of consumer-led strength, had weakened. In the third quarter, however, final domestic demand strengthened considerably, while both inventory accumulation and net exports softened, giving rise to a 4.1% annualized real growth rate.

During the next two years, the focus of U.S. economic growth is expected to shift toward net exports, complementing buoyant business investment. We expect the U.S. economy to expand by 2% in 1988 and 2.4% in 1989. Growth, however, will be very slow in the first half of 1988 as the stock market crash manifests itself through weaker increases in consumer and business spending. By the second half of 1988, however, most of the negative consequences of the crash should have abated. Consumption should begin to expand, albeit slowly, reflecting moderate income growth and continued balance sheet restructuring. A gradual pick-up in consumer-goods production should combine with brisk activity in export-oriented industries, the latter already firmly underway. Business spending on fixed investment should then begin to increase, reflecting rising utilization rates and the re-activation of investment projects shelved following the crash.

Meanwhile, U.S. inflation has slowed significantly since earlier in the year and is expected to remain moderate over the near term, hovering under the 5% mark. Interest rates are expected to rise only moderately as the Fed gradually withdraws the strong dose of liquidity injected after the stock market crash. The outlook for the U.S. dollar remains bearish during the next two years, since the current account deficit is expected to decline only gradually from US$155 billion this year to US$140 billion in 1989. Although the trade deficit will almost certainly show an improvement due to cumulative declines in the U.S. dollar and a combination of lower domestic demand growth in the United States and higher domestic demand growth overseas, some of the improvement will be offset by higher service charges related to the rising foreign indebtedness. The U.S. government deficit reduction package recently announced will not likely be sufficient to bring the deficit down to its $144 billion Gramm-Rudman target in fiscal 1988, particularly in light of the economic slowdown expected in 1988. The persistence of these twin deficits — budget and trade — will continue to exact a toll on financial market stability. Consequently we believe that the major risk to the forecast is on the downside and that there is a one in three chance of recession occuring during the next two years.

During the first three quarters of 1987, the Canadian economy expanded at a annualized rate of 5.5%. For the most part, Canada's economic growth has been much more balanced than that in the United States. Consumer spending has been brisk, particularly on durable goods such as household furnishings, appliances and automobiles. Residential construction has been very strong, particularly in central Canada and British Columbia, and business investment has been buoyant with outlays on plant and machinery expanding briskly after several years of weakness.

During the next two years, the focus of Canadian economic growth is expected to mirror closely that of the United States; improving net exports, strong business investment and constrained consumer spending. In addition, business investment is expected to become increasingly expansion-oriented instead of modernization-oriented, reflecting rising utilization rates and expanding export opportunities. Consumer spending is expected to soften, although not to the same degree as in the United States, since household balance sheets are in better shape than their U.S. counterparts. As well, with Canadians holding less wealth in the form of equities than Americans, consumer confidence has likely been less affected by the stock market crash. On balance, real economic growth is expected to decline from an estimated 3.6% in 1987 to an average close to 2.5% a year in the next two years. Meanwhile, inflation is expected to remain below the 5% mark and the Canadian dollar is expected to trade in the 75 to 77 U.S. cent range.

CHAPTER 3

Betty Lee

Spacious New Brunswick offers good life and business prospects

Betty Lee came to Canada in 1963 from Singapore to study at Montreal's McGill University where she met and married a Malaysian Chinese. The couple decided that prospects were better in Canada than in Asia and they decided to stay.

After graduation they lived for four year in Quebec City but by 1974 had arrived in Fredericton, New Brunswick where they live today.

When the Lees lived in Quebec City they took a six-week camping tour to New Brunswick and liked the countryside so much they decided to try to move there and leave "big city" life behind.

"Both my husband and I come from big city backgrounds and after we had seen New Brunswick we thought that maybe city life, with all its many attractions and diversions, was not so good for the family."

"Then a career opportunity came up at the University of New Brunswick and that really made our decision for us. Also at that time in Quebec were the most turbulent years of the separatist movement and that was another reason why we decided to leave."

"We liked Montreal and Quebec City very much, especially the cosmopolitan atmosphere in Montreal, and we still like to go back for visits."

"I don't honestly think Chinese people value outdoor life but a lot of them value spaciousness; we lived in Hong Kong for three years and we certainly know what crowdedness is like; you can hear what your next door neighbour is talking about or even neighbours two apartments away because everyone lives so close together."

"Here in New Brunswick no matter how well off you are or how poor you are you still have so much space to be on your own and to have your privacy."

"And if you live in a big city you tend not to have close friends but in a smaller city like Fredericton people are very close: I know almost everyone on my street and we keep in touch; all the women have a coffee group and at New Year we even have a dance in one of the people's homes. In Hong Kong or even Singapore you don't have this closeness."

"If I go on holiday I don't have to worry: I just drop my keys off at a neighbours; in fact I am holding several bunches of keys at the moment for neighbours who have gone away."

"This is a kind of life we really enjoy and in the big city you don't have this kind of thing."

"I have been in contact with a lot of new immigrants who come to

Fredericton and they really don't have any trouble getting along; everyone is so very, very close and friendly."

There are approximately 200 Chinese Canadians in Fredericton and an estimated 2,000 province-wide and so Chinese immigrants live in predominantly non-Chinese communities.

"Whether new immigrants are happy in these communities where there are relatively few Chinese people depends on their philosophy and outlook."

"If they say they don't want to leave the Chinese community and they still want typical Chinese food then they won't be able to get that here."

"But if they think they are coming here to earn a living and raise a family and to try to adapt to a new environment then I think it's a good idea to come to New Brunswick and the Maritimes." (The Maritimes are Canada's east coast provinces of New Brunswick, Nova Scotia, Newfoundland and Prince Edward Island).

"I feel the Maritimes is a land full of opportunities; rich in resources — you name it and we've probably got every kind of resources here — and especially for Asians who are mostly very hard working people I would say this is the place to be."

New Brunswick is the second largest of Canada's four Atlantic provinces; resource rich; a major port; eager to diversify its industrial base.

"A lot of Hong Kong people have been involved with the garment industry and a lot of New Brunswick people are very good with their hands — they make a lot of craft products. I am trying to relate garment making and craft manufacture to show that New Brunswick has ample skilled labour on hand if people from Hong Kong want to come here and get involved in the garment industry."

"In Hong Kong many women were engaged on a piece-work basis in knitting clothes for sale in North America and here there are many women who knit beautifully."

"I can't speak for other provinces but I can say that here in New Brunswick there are a lot of skilled people available just waiting to serve you; because of competition for labour it may not be like this in other provinces such as Ontario."

"And since they have the basic skills the people are very trainable.

"Also the provincial government and the federal government help so much with different programs to assist new business."

"For example, I myself am trying to set up a small food processing business myself but because of the cost involved it makes me wonder if I should risk all my savings all at once. If I lost I would lose my whole life but if I get some kind of incentive from the government which means that I don't have to take 100 per cent risk it gives me more encouragement to go ahead and invest and start my business."

"This is especially important for someone coming from overseas to a new environment where they are being asked to invest a quarter of a million dollars all at once. There is so much uncertainty and the risk is very high."

"Actually I think an investment of C$250,000 from a new immigrant is rather a lot for Hong Kong people; if you multiply by six to arrive at the Hong Kong equivalent it's one-and-a-half million Hong Kong dollars; it's really a lot of money. When you ask for such a high amount people will have second thoughts about it. It might be better if the sum asked of new investors was closer to C$100,000 so that the risks are less. With a hundred thousand you can do a lot in a small business."

"For investors who decide to come here to make and sell products the markets are not really here in New Brunswick because we don't have even one million in population but they can aim at the whole of Canada or at export markets like the United States."

"We have unemployment in Canada but there are lots of things we import which could be made here so definitely there is a market and an opportunity if people want to come here and invest."

"Overhead costs will be much lower in New Brunswick than in Ontario because land is less expensive and all kind of other costs are cheaper."

"There is even an over-land freight subsidy from the Atlantic provinces to the major central Canadian markets although things like garments or electronic products which are light weight are not likely to be sensitive to freight costs anyway and may even be able to be shipped by air."

"Real estate development is another area of opportunity in this province but if I have to make a list of possible investment areas I would say garments, wood working — we have plenty of wood around here and a lot of skilled craftsmen. In Hong Kong there are many furniture manufacturers and some of them may want to come here."

"And I think there could be a future here for high technology industries because we have excellent universities here and lots of scope for industry-university co-operation."

"Steps are being taken to get an incubator mall in Fredericton to allow us to establish a base to feed off the universities and build "high-tech" industries here for the benefit of the region."

BUILD A PROSPEROUS NEW FUTURE IN NEW BRUNSWICK, CANADA

在新伯倫瑞克省創造您美好的將來

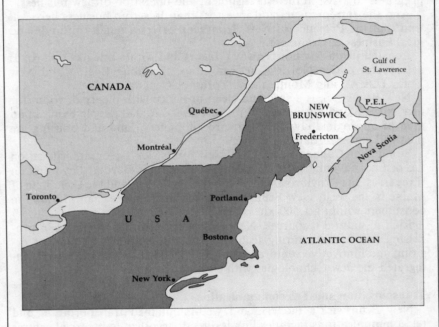

Business oriented . . . room to grow . . . plenty of low cost land and housing . . . ample energy . . . and SAME DAY ACCESS TO ONE OF NORTH AMERICA'S RICHEST MARKETS!

「天時、地利、人和」
三者兼而有之。

63

New Brunswick Committed to Attracting Entrepreneurs

Overview

The Government of New Brunswick has made a firm commitment to attracting entrepreneurs and investors to the province. Through the Department of Commerce and Technology it offers a variety of incentive programs to assist in the establishment and operation of new business.

And the entrepreneurs and investors that do set up business here will find that the Province of New Brunswick offers a quality lifestyle and ideal business environment.

Located just a few hours away (via air) and within one day (via road) are several major North American cities, including Boston and New York, U.S.A., and Montreal and Toronto, Canada.

New Brunswick is a safe and clean province with plenty of room for new citizens and businesses. With just over 720,000 people living in an area of approximately 72,000 square kilometers, land and housing are plentiful and affordable.

Situated on Canada's east coast, New Brunswick's geographic location has distinct advantages for its business community. Bordered by water on three sides, the Province of Quebec in the northwest, and the U.S. State of Maine in the west, New Brunswick has access to more than 110 million consumers within a 1,600 km radius.

Rich in natural resources, New Brunswick also has the latest in processing and manufacturing technologies; and examples abound of exciting and innovative ventures in the Province which have effectively integrated the new technologies with existing resources.

Transportation and Telecommunications

New Brunswick's modern and well-maintained transportation and telecommunications facilities link it directly to other commercial centres across North America and around the world.

The transportation system ensures that people and products reach their destinations quickly and efficiently. New Brunswick highways are connected to all major transportation routes in adjoining provinces and in the United States. New Brunswick is served by year-round deep water ports, and the Port of Saint John is one of the busiest and best-equipped ports on the Atlantic seaboard, serving as a regular stop for many international shipping lines. New Brunswick has 10 airports, five of which are serviced daily by commercial carriers, with both passenger and freight service.

New Brunswick is directly connected to Canada's state-of-the-art national and international telecommunications networks, including sophisticated voice, image and data facilities. The Province's Fibre Optic Transmission System (FOTS) should be completed by 1990.

The Business Environment and Incentive Programs

The Government of New Brunswick fosters an environment conducive to the establishment and operation of new businesses, and believes very strongly in the free exchange of investment across provincial and national borders.

It promotes outside investment while encouraging local entrepreneurship. This has meant that while New Brunswick has a flourishing homegrown industry, it has also attracted investment from other parts of Canada, the United States, Europe and Asia.

In addition, with direct land access to major United States markets, and excellent air and sea connections to other key markets around the world, New Brunswick is a key exporter. Nearly 30% of its production is destined for foreign markets, with the U.S. accounting for 70% of total exports.

The New Brunswick Department of Commerce and Technology is responsible for the promotion and development of the manufacturing and processing sectors of the provincial economy.

While the maintenance and expansion of the existing industry base continues to receive much attention and promotion, the Department also directs its attention to the development of new products and technologies, and to expanding markets. Specific sectors of interest for new investment promotion are the pharmaceutical, medical, electronic and garment industries.

To encourage business development in the Province a variety of incentives is offered in the form of grants, loans, bond and loan guarantees, and venture capital financing.

The Department also provides various other services designed to cut red tape and facilitate smooth and quick completion of projects. The Department is able to provide business contacts, plant location analysis, information on joint ventures, licensing arrangements and patents, assistance in dealing with the necessary government departments, and access to specialists in all aspects of business, including financial planning, energy management, tariff documentation, and marketing.

Education and Training

Responsive to the demands of the labour-market, the Province's post-secondary education system, composed of four universities and nine community college campuses, has made available a wide range of professional and technical training programs.

These programmes, together with the traditional arts and science programmes — many of which are offered to the graduate level — are easily accessible to New Brunswick residents at the 17 post-secondary centers located throughout the province. This, coupled with an excellent primary and secondary school system, has resulted in a labour force that is well-educated, adaptable and productive. In addition, New Brunswick's pool of human resources is one of the most stable and dedicated in North America.

Language and Culture
New Brunswick is Canada's first officially bilingual province, and offers services in both English and French. Because of its long history of linguistic and cultural quality, its citizens are very open to new ideas, new cultures and new friends.

There is a province-wide multicultural association which aims to facilitate communication and understanding between persons of various cultural backgrounds. It assists new arrivals in the community by providing material assistance, referral service and language and citizenship orientation, and it also encourages and promotes the concept of multiculturalism.

Lifestyle
When the business day is done, New Brunswick offers its residents a variety of lifestyles. Known as Canada's 'Picture Province', New Brunswick is characterized by deep forests and rolling hills, interspersed with countless rivers, lakes and streams.

New Brunswick has all the advantages of a large centre without the accompanying problems. Urban centres provide all the amenities of any modern city including art and cultural centres, theatres, museums, excellent shopping facilities and transportation systems. The lush countryside is just minutes away from the cities, and more than 163,000 acres is designated parkland where sandy beaches, hiking, canoeing, golfing and sea or fresh-water fishing can be enjoyed.

All in all, New Brunswick is the ideal place in which to build a prosperous new future. We have the resources, the technology, and the people; in addition, we have the lifestyle. Come and join us and build your new future in New Brunswick — Canada.

新伯倫瑞克省全力吸納投資移民

綱要

　　新伯倫瑞克省政府對吸納投資移民不費餘力，省府的商業及科技部特設有各類的支助計劃以協助新成立的工商業。

　　新省位於加拿大東岸，三面環海，魁北克省鄰於西北，而西接美國緬因州，面積有七萬二平方公里，而人口約七十二萬，新省各地皆可以"市容整潔"冠之。

在新省方圓1,600公里的消費者數目達一億一千萬，鄰近的北美洲主要城市如波士頓、紐約、滿地可、多倫多皆可從新省以空陸交通直達。新省除有豐富的天然資源外，更有先進的工業及製造業。

鑑於新省具有以上理想的居住及經商環境，所以工商業成功的例子屢見不鮮。

交通及通訊

新省的先進交通與電訊系統可媲美世界各地。陸路方面，公路網與鄰近城市及北美各地貫通無阻。海路運輸則四季運作如常，而聖約翰港更是大西洋海岸最繁忙的深水港之一，國際船務運輸絡驛不絕。新省共有機場十個，其中半數每日皆有乘客及貨物往來。

新省的電訊系統乃加拿大及全球通訊網的一部份，設備先進，與世界各地的電訊交通片刻無斷。而新裝置的光學纖維傳達系統專於1990年落成啓用。

商業與投資環境

新省政府現正碣力為投資者締造理想的商業環境。省府更強調自由貿易及資金交流的重要，積極推廣外貿及鼓勵本地企業乃省府一貫措施。因此，新省可吸收到從加拿大各省、美國、歐洲及亞洲各地的投資。

由於海、陸、空各路交通方便，新省出口貿易蓬勃，外銷額近生產總值的三成，其中七成銷往美國。省府的商業及科技部乃負責工商業發展的官方部門，除加強現有的工商業外，此部門更註重市場拓展和發展新科技及新產品。現受省府註視的工業計有藥品及醫療工業、電子和製衣業。

由於鼓勵工商業發展，省府特設有各項的資金援助、貸款、債券集資及貸款擔保等。商業及科技部還設有其他服務以確保投資計劃可順利及快速完成，其中包括提供客戶及生意聯絡、經營地點分析、台資、生產執照及專利等的援助。省府更樂於協助投資者與政府及有關部門聯絡及安排其與專業官員商討一切有關財務策劃、能源管理、進出口文件及市場推廣等事宜。

教育與在職進修

除一般中、小學教育外，新省有四所大學及九所工專學院提供各項文憑、學位及研究院課程以供應當地對高等教育的需求及為居民提供進修機會。因此，新省擁有高質素的人力資源。

語言與文娛

新省乃加拿大最早接受英、法雙語制。因此，當地居民對新觀念、新文化及各種族皆能適應自如。省內各地更設有多元文化組織以求達到種族間的互相瞭解和溝通。爲協助新移民適應當地生活，省府設有多項語言、物質及人事的援助。

生活方式

新省享有"詩畫之鄉"的美譽，林木豐盛、山色醉人、河川湖泊、縱橫交錯，工餘之時，置身其中，別有一番意景。

此外，新省具有現代化都市的一切文娛、交通及購物設備，而城市與郊外相隔祇是咫尺之地，全省共有163,000公畝之地被劃爲公園、海灘、高爾夫球場、划舟及垂釣等地點。

總括來說，新省乃建立你美好將來的理想地點，我們的生活方式、天然資源、人力及科技皆爲你所用。在此我們衷心歡迎你。

CHAPTER 4

Oscar Wong

Lack of information conceals numerous opportunities in Halifax and Nova Scotia

The economic outlook in Nova Scotia and the prospects for immigrants from Hong Kong and the Far East are extremely good according to Halifax physician Dr. Oscar Wong, a prominent leader of the Nova Scotia Chinese Society.

"I first went to Toronto 20 years ago when I look at a city like Halifax today I can see similarities. Toronto then was not like it is today and I can imagine that five or 10 years down the road Halifax will become a boom city."

"People who want to invest always like to be the first ones in because when something becomes well established you face a lot of competition and a lot of obstacles so as far as Halifax is concerned I would suggest that now is the time to come."

"For Halifax to become a boom city, first, the government has to be willing to help the new immigrant or investor and I am quite sure that our government has this will; second, you have to look at the people; I think the people here are ready for a boom; they are extremely friendly and helpful and this is an essential part of a city becoming a good place for people to live; third, our education system is very good here; we have 10 or more institutions of higher education in a province of 875,000 people so per capita we have more opportunities for people to have higher education than in the bigger cities."

"Halifax is not an isolated city as some people think; we are only two hours by air from Toronto or New York, one hour from Boston and Montreal and only six hours from London, England."

"We also have a harbour that's never frozen and we are the closest port to Europe in North America."

"We have the geography, we have the people and we have the government to help this place to become really a boom area in the future."

"I always tell my relatives and friends in Hong Kong that Halifax is not as bad as they think; in fact it's similar to Hong Kong in the sense that we have hills and mountains, we have water and our harbour looks like a small Kowloon. In many big cities you just see blocks and blocks of buildings. In a way the scenery is similar to Hong Kong but on a much smaller scale."

"Because we are on the coast we don't have extreme cold here or extreme heat and we don't have constant rain."

"No particular sectors have been earmarked for new investment. Of course we would like to develop the fishing, forest product and mining industries but on the other hand there are numerous opportunities for almost any small or medium size manufacturing company would be successful here."

"There are many service trades that we don't have here even including sophisticated restaurants or tailoring."

"You can't compare labour costs in Canada with the Far East because certainly labour there is much cheaper; on the other hand living standards here are much higher and when you sell your product you sell it at a higher price too."

"Neither can you compare our taxes with those in the Far Eat because just look what we get; we have super highways, we have excellent education facilities with children attending up to high school without paying a penny and university education highly subsidized; we have a good pension plan and unemployment insurance and all this money comes from our taxes."

"People have to decide whether they want this kind of society or some other kind with fewer benefits and I myself having lived in both worlds think Canadian society is more fair and better. Sure we do pay more taxes but most of the money is put to good use."

"Halifax and the province of Nova Scotia does not depend on one industry only. Of course we love to have barrels and barrels of oil coming ashore but we don't depend on that alone."

"If you look at the history of Halifax it started out as a fishing port and then, during the Second World War it became a naval base."

"Today we are the political, economic and education centre of the four Atlantic provinces but we are not like some of the big cities in the West which went up so fast and came down so quickly. We love to have oil, we love to have gas but if we don't have it it doesn't affect our daily life. We have many military personnel here; we are the east coast headquarters for the military; we are the seat of the provincial government and the capital city of Nova Scotia. We don't have the high fluctuations, the boom and bust syndrome that they have in some other Canadian cities. We may be slow but we are steady."

"Not counting students we have about 5,000 or 6,000 people of Chinese origin in Nova Scotia and other than dependent relatives and some independent immigrants only one or two Chinese investors have come here recently."

"Information is the number one reason. I went to Hong Kong a couple of times last year and tried to do some public relations work for the government appearing on television, sending out brochures, helping the provincial government to make a promotional film and meeting people."

"Most of the people there don't know about Halifax or Nova Scotia. They think Canada stops at Montreal or they have the idea that Halifax is in the Arctic. They just don't have the information. If you tell a Hong Kong person that they should go and live in Nova Scotia they think you're nuts. I'm not exaggerating."

"To increase the numbers of Chinese investors coming to Nova Scotia we must increase the availability of information; for example almost all Canada's other provinces, except the Atlantic provinces, have an office in Hong Kong and Quebec has attracted quite a lot of people with its special new regulations minimizing red tape and making immigration to the province more attractive.''

"From government's point of view it's a chicken and egg problem; the statistics do not justify us spending money in Hong Kong to have an office or a desk at the Canadian High Commission; on the other hand without an office or a desk we are not producing anything.''

"Right now we are relying on people from the Maritime Premiers Council to go to the Far East two or three times a year but that is not enough and not only not enough but not the proper way to do it.''

"I think if we had an office or a desk in Hong Kong there would be very substantial benefits to the province and to the city of Halifax because even now we have enquiries to handle by long distance telephone or telex and it seems to me one can never explain adequately in this situation. Back and forth by telephone or telex, wasting time and wasting money!''

"But if we had a person there who understands the situation here and can help people to fill out an application form or prepare a proposal it would be a tremendous help.''

"I went to Hong Kong as a private citizen but I have limited resources. Timewise and financialwise I just don't have the facilities. I think it's about time the government itself takes up this work helping and promoting but not interfering directly with private business or private deals because sometimes this sort of involvement alarms people.''

"I would like to see our Chinese community in Nova Scotia grow a little bit more to join us and help us develop the city and province because I believe it is a good place to live, a good place to bring up children and with a bright future for those who really want it.''

"I was practicing in Hong Kong and I was extremely successful. Moneywise there is no comparison but for the quality of life I have no regrets about coming here; I feel much more relaxed.''

"Come and look; that's my advice.''

Nova Scotia:
A step ahead of today

Nova Scotia, Canada's easternmost mainland province, is an ideal location for your business.

For all sorts of very good reasons.

Consider location, Nova Scotia is not only strategically located on the edge of all major North Atlantic shipping routes, but it's a full day closer to the materials and markets of Europe than either Boston or New York. Not to mention just a few convenient days' journey by truck or train from nearly 100 million potential customers in Central Canada and the Northeastern United States.

While Nova Scotia can offer you the cosmopolitan cultural pleasures those huge centres claim, we also promise you the best of natural beauty, outdoor pleasures and old-fashioned values to go with them.

As well as being a workforce that's second to none, our people are keen, energetic and committed to helping you achieve success. They're also well-educated and highly skilled.

Nova Scotia's sophisticated, world-class universities, along with our network of scientific and medical research institutes, modern vocational schools, technology institutes, apprenticeship training programs and continuing education help us provide the variety of skills a growing and modern industrial society needs. In fact, if we don't already have the skills your company needs, we may be able to help develop them for you.

We are committed to training people for jobs and also to achieving excellence in research and development as the cornerstone of our future prosperity.

And we are committed to you. We have a variety of loan and incentive programs to help you locate or expand in Nova Scotia.

Ask us to tell you how we can help your business.

Selected Economic Indicators, Nova Scotia, 1986

Population (at June 1	883,800	Total Capital & Repair Investment	$3,546,700,000
Labour Force	398,000	Total Value of Construction	$2,039,800,000
Unemployment Rate	13.4	Housing Starts	7,571
Consumer Price Index (1981 = 100)	131.7	Value of Manufacturing Shipments	$4,738,100,000
Personal Income Per Capita	$13,610	Total Exports	$1,915,964,000
Minimum Wage (Per Hour)	$4.00	Value of Mining	$356,673,000
GDP At Market Prices	$12,005,000,000^e	Value of Fish Landings	$407,792,000
Retail Trade	$4,794,600,000	Total Forest Production (m^2)	3,295,000^e
Net Power Generation (MWh)	7,411,398	Tourist Expenditure	$252,700,000^e

^{e} = estimated

The **Small Business Development Corporation Program** makes term financing of up to $250,000 available to small enterprises wishing to start up, expand or modernize. By definition, a small business is one having less than 50 employees and less than $2 million in sales.

The **Trade Expansion Program** encourages Nova Scotia manufacturers to seek out and realize national and international business opportunities not eligible for assistance under federal marketing programs. Assistance is available in the form of reimbursable costs associated with attendance at trade fairs and exhibitions, market identification, and market education courses.

Other Provincial Departments administer financial assistance programs to those businesses and industries in their particular sector (i.e. Agriculture, Fisheries, Lands & Forests, Mines & Energy, etc.).

Vocational Training — Nova Scotia's exciting apprenticeship programs, as well as trade training and vocational institutes, offer a wide variety of training to all sectors of the economy. In addition, when new and/or unique skills are required, the Nova Scotia Department of Vocational & Technical Training will organize special technical training arrangements to meet client's requirements. Financial assistance for training is available.

Tax Incentives

Nova Scotia's R&D income tax credit is equal to 10 percent of expenditures eligible for credit under the Federal Income Tax Act and is offered against the Provincial part of the income tax payable.

Nova Scotia provides 100 percent refund of Health Services Tax (Sales Tax) paid on machinery and equipment used in research and development.

Machinery, equipment, apparatus, materials and goods purchased by a manufacturer used directly and exclusively for the manufacture of goods for sale are exempt from the 10 percent Health Services Tax (Sales Tax). Non-renewable resources industries pay a reduced 4 percent tax.

& Federal Development Incentives

Another illustration of the service the Department of Development can provide to new business ventures is the ability to identify, interpret, and access a variety of federal incentive programs, and integrate these with Nova Scotia programs. Examples of the federal programs available are:

Income Tax Incentives

The **Investment Tax Credit** (ITC) in Canada currently at 5 percent (1987) is to be phased out over the next two-year period except in Atlantic Provinces and the Gaspe Region.

In the Atlantic Provinces (i.e. Nova Scotia) the Investment Tax Credit will continue at the rate of 20 percent and is available as a direct reduction of federal tax payable. This credit reduces the cost of most new buildings, machinery and equipment used in manufacturing, processing, mining, etc.

Research and Development Investment Tax Credit in Canada is 20 percent. In Nova Scotia it is 30 percent of the current and capital scientific research expenditures incurred in a taxation year. The tax credit is available as a direct reduction of federal tax payable, when the corporation does not have tax payable, at least 20 percent of this tax credit is refundable in cash. (In some cases, the refundable portion is higher, with a maximum of 40 percent). Any unused credits may be carried back three years and forward for seven years.

The Accelerated Capital Cost Allowance allows taxpayers to charge up to a 50 percent straight-line depreciation on most new machinery and equipment to be used in manufacturing and processing, thus allowing for the writing off of such assets in 2-3 years.

Employment & Immigration Canada
The Canadian Job Strategy offers financial and consultative assistance to help employers initiate training or expand their working capability. The objectives are to hire and train new workers and upgrade the existing workforce or retain employees who might otherwise have to be laid off because of technological or economic changes.

Atlantic Canada Opportunities Agency (ACOA)
The Industrial and Regional Development Program (IRDP) can provide financial assistance through incentives and repayable contributions. The program assistance for eligible projects is available over four elements of a product or company cycle.

The Atlantic Enterprise Program (AEP) is available in Nova Scotia and provides two types of support; (1) up to a maximum of 6 percentage points interest rate buy-down on new-term loans and/or (2) 85 percent special loan insurance guarantees.

Cape Breton
Cape Breton Tax Credit is a special income tax incentive for the Cape Breton area of Nova Scotia. Under the Cape Breton Investment Tax Credit (CBITC), new investments are entitled to a 60 percent investment tax credit. The CBITC applies to major activities including manufacturing and processing, farming, logging, oil and gas and mineral resources, technical services to business, certain tourism facilities, certain specialized oil and gas service vessels and facilities for the receiving, storage and distribution of goods. Tax credits may be carried forward to 10 years and back for three years. Forty percent of the CBITC is refundable in cash.

Special Assistance For Cape Breton — Assistance under IRDP and other DRIE/ACOA programs, including the Canada/Nova Scotia Tourism or Technology Subsidiary Agreements, may be raised up to a 60 percent contribution level. For example, if a maximum 30 percent IRDP contribution (plus 60 percent investment tax credit) appears insufficient to enable a worthwhile project to proceed, the Cape Breton Topping-Up Assistance (TUA) can provide up to a 30 percent extra contribution — bringing the total level of direct assistance available in Cape Breton to 60 percent.

ACOA Program Summary
Industrial and Regional Development Program (IRDP)

Program Element	Eligible Projects or Activities	Maximum Contribution Level			
		Tier I	Tier II	Tier III	Tier IV
Innovation	• Consultant studies, development of new products or processes, technological capability, development and demonstration, design	33.3%	40%	50%	50%
Establishment	• Consultant studies*	33.3%	40%	50%	50%
	• Establishment	Not Eligible	17.5%	25%	30%
Modernization/ Expansion	• Consultant studies	Not Eligible	30%	37.5%	37.5%
	• Modernization/expansion	Not Eligible	17.5%	25%	25%
	• Adaptation of microelectronic/ electronic technology	Not Eligible	30%	37.5%	37.5%
Marketing	• Market research and events to promote Canadian products for non-profit organization	45%	45%	45%	45%
	• Studies	25%	30%	37.5%	37.5%

*Maximum goes to 75% (all tiers) if either the study is requested by ACOA or if ACOA gets free and unrestricted use of it.

Minister of Development
Nova Scotia Department of Development
7th Floor, World Trade & Convention Centre
1800 Argyle Street
P.O. Box 519
Halifax, Nova Scotia
B3J 2R7
Telephone: (902) 424-5320
Telex: 01922548
Telecopier: (902) 424-5739

諾維斯高沙省：與您邁進明天

諾維斯高沙省乃加拿大內陸最東的省份，人口約九十萬，每年生意總值約十二億，為商業的理想地點。

諾省鄰近北大西洋航線，往歐洲的貨運可比紐約或波士頓短一天的航程。陸路方面，祗須數天的行車時間，便可直達十億人口的加拿大中部及美國東北部。

除一般大城市的享受外，諾省還有秀麗的大自然景色及故舊的風土人情。

諾省工人訓練有素，幹勁十足。

諾省更設有達世界水平的大學數間，再加上其他的科學及醫療研究機構，技能訓練中心及在職訓練中心等，為諾省造就了不少人材。

諾省還設有多項的工商貸款及促進計劃以助經濟發展。簡列如下：

諾省發展促進計劃

諾省經濟發展部

諾省的經濟發展部為工商業提供一連串的發展促進計劃以確保經濟得以迅速成長。舉例如下：

- **Nova Scotia Business Capital Corporation (BCC)**
  是在一九八六年成立的省府機構，專為工商業提供：

  - 貸款
  - 工商業貸款擔保
  - 有關廠房的各種援助
  - 十年免息投資貸款計劃

  可為少額生意提供高達二十五萬元的資助。凡顧員不多於五十名或每年營業額不足二百萬者皆被列為少額生意。

- **Small Business Development Corporation Program**
  是為鼓勵廠商發展出口市場。援助包括資助廠商參加貿易展覽會、市場研究及出口進修課程等。

- 其他省府部門也設有多項計劃以助農業、漁業、林木、礦務及能源工業的

77

發展。
– 專業技能訓練計劃為諸省提供多方面不同的技工以應工商業之需。

稅項特惠計劃

諸省設有多項的稅務優惠以鼓勵投資生產，如購買廠房設備可享有多種免稅及減稅辦法，用於投資或研究用的資金可退稅及加速折舊等。

加拿大就業及移民部

政府就業部門可為顧主提供資助或諮詢性服務以加強就業及現有勞工質素。

此外，還有很多不同的工業發展及免稅計劃可使投資者直接受惠。欲知詳情，請與我們聯絡：

Minister of Development
Nova Scotia Department of Development
7th Floor, World Trade & Convention Centre
1800 Argyle Street
P.O. Box 519
Halifax, Nova Scotia
Canada B3J 2R7

Telephone: (902) 424-5320
Telex: 01922548
Telecopier: (902) 424-5739

Canada's best kept secret is about to be made public

It is Halifax, Atlantic Canada's Capital City, where a new East is unfolding.

In your search for the right location for development opportunities, you will try to find the location which has specific factors. Stable government, strong economic growth, top-notch labour force, and the right environment for investment.

Halifax is the right location.

This city of 350,000 people (Metropolitan area) is located on the East Coast of Canada in the Province of Nova Scotia. The province has always had a stable political climate, with a basic three-party system of Parliamentary democracy.

Inflation and the Consumer Price Indexes places Halifax in the lowest levels of the cities in Canada.

This city has had solid economic performance in the last ten years with capital development projects topping the $100 million mark annually for all except one of the past seven years. The anticipated activity for 1987 will be in excess of $130 million.

WHY HALIFAX?

Its strategic location on the "Great Arctic Shipping Route" offers an excellent stepping-off point to the North American market. Two container piers and break bulk facilities can meet any company's requirement to move materials or product for assembly or trans-shipment to the inland North American market.

The options for transportation include road, rail, water or air.

The Halifax International Airport, on all-weather highway system, and coastal feeder shipping services provide quick access to over 48 million consumers within 24 hours from Halifax.

All your needs for skilled labour can be met with our stable, well trained, and hardworking labour force.

Seven universities and numerous technical institutions provide excellent training which develops the skills required today, as well as adapting to the needs of the future.

Halifax has the second largest concentration of scientists per capita in Canada, and a number of world class research facilities make it the place to be.

The availability of skilled labour and all the support services which a company requires makes our city the logical place to establish.

When considering other investment opportunities, Halifax, with its continued growth, will provide a need for new office, commercial, and industrial building.

A strong financial community exists with full international banking services available, including a branch of the Hong Kong Bank.

When you add up all the points indicated above and couple them with excellent cultural, educational, medical and recreational facilities, you will find out why Halifax is fast becoming the place to be in Canada.

你們知道嗎？哈利法克斯市

加拿大東岸的主要城市哈利法克斯現已漸露鋒芒。

當你想找尋適當的地方發展，你定會要求一個政治穩定，經濟繁榮及人力水準高的地方。哈市便是你要找尋的適當地方。

哈市你於諾夫斯高省內，人口有三十五萬。諾省三黨分立，民主政體十分穩定。

諾省在以往五年間的經濟表現皆能高出或平全國水平，而哈市的表現則最爲突出。哈市的通脹率乃全國各城市中最低的。

十年來哈市的經濟皆能以穩健見稱，除其中一年外，其餘每年的投資增長均過的億。預料一九八七年的投資增長可達一億三千萬之鉅。

還有其他理由今你選擇哈利法克斯市嗎？

哈市你於‘大北極航線’中的要點，與北美市場連貫無阻。海港設有兩個貨櫃碼頭及完善的貨運裝設，今貨過至北美各地，極爲方便。

除海運外，公路、鐵路和空路交通也極之完善。哈市的國際機場，全天候公路網及沿海船服務，可在二十四小時內與超過四千八百萬名消費者聯系。

哈已有訓練優良、勤奮安份的營工可供聘用。

我們有七所大學及多間工專學院培訓人材，以應未來社會之需。

在哈市，科學家與人口的比例在加排列次席，更有具世界一流水準的研究設備。

鑑於哈市在人力及設備上的優厚條件，哈市自然成爲商界理想的地方。

因經濟的發展，工商樓宇的需求亦隨之而上升，所以不乏投資的機會。

哈市的財經界也很熱鬧，有國際性的銀行業務，香港匯豐銀行在此也設有分行。

Investment in the Canadian Province of Newfoundland

Newfoundland is Canada's most easterly Province. It consists of the island of Newfoundland (111,390 km) and Labrador, the mainland portion (294,330 km).

The Province has a resource based economy, the major sectors of which are: the fishery, forestry, oil and gas, mineral production (iron ore, fluorspar, limestone, gold, asbestos, gypsum and shale), and hydro electric power.

Newfoundland exports average $1.6 billion annually. The major commodity groups of these exports are fish products, newsprint, and iron ore. The markets of major interest for Newfoundland exports include the United States, the United Kingdom, West Germany, Japan, and the People's Republic of China.

THE FISHERY

Newfoundland as one of the major fish producers in the world has demonstrated an ability to anticipate world demand and to provide a versatile product for the international seafood markets. The landed value of fish is $150 million per year and the annual processed value of fish products exceeds $400 million.

Cod has traditionally been the mainstay of the Province's fishing effort. In the last decade, however, other groundfish species such as turbot, flounder, redfish and catfish have been offering attractive investment opportunities for the export market.

Species such as scallops, lobster, and crab continue to be in high demand in Europe and North America. The growth potential for herring and mackerel offers a promising market prospect in Asia and the Far East. Newfoundland delicacies such as capelin, squid, shrimp and eel are making significant market penetration.

In addition investment opportunities are available in the following areas:

- Aquaculture — the farming of aquatic plants and animals has made great progress over the past decade. In Newfoundland several species such as trout, salmon and blue mussels are moving toward commercial production.
- A joint venture opportunity exists to manufacture leather from fish skins. The process, which utilizes fish skins that are a by-product of the existing fishing industry, results in a leather that has a high potential to be used in the fashion leather industry to replace products such as reptile skins which are in increasingly short supply.

The sealing industry offers new business opportunities in the production of leather, oils, meat and organs.

- Opportunities exist for Canadian companies to harvest and commercially process underutilized fish species, such as hake, grenadier and argentine, mackerel. Under the Law of the Sea Conference 150,000 metric tons are available for utilization.

FORESTRY

Newfoundland's forestry sector generates approximately $400 million annually for export from the three paper mills in Newfoundland which have at their disposal approximately 100,000 km² of productive forest land.

Opportunities exist for paper companies seeking an incremental long-term source of high quality wood fibre. The wood resource available, of black spruce and balsam fir, will support the establishment of a mechanical pulp mill operation.

The Labrador portion of the Province contains a substantial forest reserve which has yet to be tapped. These forests are as yet uncommitted to industry, and with hydro-electric power close by and short shipping distances to European and American markets, an excellent investment opportunity exist.

MINERALS

Newfoundland and Labrador's mineral wealth is a significant component of the economy of the Province contributing 30% of the Province's net value of goods. It accounts for 10% of the Province's workforce in both direct and indirect employment related to the mining industry.

Mineral exploration activity is increasing at a faster rate every year due to recent legislation which has opened large tracts of land both to the small entrepreneur and large multinational mining companies. Investment opportunities both in mineral exploration and mining production and processing exist for a variety of minerals.

OFFSHORE OIL AND GAS

Newfoundland's already discovered and potential reserves of oil and natural gas offer the potential to make the Province a world leader in the supply of petroleum reserves.

Development of the offshore Hibernia field will create a wide variety of opportunities for investors.

The major marine offshore construction project offers potential opportunities.

A joint venture opportunity exists for the development of long-term offshore steel fabrication yards. Sub-contractor and capital investment opportunities exist with the potential of long-term profitability.

Opportunities exist in the areas of cold ocean research activity and marine consulting and engineering projects associated with offshore development.

Joint venture opportunities exist in support of major construction and fabrication; in the materials handling field. A wide range of capabilities are available.

The Government of Newfoundland and Labrador has given priority to the development and use of technology and research in areas fundamental to the long term development of the Provincial economy.

Newfoundland and Labrador intend to build upon the marine experience gained from 400 years of fishing and sailing in our cold and ice-infested waters. The Province is rapidly becoming a leader for research in marine related areas and this trend will accelerate with the pace of off-shore oil and gas development.

Newfoundland is on the verge of the greatest growth and development it has ever seen. Development of industrial infrastructure based on the prosecution of natural resources is the key to our future prosperity.

As a Canadian province we welcome your participation in the exciting prospects of our future. Many investment opportunities have already been identified, and many more exist. Direct inquiries to:

Director, Prospect Development,
Department of Development and Tourism
P.O. Box 4750
St. John's Newfoundland, Canada
A1C 5T7
Telephone (709) 576-2781
Telex 016-4949

紐芬蘭省的投資機會

紐芬蘭是加拿大極東的省份，包括有紐芬蘭島及本土兩部份。[紐省經濟主要依靠其天然資源，其中以漁業、林業、石油、及礦業（鐵、螢石、石灰石、金、石綿、石膏及頁岩等）爲主。][紐芬蘭每年外銷額平均爲十六億元，其中主要貨品有海產，新聞卷紙及鐵礦。主要市場包括英、美、德、日及中國等。]

漁業

紐芬蘭是世界主要漁類生產地之一，每年漁獲達一億五千萬元，而海產製品總值則超過四億元。

一向從來，鱈魚是紐省漁業的主要漁穫。但於近年間間，其他魚類如大鰈、比目魚、紅魚、及鯰魚等也有出口市場。帶子、蟹及龍蝦，在歐洲及北美都有很大的市場。而鯡魚及鯖魚亞太區的市場潛力甚豐。其他如蝦、鱔及魷魚等亦開始受到重視。

除此以外，以下各行業也可為投資者提供良好的機會：

——人工栽培水產的科學在過去十年來大有進展。鱒魚、鮭魚及貽貝等已將可以用人工方式繁殖及大量生產。

——利用魚皮加工製成皮革，質地柔軟耐用，可取替日益短缺的鱷魚皮以供時裝界作用。

——把漁穫加工，以供應出口市場的需求。

農林業

紐芬蘭擁有大量木材以供造紙業之用。省內三間紙廠佔林地十萬平方公里，每年出口達四億元之鉅。在Labrador的優質林木現正有待開發。投資者可乘紐省有充足電力之便及其離歐美市場之近，在紐省設廠投資。

礦產

紐芬蘭的礦產產量佔總生產的三成、而與礦業有關的就業額就佔總數的一成。而最近政府所通過的工地開法案更可為礦業帶來更進一步的發展。

離岸石油開採及其他投資機會

紐芬蘭的離岸石油蘊藏量豐富，實為良好的投資機會。與石油開採相息相關的海洋工程及煉鋼業等也可在紐省發展。

鑑於紐芬蘭有四百年的捕魚及航海歷史，所以其在海洋研究學上常處領導地位。隨着離岸油田的發展，這方面的研究將會更砸進一步。

由於紐省的經濟與其資源息息相關，所以省府對資源的開採及有關的工業架構尤為重視。現省府正積極吸納外資、與投資者並進，以收其經濟效益。

各位若有任何疑問，請與我們的貿易發展主任聯絡：

DIRECTOR, PROSPECT DEVELOPMENT
DEPT. OF DEVELOPMENT AND TOURISM
P.O. BOX 4750
ST. JOHN'S, NEWFOUNDLAND, CANADA
A1C 5T7
TEL: (709) 576-2781
TELEX 016-4949

CHAPTER 5

Opportunities in industrial, commercial and residential real estate

Extracted from 'Canadian Real Estate 1988: the Royal LePage Market Survey' by kind permission of Royal LePage Ltd.

Less volatile market conditions for resale homes will prevail in 1988

A healthy economy and relatively moderate interest rates are expected to continue to stimulate resale home buying activity across the country in 1988.

Overall, national housing resales in 1988 are forecast to increase by 7 per cent, rising from the estimated year end 1987 level of 300,000 units to 321,000 units.

The value of resale homes across Canada is expected to increase as well, with average prices rising 6 per cent, from the estimated 1987 figure of $110,000 to $116,500 in 1988.

Moderating influences noted

The first six months of 1987 were periods of exceptional activity in many major Canadian cities.

The first quarter saw record-breaking sales in many centres, followed by slowdowns to more normal levels of activity. These slowdowns ranged from moderate adjustments in most centres, to dramatic corrections in cities like Toronto and Hamilton.

In many parts of the country, it was the year of the recovery in residential real estate markets. Vancouver, Montreal and Ottawa joined Calgary and Edmonton in experiencing significant increases in both housing sales and the value of homes. Only a few major communities, including Regina and the Halifax/Dartmouth area, had sluggish levels of real estate activity. And even though the increases were modest, home buying activity in 1987 in both these cities was higher than it was in 1986.

Given the robust economy of southern Ontario, real estate markets in Hamilton and Toronto are expected to see renewed activity in 1988. No major centre is forecast to see a downturn in housing sales. Calgary, Edmonton, and, to a lesser degree, Halifax/Dartmouth, are expected to enjoy the fruits of renewed oil industry activity.

Housing markets in Ottawa, Montreal and Vancouver are expected to continue to be healthy, and market trends should be considerably less volatile than they were in 1987. Winnipeg is again expected to be the most active of major centres on the Prairies, although the forecast calls for a relatively strong year for Saskatoon.

Note: The following forecasts refer to residential resale housing markets. 'Sales' refer to total residential resales in a given market during the full-year period, and 'prices' or 'values' refer to the overall, full-year average price of all residential resale properties.

Vancouver

Foreign investment and continued strength in the service, tourism, forestry, and fishing industries are responsible for Vancouver's healthy resale housing market. These factors, combined with relatively moderate interest rates, are expected to continue to produce an active residential market.

Sales: Residential housing sales are expected to increase 8 per cent in 1988, rising from the estimated year-end 1987 level of 24,000 units to 26,000 units.

Prices: The overall selling price of residential properties in Vancouver is forecast to appreciate 6 per cent in 1988 to $139,000. single family detached homes are expected to increase a similar amount, rising from $143,000 in 1987 to $151,500 by year-end 1988.

Edmonton

The residential resale housing market in Edmonton is on the rebound as a result of the relative stabilization in the price of oil. Continued interest rate stability and reasonable levels of available mortgage funds are expected to encourage more potential buyers to enter the housing market in 1988.

Sales: Housing unit sales in 1988 are forecast to reach 9,173 units, a 10 per cent increase over the estimated year end 1987 level of 8,830 units.

Prices: The typical selling price of a home in Edmonton is expected to climb 4 per cent in 1988, rising from the 1987 figure of $78,350 to $81,500.

Calgary

For much of 1987, the residential resale housing market in Calgary was characterized by high demand and a relatively short supply of homes listed for sale. Combined with rising oil prices, The 1988 Winter Olympics, and the relocation of many major corporate head offices to the Calgary area, these conditions are expected to continue. Although residential real estate in Calgary is forecast to experience another healthy year in 1988, it is unlikely the number of unit sales will exceed the record number of homes sold in 1987.

Sales: Residential housing sales are expected to remain strong in 1988, matching the estimated 16,000 units sold in 1987.

Prices: The strong demand and limited supply of listings pushed the price of homes in Calgary up an average of 8 per cent in 1987 to $93,400.

The average price of a resale home in Calgary is expected to climb another 8 per cent in 1988 to $100,850.

Regina

Weakness in the agricultural sector, combined with cutbacks by the Saskatchewan Government that have caused uncertainty in the public service sector, produced a sluggish residential housing markert in 1987. Both influences are expected to continue in 1988, producing another flat year in the resale housing market in Regina.

Sales: Residential housing sales are forecast to increase 1 per cent to 3,250 units in 1988, topping the 1987 estimated level of 3,225 units.

Prices: Selling prices in Regina are expected to increase 3 per cent in 1988, rising from the estimated year-end 1987 figure of $65,750 to $67,750.

Saskatoon

Relatively strong levels of activity characterized the Saskatoon residential real estate market in 1987. The reduced price of grain paid to Prairie farmers and cutbacks in provincial Government expenditures, and a depletion of potash reserves have caused some concern. However, growth in the high technology, retail, and service sectors are expected to provide offsetting influences in 1988.

Sales: Housing sales are forecast to rise 3 per cent in 1988 to 3,200 units, up from the 1987 estimated level of 3,100 units.

Prices: Residential real estate prices in Saskatoon are expected to experience a typically moderate 3 per cent increase in 1988, rising to an overall average of $77,250. This is $2,250 higher than the estimated 1987 figure of $75,000.

Winnipeg

Winnipeg's resale housing market was fuelled by a strong and diverse local economy in 1987. Relatively moderate interest rates and a growing retail sector are expected to continue to help produce strong buyer demand in 1988.

Sales: Housing sales are expected to increase 5 per cent in 1988, to 12,400 units, compared with the estimated 1987 level of 11,750 units.

Prices: The value of homes in Winnipeg is expected to climb 6 per cent in 1988, rising to $82,600, an increase of more than $4,500 over the 1987 estimated figure of $78,000.

Hamilton

After experiencing an exceptionally strong first quarter in 1987, the residential resale housing market in Hamilton returned to more normal levels of activity for the remainder of the year.

Also, selling prices returned to more moderate levels. Although the closing of the Firestone plant and the resulting loss of 1,300 jobs created some concerns, real estate market activity in Hamilton is still expected to increase marginally in 1988.

Sales: Residential housing sales are forecast to rise 2 per cent to 11,225 units in 1988, an increase of 225 units over the estimated year-end 1987 level.

Prices: Overall selling prices in the Hamilton area are expected to climb 5 per cent, from the estimated 1987 figure of $106,000 to $111,300 in 1988.

Toronto

After an exceptional first quarter in 1987, the residential resale housing market in Toronto entered a correction phase. Prices declined to more realistic levels, in response to buyer resistance and an increased inventory of homes listed for sale.

A continuation of the strongest local economy in the country, relatively moderate interest rates and more realistic price levels are expected to encourage purchasers to enter the marketplace in 1988.

Sales: Housing sales in Toronto are forecase to increase 4 per cent in 1988, rising to 46,800 units. This compares with the estimated 1987 level of 45,000 units.

Prices: The value of homes in Toronto is expected to appreciate 7 per cent in 1988, rising to $192,500. This is an increase of more than $12,000 over the 1987 year-end estimate of $180,000.

Ottawa

Ottawa's residential resale housing market recovered strongly during 1987, with unit sales close to 20 per cent higher than in 1986. Much of the strength occurred in the first half of the year. Although some of the pent-up demand that developed during recent years has been satisfied, market activity is expected to continue at relatively healthy levels in 1988. The Federal Government restraint measures that slowed market growth have been largely discounted, and the high technology industry is expected to show at least a partial recovery.

Sales: By year-end 1988, residential housing unit sales in Ottawa are expected to climb 5 per cent to 9,825 units, topping the estimated 1987 levels of 9,350 units.

Prices: Overall selling prices in Ottawa are forecast to rise 4 per cent to $122,200 in 1988, an increase of more than $4,500 over the estimated 1987 figure of $117,500.

Montreal

Pent-up demand caused an increase in residential housing prices in Montreal and fuelled speculation in the market during the first quarter of 1987. The market returned to more normal levels of activity as the year progressed, but still remained very healthy. With a strong provincial economy and two years left in the mandate of the current Provincial Government, the housing market in Montreal is expected to experience another year of steady growth and active buyer demand.

Sales: Residential housing sales in Montreal are expected to increase 5 per cent in 1988, reaching 24,675 units, compared with the 1987 estimate of 23,500 units.

Prices: Overall selling prices in Montreal are forecast to increase 8 per cent to $97,038 in 1988. This represents a rise of more than $7,000 over the 1987 figure of $89,850.

Halifax/Dartmouth

The residential housing market in Halifax/Dartmouth was relatively soft in 1987, especially during the first six months. Federal Government restraint programs, including spending cuts by the Department of National Defence and others, as well as minimal offshore drilling activity, have had a dampening effect on consumer confidence and home buying activity.

However, proposed capital spending on highways, hospitals, and the potential for renewed interest in the oil and gas sector as world prices stabilize, are expected to have positive impacts on the local economy in 1988. Both real estate sales activity and residential selling prices are expected to recover from 1987 levels.

Sales: By year end 1988, housing sales in the Halifax/Dartmouth area are expected to climb to 4,525 units, an increase of 5 per cent over 1987's estimated level of 4,300 units.

Prices: Overall selling prices are expected to appreciate 4 per cent in 1988 to $89,300.

Commercial
Increasing globalization of world economy is impacting all market sectors

M. Wayne Mondville
Senior Vice President & National General Manager — Brokerage,
Royal LePage Commercial Real Estate Services

Last year in this space we spoke of the increasing globalization of world market forces and their impact on Canada in general, and the Canadian real estate sector in particular. In the last 12 months, we have seen this trend continue at an ever-quickening pace; more than ever before, we have learned that Canada's status as a significant world economy has placed it in a position both to take advantage of, and to be affected by, global forces. Several significant events have recently occurred, and have begun to have impact on the way we do business in Canada.

The deregulation of the world's financial services industry in general has broken down many of the old barriers to the movement of capital between political jurisdictions. In essence, this has enhanced the ability of world-class financial institutions to effectively export their expertise and financial strength to other countries. The City of London's "Big Bang" in 1986 and a similar lifting of restrictions which occurred in

June, 1987 in Canada, have placed two of the world's top five financial capitals much more directly in competition within the international marketplace.

Restrictions have been lifted

The removal of the Foreign Investment Review Agency and the establishment of Investment Canada, have lifted previous restrictions on foreign investment in our country, and have encouraged the interest of foreign governments and corporations in Canadian investment opportunities. While the detractors of these liberalized policies have indicated that this now means that "Canada is for sale", others have argued that we are simply taking advantage of the reality of world financial markets.

The health of the Canadian economy, and our country's relative economic and political stability, have combined to enhance international recognition of the merits of investing in Canada. Certainly a significant discount of our currency over the U.S. dollar has given us a competitive advantage in some sectors, as compared with our neighbours to the south.

Large sums of foreign capital are being attracted to our country. But even without this influx of foreign funds, economic indicators within Canada are extremely positive. Canadian stock exchange advances have outstripped even those in the United States and have been fuelled in large measure not by rampant speculation, but rather by impressive corporate profit increases and anticipation of continued gains.

A Financial Post survey of over 100 corporations listed on The Toronto Stock Exchange indicated that second-quarter 1987 net income was, on average, 32 per cent greater than for the same period in 1986; corporate profit margins for the second-quarter were 25 per cent greater than last year. Despite five years of soaring prices on The Toronto Stock Exchange, the short to mid-term outlook shared by most analysts is positive.

The devaluation of Canadian and U.S. currencies relative to worldwide exchange rates has made North American assets attractive to foreign investors. Canada, in particular, will continue to benefit from this as demand for our natural resources increases to satisfy world markets.

The mining sector remains similarly bullish as Canadian mining firms have survived and attuned themselves to low industrial metals prices in recent years. In addition, they are excellently poised to take advantage of the recent drawdown in inventories, as increased production of such metals is beginning to be demanded.

Canada's oil and gas sector has similarly shown continued improvement over the last year. Oil prices have increased from their 1986 low of $11 U.S. a barrel to current rates in the range of $18 U.S. a barrel. Expectations are that prices will continue to increase through 1988, although they are unlikely to reach levels high enough to trigger another recession.

Additionally, it has been reported that, as a result of changes in royalty and taxation schedules affecting the oil industry, the net dollars achieved by oil-producing companies in Canada is the same at current price levels as it was when oil was $30 U.S. per barrel. This has been reflected by renewed capital expenditures and employment growth in the oil patch.

Further investment opportunities will arise as a result of Canada's Crown Corporation privatization program.

While a privatization program in Britain has been based on general public share offerings, Canadian privatization has tended to focus on the sale of Crown corporations to existing third-party operating companies. The intent is to increase corporate operating efficiency by lifting public controls, removing decisions based on political expendiency, and allowing more direct market response.

While the primary thrust of these initiatives has been at the Federal level, provincial governments in Ontario, Alberta and British Columbia are also pursuing similar programs. Significantly, these privatization initiatives send a signal of "non-interference" to foreign investors seeking opportunities in Canadian companies.

A form of free trade already exists

The considerable focus placed on free trade discussions between Canada and the United States over the past year has clouded the realization that, in fact, a form of free trade between our countries exists now. This is not in terms of lack of tarrifs, but certainly in terms of the flow of raw materials and finished products back and forth across the 49th Parallel.

With an almost total absence of trade barriers and protectionist measures, Canada and the United States enjoy perhaps the freest trade of any two nations outside of the European Economic Community.

It is an irony of these free trade discussions that the most significant trade disputes between our countries in many years arose in their midst. Last winter, softwood lumber difficulties and the attendant reverberations through Canada's forest industry, demonstrated the severe impact on a single industry sector that can arise as a result of trade restrictions, or protectionist or isolationist policies.

It is important to remember in all of this that Canada is competing in an increasingly world-oriented financial environment. Each of the technical and economic considerations discussed, in addition to specific geo-political considerations throughout the world, affect the international view of Canada and its investment potential.

Much of the media attention paid to foreign investment has ignored the competitive strengths and basic attractions of the Canadian marketplace. In a manner typical of Canadian self-denegation, too much interest has been placed on the source country of foreign investment.

In the 1960s and 1970s, we talked about the U.S. invasion; in the early 1980s it was the Chinese invasion; and now, there is the much discussed Japanese invasion. All of this, with its overtone of xenophobia, has provided a convenient external focus for our attentions. More importantly, it has masked much of the real rationale for foreign investment in Canada.

In dissecting and quantifying the nationalities of investment source, we have spent far too much time rationalizing the "flight of capital" from the country of origin and have attributed such investment to problems or deficiencies in the economic or political realities of the source country.

"Pull", not "Push" is key

It is convenient, and to some extent true, to suggest that interest in Canadian investment from Hong Kong, for instance, is due to the impending reversion to Mainland Chinese rule, or that Japanese interest is rooted in Japan's domestic trade surplus and currency appreciation difficulties. However, such rationale misses the point. The point is: Canada is a good place in which to invest.

While there is some "push" of capital away from these centres, that capital has the opportunity to seek placement virtually anywhere in the world. The "pull" exerted on foreign capital by the basic attractions of Canada and its investment opportunities brings that investment here. It is this reality which is more to the point, and we must learn to continue to capitalize on our strengths.

All of this has meant significantly increased interest in Canada and increasing levels of foreign investment. In 1985, total direct foreign investment in Canada was a healthy $3.4 billion. But in just one year, that almost doubled to some $6.7 billion. We must recognize that this investment does not mean the pillage of Canada. This investment, in part, has contributed to a strengthening Canadian economy with attendant spin-off benefit to Canadian corporations. It has provided additional opportunities for Canadians, not only here, but also abroad.

This strength has allowed Canadians themselves to seek attractive investment opportunities in the international arena; in 1986, Canadian investment abroad of $7.9 billion more than offset the foreign direct investment in Canada of $6.7 billion. The pace of this offsetting investment is outstanding. It has been estimated by some analysts that by 1991, Canadian corporations will own as much abroad as foreign companies will own in Canada.

Notable examples through 1987 of significant acquisitions or investments by Canadians in the international marketplace include Campeau Corporation's acquisition of Allied Stores, and Peoples Jewellers' acquisition of Zale Corporation.

The benefits to Canadians at home, and to their participation in the world's increasingly homogeneous financial markets, cannot or should not be disputed. An isolationist policy in the face of the reality of today's world marketplace would preclude growth in an economy of only 25 million people and abundant natural resources and potential. This increasing globalization of the world economy directly impacts Canadian commercial real estate markets. In turn, it helps to strengthen those markets, thereby enhancing their attraction to investors, both domestic and foreign. Toronto, for instance, with some 100 million sq. ft. of office space, is one of North America's leading office markets. Significantly, with a vacancy rate of only 6.5 per cent as of mid-1987, Toronto has the healthiest office market of any major North American city. It is interesting that, while the City is the envy of any office market investor or participant throughout the continent, there is some local (mis)conception that the market is overbuilt. Opportunities continue to exist in the office segment within Toronto and projections indicate that strong market conditions will continue well into 1989, even given aggressive project completion schedules.

Similar health and vitality is seen within the industrial sector in the greater Toronto area. Here, considerable media attention has been placed on the shift from a manufacturing to a service economy. Also viewed as noteworthy is a steady net decrease in manufacturing and warehouse employment from a high of some 284,000 jobs by 1981, to 257,000 jobs in 1986, and a projected decrease to 248,000 jobs by 1991.

However, these statistics ignore some basic market fundamentals. Smokestack industries have declined; large manufacturing facilities employing hundreds of workers are giving way to a demand for smaller, more concentrated and more productive specialist industries, stimulating demand for modern facilities in new industrial subdivisions. Demand for serviced industrial land in our suburbs has risen, giving rise to significant price increases in this increasingly scarce commodity.

A rebirth of Montreal's downtown is taking place as projects currently under construction will add another 550 stores, comprising 1 million sq. ft. of retail space. New projects including Les Cours Mont-Royal, the renovation of the historic Mount Royal Hotel, and Le Windsor, the renovation of the former Windsor Hotel, both to accommodate retail and office uses, are indicative of the attractions of this market. Demand for land in the core and in the suburbs remains strong. Overall, office vacancy rates are declining, and our analysis of the investment market over the past two years shows that prices for properties of all types have risen sharply, reflecting great demand on the part of investors.

Western Canadian markets have strengthened, along with increased vitality in both the oil and gas, and forest products sectors. Signs of recovery were evident in Calgary throughout 1987, and sales and leasing activity in the City's industrial, investment and office leasing sectors were stronger than they had been in over a year. Vancouver's office leasing and industrial markets are experiencing healthy growth. Concerns that economic activity that rode on the coattails of Expo'86 would come to an end with the closing of the Fair's gates have proven to be unfounded.

Tax reform, or at least a version of it, came to Canada in the Summer of 1987. It is evident that the serious impacts that were experienced in the real estate industry south of the border with realignments of their tax legislation have not, and are not likely, to materialize in our country. Land development companies will be most adversely affected as a result of a requirement, commencing in 1988, to capitalize interest and other soft costs in respect of undeveloped land. However, investment properties and current returns from them should not be materially affected. If anything, it can be argued that investment properties will hold greater appreciation potential, due to the added cost factor of non-deductible land carrying costs incorporated in new buildings.

Additional charges such as decreasing the Capital Cost Allowance to 4 per cent from its current 5 per cent on a declining balance basis, and eliminating CCA on real estate assets until the year in which the asset is put into productive use, should have only minor impacts on the operation of the industry.

Canada viewed as a safe haven

Canada will continue to provide attractive real estate investment opportunities to the Japanese. Their currency has appreciated against the dollar by about 80 per cent in the past five years, and 40 per cent in the last two years alone, and they face a property market with central Tokyo land prices of $20,000 per sq. ft. and investment property yields of 2 per cent or less.

Canada will remain attractive to the investors from The Far East who may be looking for a safe haven for the placement of family or corporate assets, and it will remain attractive to the Americans whose domestic investment opportunities may be limited by weak real estate markets and adverse taxation legislation. Most of all, it will remain attractive to anyone, especially to Canadian individuals and corporations, looking for a sound and stable economic and political environment in which to participate in real estate investment and land development activity.

While much international focus has been placed on Canadian real estate markets in the past 12 months, this focus is likely to become much sharper and reinforced during 1988. With The 1988 Winter Olympics occurring in Calgary early in the year, and a major International Economic Summit to be held in Toronto in the Summer of 1988, world media attention will be placed on Canada, its people, its cities and its political and economic institutions for a sustained period.

Global forces will continue to present opportunities and challenges within the Canadian commercial real estate sector, as with all sectors of our economy, well into the 1990s.

Toronto Commercial Market Outlook
Business diversification is a key factor in maintaining market growth

The widely recognized and much envied diversification of its business base is a major factor determining the health of the Metropolitan Toronto economy. In turn, this positively impacts the Region's commercial real estate markets. Forecasts for a slowdown in economic growth ultimately will prove to be correct. When this happens, and it may not be in 1988, the benefits of diversification, together with Metro's other strengths, will continue to maintain acceptable activity levels in all real estate sectors.

Throughout 1987, the Ontario economy continued as the most robust in Canada. This largely was the result of strong performance in the services, automotive, housing and general manufacturing sectors and a consistently high level of consumer spending. Due to its strategic position in the economic epicentre of southwestern Ontario, and recognized status as Canada's financial, banking and general services centre, Metropolitan Toronto prospered as never before. The rate of business growth was outstanding. Existing firms expanded their operations and numerous new companies were attracted to Metro by their desire to key into the growth machine. In addition, large increases in population, one of the lowest unemployment rates in Canada and strong income gains propelled consumer spending to new heights.

It is not surprising that Toronto's commercial real estate market prospered in this environment:

□ the demand for business accommodation translated into high levels of leasing activity in the office market. During the first half of 1987, there was a 25 per cent decline in the overall vacancy rate, to a five year low of 6.5 per cent

□ individuals, institutions, and offshore investors created a frenzy in the marketplace as they pursued a dwindling supply of prime commercial real estate investments

□ demand for industrial premises exceeded supply throughout the market, forcing lease rates plus land and building prices up dramatically

□ high demand, combined with lack of product, resulted in a substantial increase in quoted retail rental rates in nearly all product categories and locations

In 1988, it is probable that a number of key sectors will continue as sources of strength for the Ontario economy and hence for the Toronto commercial real estate market. Capital spending on non-residential construction should continue to grow, particularly in the manufacturing and service sectors. Investment in machinery and equipment also should be strong, in line with on-going modernization and expansion plans in many businesses.

However, a number of forecasters have suggested that not all sectors of the Ontario economy will be equally strong in 1988. Beginning in mid-1987, it was apparent that the production of automobiles and parts and related intermediate parts was beginning to slow and that the boom in new housing construction was losing steam. For some, but certainly not all, this is an indication that Ontario's overall economic growth will slow in 1988.

This may indeed be the case for the Province, but Toronto's highly diversified economy suggests that the City and its commercial real estate markets will continue to enjoy generally positive conditions. As experience has shown, any downside largely is balanced by growth from other areas.

A case in point was the concern registered from many quarters early in 1987, when Toronto was bypassed by Ottawa which designated only Montreal and Vancouver as international banking centers. However, an upside development was quick to surface. Deregulation of the financial services sector has been positive for Toronto in that it has encouraged a number of major financial services firms, both from the United States and offshore, to establish operations in the City. This is understandable, as Toronto is the financial services capital of Canada.

In essence, Toronto is able to rely upon its diversified economy to maintain a relatively stable keel in the wake of any sector downturns. Royal LePage believes that this attribute will largely ensure the continuance of a healthy commercial real estate market in 1988.

The "insurance" provided by business diversification, an environment conducive to commercial development and an ability to continually attract new business and investment explains why Toronto continues to be the envy of most other North American cities. Using these indigenous strength as a starting point, the Royal LePage Survey Team has formulated detailed forecasts for Metropolitan Toronto's key commercial real estate sectors.

□ *Office Leasing.* It could be pointed out that the pace of office market activity in the second half of 1987 was down from that of the first half. But one would be accused of being "picky". The bottom line is that overall absorption of 8.3 million sq. ft. means that 1987 was the best year for the Metropolitan Toronto office market since 1981.

Royal LePage research indicates that the majority of leasing activity, over 90 per cent, was sourced from the private sector. Because of Toronto's strong economic base, all business sectors continue to expand and are requiring space in all size categories.

A key point to note is that no major shifts in leasing activity have occurred within the various space classifications. With the market for space becoming tighter and less competitive among landlords, the ability to acquire class A space at effectively class B rates is disappearing.

The tightening of the market is underlined by the major decline in vacancies. Within the financial core, the vacancy rate has dropped to 4.7 per cent at the end of 1987, from 6.2 per cent at mid year. In the downtown fringe area, the decline in the vacancy rate has been even more dramatic — from 5.6 to 3 per cent. Concurrently, inducements offered by landlords have declined to a dollar figure that approximates 1-1 1/4 years net rent. With the continuing tightening of the market, it is forecast that inducements in the downtown area will be less than one year's net rent in 1988.

While activity in the office market during 1988 will not match the pace witnessed in 1987, it will be another good year as the Metropolitan Toronto economy continues in a steady, stable phase of growth.

On an overall basis, the Royal LePage 1988 office leasing forecast is calling for 6.9 million sq. ft. of absorption and a vacancy rate of 6.3 per cent, down slightly from the 1987 vacancy of 6.8 per cent. The estimate for new supply in 1988 is 7 million sq. ft., compared with 7.4 million sq. ft. in 1987. This will bring the supply of office space in the Toronto Census Metropolitan Area to 111.9 million sq. ft. by the end of 1988.

Declining vacancies in the financial core, downtown fringe and midtown areas suggest that rental rates will be under increasing pressure. Quoted net rental rates for class A space in the financial core, which ranged from $24-32 per sq. ft. in mid-1987, are forecast to rise to $31-39 by the end of 1988. The forecast for the average full floor net asking rate for the top ten core buildings is $36, compared with $32 in 1987. Rents for similar space in the downtown fringe and midtown areas are expected to move to a range of $25-29, compared with $20-24 at mid-1987. The Survey Team notes that the increase in rental rates in suburban locations will be proportionately less, as vacancies are expected to increase.

Royal LePage cautions that the Toronto Metropolitan Area office market is increasingly complex, with numerous districts, concentrations and dispersed areas. While the following discussions are grouped into three broad categories — the downtown, midtown and suburbs, because of space considerations, specific areas of interest should be investigated in detail.

Absorption of space in the downtown area during the first half of 1987 was slightly more than 2 million sq. ft., nearly twice the average over the last several years and a record for a six month period. Although preliminary figures from Royal LePage's office leasing data base indicate a slowing of demand in the second half, full year absorption in the downtown will be a strong 3.1 million sq. ft.

This level of demand explains why developers are extremely eager to initiate new projects. Royal LePage has identified 43 downtown projects that could accommodate a tenant with a 150,000 sq. ft. requirement prior to 1992. It should be noted that construction would not start on many of these projects without a core tenant.

Completions in the downtown core in 1988 will total 1.8 million sq. ft., compared with 1.15 in 1987. The key project is Campeau Corporation's 1.5 million sq. ft. Scotia Plaza at 40 King Street West, with the Bank of Nova Scotia as lead tenant. Because it will be one of the few buildings offering relatively large blocks of space in a very tight financial core market, Scotia Plaza seems reasonably certain of leasing success, even at average net rents of ¢35 per sq. ft.

Absorption in the downtown area in 1988, forecast to reach 2.4 million sq. ft., will be greater than the new supply. As a result, the vacancy rate will continue to decline, reaching 2.5 per cent by the end of 1988. The office forecast notes that there will be shortages of space in the downtown core throughout the year, due to lack of adequate supply levels in mid price ranges.

In the future, the development requirements of the downtown market increasingly will be fulfilled by the area west of the financial office core. Several large developments such as the CN Convention Centre and the

World Centre for Automated Banking have extended office development well to the west of the University Ave. area. Development of the CBC lands between John and Simcoe Streets south of Wellington Street and a large office development in the block immediately north of the CBC site will accelerate this trend. In addition, redevelopment of the railway lands south of Front Street between Bathurst Street and the financial core is planned.

A notable aspect of the office market in 1988 will be the start of construction of a number of exciting projects. Within the financial core, two major projects are planned. BCE Place, being developed by Bell Canada Enterprise Development Corporation, will occupy the block bounded by Bay, Front, Wellington and Yonge Streets. The first building in BCE Place will be in excess of 1 million sq. ft. and will be named for Canada trust, the core tenant. The other major project, a 1.5 million sq. ft. office/retail complex, will be developed by Trizec Corporation Ltd. and Markborough Properties on a site that comprises most of the two city blocks bounded by Adelaide and Richmond Streets between Yonge and Bay Streets.

Activity will be equally strong in the area surrounding the core, with construction starting on several major office projects including Phase III of College Park, York Hanover's World Trade Centre, Cadillac Fairview's CBC Broadcast Centre and the second phase of Campeau Corporation's Waterpark Place.

Absorption in the midtown office market, projected to reach only 660,000 sq. ft. in 1988, will continue to be constrained by lack of new supply. New supply largely will be provided by the 300,000 sq. ft. Crown Life Place at 175 Bloor Street East. As a result, midtown vacancy will decline to 2.9 per cent by year end. Because of the shortage of sites, the midtown districts of Bloor Street, St. Clair Avenue and Eglinton Avenue which have always been popular with tenants preferring moderate rental rates, will increasingly be bypassed in favour of the North Yonge corridor and the suburban districts.

The suburban office districts now account for approximately 40 per cent of all space in the Toronto CMA. This percentage is rising every year as the suburbs have regularly been accounting for more than 50 per cent of the Toronto area absorption. During 1988, new supply will total 4.3 million sq. ft., while absorption is projected to reach 3.8 million sq. ft. This means that the vacancy rate will increase slightly, to 11.2 per cent, up from 10.4 per cent at the end of 1987.

Most of the future development activity in Metro North will be in the North Yonge corridor, from York Mills Road to Steeles Avenue. Activity in Metro East is focused in Scarborough, north of Highway 401 and in Markham, where the northern limit of substantial office development has pushed past Highway 7. There will be continued strong growth in Metro West, notes the Survey Team, as the area is well served by a good road system and has an abundance of attractive office sites close to Toronto International Airport.

□*Industrial.* The impact of a healthy manufacturing sector, consumer demand for durables and big ticket items and investor interest continues to generate strong demand for manufacturing and distribution facilities. As a result, sales and leasing activity is at a record level in the Greater Metro Toronto industrial market.

A key trend throughout 1987 has been the emergence of an owner-oriented market, reflecting readily available financing, prosperous manufacturers and relatively stable interest rates. With strong demand and a shortage of product for sale, buildings are turning over quickly. The majority of buyers are investors and large manufacturers who have special needs that cannot be met in leased premises. Average cost per sq. ft. for freestanding buildings range from approximately $35-65, equal to replacement cost.

Strong demand for leased premises is being sourced from all types and sizes of users; small units in the suburban fringe are particularly in demand. Average rental rates range from $3.25-5 per sq. ft. net.

Increasing tenant mobility also has become apparent for non-capital/equipment intensive users, as firms move to areas of lower costs, both from a standpoint of rents and taxes, and to areas where there is a better selection of leased premises.

Developers have responded to the demand for industrial premises by increasing construction. In terms of development, speculative construction has been slightly more prevalent than build to suit. A small portion of this construction will be related to condominium projects; small space users are considering condominium purchase as an alternative to leasing because of the equity position it offers.

Royal LePage research indicates that land for industrial use within the Metro boundary is increasingly limited in supply. While more land is available outside the Metro boundary, price increases throughout 1987 have had a slowing effect on the purchase of serviced land. There is no question that there is an ample supply of vacant land designated for industrial use in the suburban markets. However, there is some question as to the ability of the present servicing infrastructure to support more development on the suburban fringe. As a result of the severe shortage of serviced, industrial land available for sale, redevelopment of older industrial sites is expected to become more prevalent in the market.

Strong demand and dwindling supply in many size ranges and areas of Greater Metro have exerted upward pressure on rental rates throughout 1987. Overall, increases have ranged from 10-25 per cent. At the end of 1987, rents range from $3.25-5 per sq. ft. net. Generally, rates average $4.85 per sq. ft. for space in the 5,000-10,000 sq. ft. range; $4.25 for space between 10,000-25,000 sq. ft.; and $3.90 per sq. ft. for space between 25,000-50,000 sq. ft. In a number of locations, rental rates between $5-6 per sq. ft. net are being achieved.

Absorption is expected to be maintained at the 1987 rate of 16 million sq. ft. per annum, while available space (on the market for sale or lease, vacant or occupied) will be stable at approximately 30.7 million sq. ft.

Construction activity is forecast to continue strong in 1988, particularly in the suburbs to the north and west of Metro, where there is good availability of serviced industrial land and highway access. Overall, Royal LePage expects that new construction will approximate 25 million sq. ft., with more speculative and multi-tenanted buildings than in 1987.

Considering the construction emphasis on multi-tenant space, available space in this category is expected to rise, while available space in single-use buildings is expected to decline.

Royal LePage researchers say that the availability rate for single-use space will decline to 4.8 per cent in 1988, down from 5.8 per cent in 1987. The surge in multi-tenant construction means that the availability rate in this space category will reach 9.1 per cent in 1988, up from 8.6 per cent in 1987. Overall availability will decline to 6.3 per cent, compared with 6.8 per cent in 1987.

It is expected that the upward pressure on industrial rental rates witnessed during 1987 will abate somewhat in 1988. Rents are forecast to increase to a range of $3.50-5.50 per sq. ft. net.

□ *Investment.* A continuing shortage of product for sale and very strong demand are the key factors that will ensure continued competition in the Toronto-area commercial real estate investment market in 1988.

At the same time, demand increasingly will become more selective. There are two basic reasons for this.

Firstly, the Toronto investment market has witnessed a dramatic rise in prices during 1987. While demand is not expected to abate, there is a limit to what investors will pay, particularly with respect to less well-located product in metro or product situated in secondary markets.

The second major factor leading to a more selective investment approach is the overall implications of Tax Reform. With the real estate investor being subjected to increased taxation because of the reduction in the rate of capital cost allowance, a more selective, cautious approach will characterize investment decisions.

A forecast for a strong office market in Metropolitan Toronto during 1988 and steady increases in rental rates suggests that office product will continue to be a prime target for institutions and larger investors, both domestic and foreign. However, as was the case throughout 1987, the supply of quality office buildings for sale is expected to remain low. Consequently, when this type of product is available, competition will be extremely brisk.

Opportunities to acquire office product will be more readily available in secondary locations, such as the periphereal downtown and midtown areas and in suburban areas such as Mississauga, Pickering and Markham, where owners will begin to rationalize their portfolios. In large part, this rationalization will focus on buildings requiring retrofit or renovation to remain competitive in the office leasing market.

The Survey Team also believes that small to medium size users will begin to look more closely at the acquisition of office buildings, as rising rental rates cause the economics of owning office accommodation to become more attractive than that of leasing. In addition, some owners/occupiers may consider a sale and leaseback as a means of obtaining additional capital to inject into their own business. This will be especially true if interest rates should rise from their current position.

Royal LePage research has demonstrated that owners of residential buildings tend to trade amongst themselves because they understand the complexities of both market and rent review legislation. Bill 51 will intensify this trading, says the Team, because it has created an atmosphere in which a new owner is permitted to recover a variety of specified costs, including the cost of financing.

Generally, it is expected that the shortage of quality apartment buildings for sale will continue into 1988. As a result, many investors will turn their attention to large and small apartment buildings in secondary markets, such as Hamilton, London, Kitchener/Waterloo, St. Catharines and Ottawa. However, they will be highly selective in their approach.

In addition, investors will find that a number of longer-term owners who purchased residential properties under the M.U.R.B. program may release their buildings to the market. This is because M.U.R.B. tax advantages have diminished and will be phased out by 1991.

Quality retail investment product has become increasingly scarce, and is likey to remain so during 1988. Investors continue to be strongly attracted to the market because of the continued strength in consumer spending and the resultant upward pressure being placed on rental rates and values.

Despite these conditions, investors continue to be concerned with quality of both retail product and its tenants. As a result, there will be a growing expectation for higher returns unless considerable upside potential exists in the medium term. Some investors may satisfy their demand for retail product by looking outside the Toronto area, but their actions will be colored by the perception that there is more risk attached to product in secondary locations.

Given the strength of the industrial sector and the requirement for new construction, strong investment activity in this market area is assured. This will occur both through the purchase of existing facilities and involvement in the development process.

□ *Retail.* The Metropolitan Toronto retail sales and leasing market continues to be characterized by a shortage of product, largely due to a lack of new construction and few renovations of existing retail stock. High demand, combined with the lack of product, has also resulted in a substantial increase in quoted rental rates in nearly all categories and locations. In a growing number of instances, higher rents have forced established traditional retailers to relocate.

Suburban locations in particular, which have experienced substantial leasing demand and a severely limited supply of space in retail strips totalling 10-30,000 sq. ft., have experienced significant increases in quoted rental rates. As an example, a lease negotiated in mid-1987 in a Bayview Avenue location in North York was at a rental rate in the $40 range. Two years previously, this space was available at approximately $10 per sq. ft.

Royal LePage's retail data base indicates that, as of the third quarter of 1987, rental rates in regional centers are averaging $45 per sq. ft. net and are expected to climb steadily through 1988. Rates in new strip centers are $20-25 per sq. ft. net and should hold in this range. Downtown retail leasing in the $45 per sq. ft. net range; these rates are forecast to climb slowly in 1988.

Strong consumer confidence and an unemployment rate which at approximately 6 per cent is one of the lowest in Canada have provided the ideal environment in Metropolitan Toronto for impressive gains in retail sales. A major strength in the marketplace reflecting the desire of developers and retailers to capitalize on strengthening consumer spending intentions is the remerchandising of established neighbourhood districts. Examples here include Bayview Avenue, Mt. Pleasant, Queen Street East and West, Avenue Road, Bloor Street West and Church Street.

Looking ahead to 1988, Royal LePage researchers stress there will be no major additions of retail space. However, there will be a number of renovations and expansions of existing facilities, infill projects and construction of a number of suburban strip centres that will serve to satisfy some of the demand for new space.

Here are the expansions identified in regional centers:

☐ addition of a number of new stores, for a total of approximately 300,000 sq. ft., in North York's Fairview Mall. Completion is expected in Spring of 1988.

☐ addition of an Eaton's department store, together with a variety of smaller shops, in the Mississauga Sheridan Mall, for completion in late 1988. The new supply will total 250,000 sq. ft.

☐ construction of a Sears department store and miscellaneous ancilliary space in the Pickering Town Centre, with completion scheduled for the fall of 1988.

Provided that economic conditions are not dramatically reversed in 1988, the Metropolitan Toronto area is guaranteed to maintain its current status as one of the country's most dynamic and growth oriented commercial real estate markets.

Montreal Commercial Market Outlook
Overall market environment largely will remain positive

For the most part, 1987 proved to be a period of significant growth for Montreal's commercial real estate markets. Developer confidence remained buoyant throughout 1987 and leasing of office, retail and industrial space was strong.

It is anticipated the overall environment largely will remain positive throughout 1988. However, it is possible the investment market will experience slight price corrections. Investor cautiousness may result in a period of price stability or possibly a slight decline in prices; but it is felt this ultimately will provide a more equitable balance between supply and demand.

The following are Royal LePage's forecasts for the various sectors of Montreal's commercial real estate market:

□ *Office Leasing.* A comprehensive analysis of office leasing activity within Greater Montreal in 1987 indicates that overwhelming demand for post-1980 class A space by a broad range of users has resulted in record-setting levels of absorption. Developers and users of office space increasingly are focusing their attention on areas outside the core, which is facilitating the growing prominence of the suburban office market.

By December, 1987, total absorption is expected to approach 2 million sq. ft. However, completion of over 2 million sq. ft. of office space in the second half, combined with the addition of almost 780,000 sq. ft. in the first six months of the year, means that overall vacancy will rise to 11.2 per cent by year end 1987.

Office leasing activity in the South Shore, St. Laurent, West Island and North Shore is particularly strong. By the end of 1987, for example, suburban absorption is expected to total 1.32 million sq. ft., representing almost 66 per cent of all anticipated absorption in the metropolitan area during this period.

To address this demand, almost 2 million sq. ft. of space is scheduled to be added to the suburban class A office inventory by the end of 1987. Significant development in this market means that suburban office space now accounts for approximately 37 per cent of the overall office market, compared with 28 per cent at the end of 1986.

An analysis of the core office leasing market reveals that the overall core vacancy stood at 9.2 per cent as of June, 1987. At mid-year, only one project — the 250,000 sq. ft. Windsor Hotel redevelopment — had come on stream. Completion of the substantially preleased Les Co-operants building in the Fall increased the core office inventory by 500,000 sq. ft. With these project completions, the core office vacancy rate is projected to increase slightly by year-end 1987.

Because demand for post-1980 class A buildings predominated in the office leasing market in 1987, this space now is in limited supply. The Survey Team notes that vacancy within these newer core buildings is only 4 per cent. Tenants seeking contiguous core office space in excess of 50,000 sq. ft. often are unable to find suitable accommodation. Consequently, user interest is shifting to the more mature core class A buildings.

Due to continued strength in the suburban market and steady demand for core class A space, overall office vacancy is expected to drop to 10.4 per cent by year-end 1988.

As office inventory tightens, quoted rental rates will rise and inducement packages will decline by up to 10 per cent. In 1988, quoted rental rates for core class A space will range from $18-30 per sq. ft. net, up from $16-27 in 1987. Quoted rates for suburban space will range from $11-14 per sq. ft. net, an increase of approximately 50 cents per sq. ft.

net over 1987.

☐ *Industrial*. Heightened demand by investors, developers and users for quality industrial buildings has resulted in a limited availability of product particularly those located in West Island and the South Shore. When product is available, the cost ranges from $30-40 per sq. ft. This shortage of available product is forcing many corporations to lease space.

The generally healthy business climate has encouraged many industrial users to upgrade and expand their space requirements. As well, a number of new firms have moved into the area, intensifying demand for rental space for freestanding and multi-tenant facilities. By the end of 1987, Royal LePage researchers anticipate that absorption of industrial space will approach 2 million sq. ft.

In response to growing demand for space, both on a sale or rental basis, developers increasingly will proceed with construction of build-to-suit and multi-tenancy buildings. In 1987, approximately 2 million sq. ft. of space was released and another 2 million sq. ft. is scheduled to be available in 1988.

Although demand for serviced industrial land will remain strong in 1988, it will be in short supply, particularly in Montreal and West Island. The majority of serviced land currently is in the hands of developers. While some owners may be willing to lease certain parcels, the majority are not inclined to release well-situated sites.

☐ *Investment*. While the investment market largely remained positive in 1987, some buyer resistance became evident during the latter half of 1987. Investment yields for properties have declined to historic lows and investors increasingly are reluctant to pay escalating prices when rental rates are not keeping pace. An assessment of the market suggests that buyers and sellers are readjusting their expectations and will continue to do so in 1988.

There also are two key changes in the Provincial and City legislative frameworks which may affect investment activity during 1988:

☐ Amendments to the Provincial legislation which currently prohibits the conversion of apartments to condominiums. While it has been proposed that this moratorium be lifted in 1988, it is Royal LePage's opinion that the conversion process will not be easy. If this proves to be the case, it is possible that values of high-rise residential units, which have been bid upwards in anticipation of profits from conversion, may stabilize or decline slightly.

☐ A review of the central area by Montreal's city planning department. The new Civic Administration has initiated this review with the objective of producing a draft of a new downtown plan for discussion early in 1988. It is possible that significant changes could be proposed.

In 1988, local investors and traders will dominate the investment market. Demand will be strongest for class A office product and regional shopping centres. At present, however, supply of both product categories is scarce and prices are high. Should market adjustments materialize, as forecast, a better balance between achieveable rents and returns may evolve. This should make it easier for investors to acquire product that satisfies their criteria.

□ *Retail.* By the end of 1987, three retail projects — Le Windsor, Le Faubourg Ste-Catherine and Les Cours Mont-Royal — totalling 223,000 sq. ft. — are expected to be completed. In 1988, completion of Place Montreal Trust and La Maison des Cooperants/Les Promenades de la Cathedrale will add another 580,000 sq. ft. of retail space to the core. Most projects have substantial preleasing commitments.

Investor preference for smaller malls is evident, with most centres changing hands at prices ranging from $40-80 per sq. ft. net. Over the longer term, it is anticipated there will be increasing investor and developer interest in convenience or "pod" centres. Mini-malls, or pods typically contain five to 15 units, totalling 5,000-20,000 sq. ft.

Pods usually are located on busy streets or highways; therefore, intensified interest in this type of product will lead to increased demand for well-located sites along transportation arteries.

With the exception of some short term corrections in the investment market, it is anticipated that Montreal's commercial real estate markets will experience growth in 1988.

Ottawa/Carleton
Commercial Market Outlook
Increased investor, developer and user activity will spur market growth

Ottawa/Carleton's commercial real estate market continues to benefit from the economic prosperity that exists throughout most of Southern Ontario.

At the local level, steady growth in the non-Government service sector, activity by Crown Corporations and the continuing influx of high technology firms is providing consistently positive levels of expansion within all market sectors.

With these factors in place, the Royal LePage Survey Team has developed these projections:

□ *Office Leasing.* Continuing employment in the private sector, expansion by high technology companies and demand by Crown Corporations is resulting in healthy demand for office space, particularly in the suburban markets.

Statistics generated from Royal LePage's computerized office data base project that total absorption will reach 1.1 million sq. ft. by the end of 1987. Additions to office inventory during the same period are expected to total 1.2 million sq. ft. This will provide an overall office vacancy rate of 10.4 per cent.

By year end 1988, it is projected that overall office vacancy will increase to 11.1 per cent. The year-over-year increase largely will be a consequence of the market's inability to fully absorb new inventory outside the core. Demand will only surpass new supply in the core.

A better balance between core supply and demand began in 1987. Royal LePage researchers note that only three downtown office projects, totalling 407,000 sq. ft., will come on stream in 1987. Strong demand for this new core class A office space was experienced throughout the year. As a consequence, core vacancy will stand at 10.6 per cent by the end of 1987.

In 1988, only one office project is scheduled to be completed in the core. Transport Canada has preleased 200,000 sq. ft. of the 275,000 sq. ft. building presently being developed by Minto Construction. Total absorption in the core should reach 350,000 sq. ft., which will result in an overall core vacancy of 9.6 per cent by year-end 1988.

While demand for core class A office space will continue to dominate the market in 1988, Royal LePage notes that leasing activity in the core class B market will strengthen. Based on this projection, it is anticipated the core class B vacancy rate will decline to 7.3 per cent by December, 1988.

As vacancy rates tighten in the core, inducements are expected to become less generous and quoted rental rates will increase. By the end of 1988, quoted rates for core class A space will range from $19-25 per sq. ft. net, while core class B space will range from $12-16.

Within Ottawa's fringe and suburban office markets, Royal LePage researchers predict ongoing demand for class A space and continued development activity, albeit to a lesser extent than occurred in 1987.

The eastern suburban office market began to strengthen in 1987, largely due to the City of Gloucester's decision to consolidate its operations in the Glenview Park of Commerce. In total, 206,000 sq. ft. will be introduced in this market during 1987 and 160,000 is expected to be absorbed. This will result in an overall vacancy rate of 10.5 per cent by year-end 1987. Although demand will remain steady in 1988, completion of three major projects, totalling 220,000 sq. ft., will cause the overall vacancy rate to increase to 12.6 per cent by December, 1988.

In the western suburbs, demand from high technology firms has encouraged substantial development and absorption. By the end of 1987, over 517,000 sq. ft. of class A space will be introduced in the market. Healthy demand for existing space, together with substantial preleasing commitments for a large portion of the newly developed space, should lead to absorption of 589,000 sq. ft. in 1987.a As a result, the overall western suburban office vacancy rate will be 8.5 per cent and availability of contiguous floors of class A space will become limited.

Completion of a number of small office projects will characterize development in the western suburbs in 1988. Anticipated absorption of 300,000 sq. ft. largely will offset additions to inventory, resulting in an overall vacancy rate of 8.7 per cent as 1988 comes to a close.

Generally, quoted rental rates in all suburban areas will increase by up to $1 per sq. ft. net in 1988. It is forecast that suburban class A space will range from $13-18 per sq. ft. net, while class B space will range from $8-13.

□ *Industrial.* Industrial sales and leasing activity achieved healthy levels of growth in 1987. As well, demand by developers and owners for serviced industrial land has resulted in significant increases in land prices in some industrial parks over the past year.

Over 70 per cent of the 700,000 sq. ft. of industrial space that was absorbed in 1987 can be attributed to leasing of multi-tenant space. Developers have responded to this demand by constructing significant multi-tenant space in many of the Region's major industrial parks.

By the end of 1987, almost 1.3 million sq. ft. of the 7.7 million sq. ft. of multi-tenant industrial space will be unoccupied. The addition of another 400,000 sq. ft. of multi-tenant space in 1988, together with projected absorption of approximately 400,000 sq. ft., will cause total multi-tenant vacancy to decline marginally during 1988.

In contrast, only 2.5 per cent of the 8.7 million sq. ft. of single-use space in the Region is available for sale or lease. In 1988, anticipated absorption of 200,000 sq. ft. will equal additions to inventory, resulting in no change in available space.

Given that the overall availability of industrial space is expected to rise only slightly from its current level of 9.2 per cent, it is likely that quoted rental rates will continue to range from $6-10 per sq. ft. net, while standard warehouse facilities will be available at $4.50-6.

Those who develop speculative or build-to-suit premises in 1988 will find it increasingly difficult to acquire serviced industrial land within municipally-planned business parks such as Rideau Heights, the Ottawa Business Park and the Queensway Industrial Campus. Limited availability of land also will force many prospective purchasers to consider outlying areas. Buildings will carry price tags in the $50 per sq. ft. net range.

□ *Investment.* The investment market is expected to remain active in 1988. While proposed tax reform is of concern to all participants, it is not expected to be a long term negative factor in the marketplace. On the positive side, vendors are capitalizing on renewed leases at higher rental levels by releasing product with higher property values.

When institutional qualilty product becomes available, demand is strong. Private investors and local syndicates also are active in the market, preferring to purchase stable rental properties in the office and industrial sectors.

An important concern of the Survey Team is the longer term limitation of prime downtown development sites. As a result, "visionary" investors and developers are aggressively pursuing the remaining downtown land opportunities.

□ *Retail.* The emergence of in-fill retail development along the Region's major transportation arteries has resulted in significant price increases for high profile, zoned retail land. Accordingly, higher rental rates are being achieved in many areas.

To achieve current market rents, many owners of existing retail plazas have initiated renovation and upgrading programs. As well, the ability to achieve higher rents is encouraging development of a number of new retail projects.

Generally, Ottawa/Carleton's commercial real estate market will be positively impacted by increased investor, developer and user activity on the part of Government and private enterprise. For these reasons, the Survey Team forecasts solid growth in the Nation's capital in 1988.

Winnipeg Commercial Market Outlook
Declining vacancies and strong demand are encouraging commercial development

While other commercial real estate markets are characterized by peaks and valleys, Winnipeg's market continues to maintain a steady growth.

Forecasts of solid economic growth can be attributed, in part, to development of the $1.94 billion Limestone hydroelectric project, one of the largest construction projects currently underway in North America. As well, the local economy continues to benefit from capital expenditures and development incentives from all levels of Government.

Given these positives, the Royal LePage Survey Team offers these forecasts:

□ *Office Leasing.* In 1987, office leasing activity largely was characterized by lateral movement generated from accounting and legal firms, national companies with core office space, and Crown Corporations such as the Federal Business Development Bank.

Only one office project was completed in 1987. Approximately 90 per cent of the 275,000 sq. ft. Canada Place development currently is leased. Leasing activity in the Portage Avenue and Main Street intersection is brisk and tenants are finding it increasingly difficult to acquire contiguous class A space in excess of 20,000 sq. ft.

As absorption is anticipated to reach 250,000 sq. ft. in 1987, it is projected that the overall vacancy rate will stand at 9.7 per cent by the end of 1987. The core class A vacancy rate will be 6 per cent at year-end 1987. To reflect the strengthening office leasing market, quoted rental rates edged upward in 1987. Rental rates for new class A space range from $14-15 per sq. ft. net, while rents for older class A space range from $10.50-12.50.

The announcement of two major office projects to come on stream in 1989-1990 is indicative of investor/developer confidence in the market's ability to absorb quality office space. As neither of these projects is scheduled to be introduced in 1988, however, total office inventory should remain static. With projected absorption of 250,000 sq. ft., it is forecast that the overall office vacancy rate will decline to 6 per cent by December, 1988.

□ *Industrial.* Leasing activity throughout 1987 was hampered by the severe shortage of space. With an industrial vacancy rate of only 1 per cent, users are finding it virtually impossible to locate available space. When movement is possible, it generally involves distribution or service related companies.

Despite the exceedingly limited supply of space for lease, very little speculative construction was initiated in 1987. Developer cautiousness should lessen in 1988, however, and some multi-tenant projects are expected to be started.

Those wishing to purchase industrial buildings also are experiencing difficulty in acquiring suitable product. Available buildings in excess of 40,000 sq. ft. often are purchased by local investors who lease the entire facility to a single user or subdivide the space into multi-tenant units. Users who wish to establish an equity position usually choose to purchase freestanding buildings of approximately 10,000 sq. ft.

In 1988, the quoted rental rate for new multi-tenant space will be approximately $4.50 per sq. ft. net. On sale/leaseback agreements, quoted rental rates will range from $5-5.50 for new, build-to-suit facilities.

□ *Investment.* Investment activity largely was nonexistent in 1987 due to the absence of product for sale. Product that was available, usually through portfolio rationalizations, was aggressively pursued by local investors, developers and pension funds.

As in many Canadian centres, local and national investors favor retail product. In large part, investors are attracted to this sector because of solid rental rates and limited lease inducements.

□ *Retail.* As 1987 progressed, it became evident there was a growing scarcity of available land zoned for retail use along the City's major arteries. The reduced availability of suitable land has caused prices to increase. As well, it is projected that owners of existing retail buildings, particularly those located close to the core, will redevelop and remerchandise buildings in 1988. Land still is available outside the core and retail development occurs in areas where residential subdivisions are being built.

Quoted rental rates stabilized in 1987 following a period of price escalations in 1986. Rates are forecast to remain firm in 1988, ranging from $14-18 per sq. ft. net for strip mall space near major transportation arteries. Retail space along Portage Avenue is being quoted at $16-18 per sq. ft. net, while rates within regional centres range from $35-40.

Projections of modest sales and leasing activity in most sectors should auger well for Winnipeg's commercial real estate market in 1988.

Regina Commercial Market Outlook
Modest growth will be largely similar to that of 1987

Regina's commercial real estate market largely was categorized by stable growth in 1987. Moderate activity in the retail and industrial sectors, plus growing interest in the investment market, helped mitigate a flattening of demand in the office leasing sector.

Looking ahead to 1988, it is likely that the proposed privatization of some Crown Corporations could create more activity in the private sector. As well, the continuation of acceptable interest rates and attractive yields on investment product should foster continued investor confidence.

□ *Office Leasing.* Limited absorption of office space and no additions to inventory resulted in a virtually flat office leasing market in 1987. Consequently, the overall office vacancy rate will decline only marginally to 4.5 per cent by December, 1987, from 4.8 per cent at year-end 1986. When Government space is excluded, the overall competitive vacancy rate is expected to be 8 per cent in December, 1987.

The vast majority of leasing activity is, and will continue to be, generated from businesses which are upgrading. While the Provincial Government appears to have satisfied its space requirements, some Federal Government leases are expiring which may prompt additional leasing activity.

Following two years of no office construction, core office inventory will expand by 100,000 sq. ft. in 1988. In January, 40,000 sq. ft. will be available in the Saskatchewan Drive Plaza. Another 60,000 sq. ft. of office space is to be released in February when the multi-million dollar Convention Centre is completed. Construction of the 48,000 sq. ft. Park Centre Office Building, located just outside the core, also will be completed in the Spring of 1988. The project is 60 per cent preleased.

Because anticipated absorption in 1988 is expected to offset additions to office inventory, the overall office vacancy in December, 1988 will fall to 3.8 per cent. The vacancy rate for competitive space will stand at 6.1 per cent.

With vacancy rates on the decline, it is likely that owners of existing office towers, such as the Lloyds Bank building and Canada Trust Tower, will contemplate plans to construct twin structures in 1988. Possible development will hinge on the ability of owners and developers to locate anchor tenants.

The declining office vacancy rate will cause quoted rental rates to edge upward in 1988. However, because of anticipated Government cutbacks in space requirements, quoted rental rates for core class A space in post-1982 buildings will be similar to rates quoted in 1987.

□ *Industrial.* Throughout 1987, Regina's industrial market was characterized by steady leasing activity and the sale of modest amounts of space to small plumbing, printing and distribution companies. Properties are selling for $20-25 per sq. ft., including land, which is 20-30 per cent below replacement cost.

As 1987 comes to a close, the overall industrial vacancy rate stands at 5 per cent, unchanged from year-end 1986. The vacancy rate for multi-tenant space will remain at 8 per cent, double the rate found in single-use space. In 1988, anticipated absorption of 200,000 sq. ft. will equal proposed additions to industrial inventory. Consequently, vacancy levels will remain static and quoted rental rates will hold at 1987 levels. Quoted rental rates will range from $3.25-3.50 per sq. ft. net for warehouse space and from $7-8 for space with a high office component.

Increasing demand for higher-end space in 1987 led to the construction of two speculative multi-tenant projects. Another 50,000 sq. ft. of speculative, multi-tenant space is expected to be released in 1988.

□ *Investment.* Favorable interest rates and lower yields on other traditional investment vehicles have strengthened demand for income-producing real estate. In general, however, the supply of available class A office, core and regional retail, and high-rise residential product remains low.

Redevelopment of the core area is spawning renewed interest in downtown land assembly. It is anticipated that completion of the 300-room Ramada Renaissance Hotel and Convention Centre, together with redevelopment of Midtown Centre, will encourage future construction.

□ *Retail.* Heightened construction and redevelopment activity will characterize the retail market in 1988. Core retail projects to be completed in 1988 include a 100,000 sq. ft. renovation to Midtown Centre and a 35,000 sq. ft. renovation to Regina Inn Mall. In addition, a 35,000 sq. ft. strip mall on Albert Street North and an 80,000 sq. ft. renovation project to Avon Shopping Centre will be completed in 1988.

Despite additions to core retail inventory, demand by national retailers will keep the core retail vacancy rate at 1 per cent. Quoted rental rates for core retail space likely will increase by approximately $2 per sq. ft., to $16-22, by the end of 1988.

Calgary Commercial Market Outlook
City's improved economic and business climates will be key positives

The recovery in Calgary's commercial real estate market is a reflection of the optimistic mood prevailing in the City. Economic revival in

Calgary began slowly in the Fall of 1986, picked up steam in the spring of 1987 and now has a positive momentum. While it cannot be termed "healthy", Calgary's economy is rebounding and well on its way to a reasonable status.

According to the Market Survey Team, ongoing improvements in the City's economy and hence the commercial real estate market largely will be the result of three positive factors:

☐ returning confidence within the oil and gas sector

☐ The 1988 Winter Olympic Games

☐ continuing progress in the diversification of the Alberta economy

With the OPEC countries maintaining production levels at close to stated quotas and the continuing war between Iraq and Iran, international oil prices have stabilized. In late Summer 1987, they ranged from $19-20 U.S. a barrel, a solid although unspectacular price for the industry.

Strengthening oil prices, which could rekindle exploration, have not been the only positive in the oil patch. Activity in the industry also is being spurred by royalty holidays of up to five years from the provincial Government, the end of the 10 per cent federal oil and gas revenue tax and the implementation of the $350 million Canadian Exploration and Development Incentive Program.

Complementing changes in the operating environment have been company initiatives to optimize internal operations: oil and gas firms in Calgary have achieved greater efficiencies and are intent on staying "lean and mean". Therefore, while the international price of oil likely will continue to fluctuate, there is a prevailing feeling that the worst times are past.

The message that Calgary is on the mend and that there is upside potential will be broadcast to a world-wide audience in 1988 when the City hosts The Olympic Winter Games. In addition, this event is expected to inject millions of dollars into the Calgary economy. This economic benefit was experienced during 1987 in the office leasing market, where Olympic-associated tenants have leased a significant amount of short-term space.

☐ *Office Leasing.* The gradual strengthening of business confidence in the Calgary economy has resulted in a modest upturn in the City's office leasing market.

Compared with 1986, the number of tenants actively seeking space increased dramatically in 1987. This is expected to continue into the new year, with tenant expansions, new companies to the City and a stable demand base in the energy sector all serving to reduce vacancies both in the downtown core and Beltline markets.

It is significant that not one area of the economy has dominated office leasing activity. Demand for accommodation has been sourced from all quarters, including oil and gas, information processing and communications, financial and other services, new business starts and outside firms new to Calgary.

114

Class A headlease space (space available directly from the landlord) is at the forefront of leasing activity after receiving very little attention in 1986. Attractive rental rates combined with still sizeable inducements have played a major role in generating this activity.

Although the changes in the office market have been gradual, it is clear that momentum is building. Absorption of space in the total market in 1987 is projected to reach 650,000 sq. ft., compared with negative absorption of 530,000 sq. ft. in 1986. The vacancy rate is forecast to decline to 19.2 per cent at the end of 1987, down from approximately 20 per cent at the beginning of the year.

The downtown core which has accounted for the bulk of leasing activity, is expected to achieve absorption of approximately 600,000 sq. ft. in 1987. However, the net decline in vacant space will be only 200,000 sq. ft. due to the completion of the 400,000 sq. ft. Cascade Tower in December. As a result, core vacancy will be relatively stable at 17 per cent.

There has been a tightening of rental rates, with most of the prime buildings quoting rates in the mid to the upper end of the $10-16 per sq. ft. net range.

Following closely on the heels of the downtown core, the Beltline market also has faired well, with absorption in 1987 expected to reach 150,000 sq. ft. This will result in a year end vacancy rate of 17.4 per cent.

In contrast, competitive pressure from the downtown core has hampered recovery in the suburban markets. Royal LePage is forecasting negative absorption of 100,000 sq. ft. in the suburbs in 1987, as tenants continue to pursue attractive opportunities in more centralized markets.

Activity in Calgary's office leasing market is forecast to continue to increase throughout 1988, as the economy strengthens and the price of oil demonstrates further stability. The Survey Team notes that the timing of lease expiries, particularly in early 1988, will lead to a substantial rise in tenants actively seeking space, and these tenants will increasingly be in an expansionary mode.

Overall absorption in 1988 is forecast to surpass 1 million sq. ft., with attention primarily on the class A market. Citywide, vacancy will increase slightly, reaching 19.4 per cent by year end. Impacting vacancy rates will be the completion of two projects, the 808,000 sq. ft. Canterra Tower and the 650,000 sq ft. Amoco Tower.

It is expected that demand in 1988 will result in a tightening of class A rental rates, to a range of $14-18 per sq. ft. net, up $2-4 from 1987. Inducements, which ranged from $25-40 per sq. ft. at the end of 1987, are forecast to recede to the $20-30 range.

The office market forecast also suggests that vacancy rates in the core and overall suburban market will show only minor change, settling at approximately 17.7 per cent and 19.4 per cent respectively by the end of 1988. The vacancy rate in the Beltline, however, will drop below 12 per cent, compared with more than 17 per cent at the end of 1987.

□ *Industrial.* Calgary's industrial market has never experienced the extreme highs and lows as did its sister office leasing market. This sector of the City's commercial real estate scene has simply moved along, quietly chipping away at the over-capacity left behind after the 1982 recession.

However, the industrial market is now starting to move at a quicker tempo. The Survey Team expects that absorption will increase slightly, reaching 1 million sq. ft. in 1988, while the vacancy rate will drop from 9.6 to approximately 7.5 per cent. With the rapidly falling vacancy rate, debate is increasing as to when Calgary will experience its first new speculative industrial construction start since 1981. The Team feels this much awaited event will occur sometime in 1988.

Indeed shortages of all types of product are now beginning to appear. Royal LePage industrial experts feel a full 3 per cent of the 9.6 per cent space vacant is only useable as dead storage, i.e. this space is not functional for a modern warehousing operation. Therefore, there is only 6.6 per cent or approximately 3.5 million readily useable sq. ft. available in Calgary's industrial market.

As vacancies continue to drop, and the shortages become more pronounced, rental rates will increase. While average rents will respond to the demand pressure and increase from $3.50 per sq. ft. to $3.75 in 1988, these rents will still not be high enough to make new construction economically viable.

Therefore, the great majority of industrial development activity will continue to be build-to-suit. If construction activity does increase in 1988, the availability of serviced land will not be a problem. Royal LePage statistics indicate that the City has approximately 20& acres, while private owners hold another 100 acres.

Calgary's industrial tenant mix is largely the same as in previous years, with a noticeable increase in new smaller businesses initiated by recently unemployed oil and gas personnel. As has been the case in the past, the market continues to be dominated by distribution companies.

□ *Investment.* Renewed confidence in Calgary has led to a dramatic increase in investment activity over 1986, as underscored by several notable sales in 1987.

Of particular note are the sale of several major office buildings including Place 800, Canada Place, the Fina Building, Project 700 and, in the Beltline and suburban markets, Mount Royal Place and Crestview Centre.

In contrast to the limited demand in 1986 for office buildings other than those which were 90 to 100 per cent leased, demand in 1987 widened to include growing interest in empty or partially empty buildings. The interest is projected to continue in 1988.

Fuelling this interest are a combination of factors. Clearly, economic considerations go beyond the recent revival in the oil and gas industry and point to the long-term viability of the energy sector and the local economy. In addition, the considerable upside profit potential available to investors, together with market prices that are generally below replacement cost, have proven attractive to investors seeking above average rates of return not available in other Canadian centres.

The Market Survey Team notes that recent transactions show an upward shift in values for well-located properties of all types. As with 1987, there remain very few fully leased office buildings for sale. Similarly, well leased industrial buildings for sale are in limited supply. A reasonable amount of apartment blocks and strip shopping centres have been trading with a good demand/supply balance. Throughout 1988, market priced properties will continue to be in demand.

The 1988 forecast calls for an active investment market. As in 1987, primary buyers are expected to be Eastern Canadian groups and individuals, with Hong Kong and Japanese investors showing increased interest. Local investors are also becoming more visible and aggressive and are beginning to seriously compete for Calgary's well priced properties.

□ *Retail.* The activity currently underway in Calgary's retail sector is a reflection of both the buoyant feeling in the marketplace and the underlying fierce competition among developers for market share.

Strengthening consumer confidence and an increase in leasing activity has meant a surge of new development. Considerable expansion and renovation of existing facilities is currently underway, as well as new major developments. Calgary now has 2.2 million sq. ft. of additional retail space being built in major shopping areas.

Large expansions/renovations recently completed or scheduled for completion in 1988 include Southcentre Mall — 120,000 sq. ft.; Chinook Mall — 130,000 sq. ft.; Market Mall — 94,000 sq. ft.; and Northland Village Mall — 440,000 sq. ft.

New projects on the drawing board include The Renaissance — 410,000 sq. ft.; Canyon Creek Centre — 560,000 sq. ft.; Banker's Hall retail component — 250,000 sq. ft.; the retail component of the new Eaton complex — 170,000 sq. ft. and the new Eaton's Store itself — an increase of 40,000 sq. ft. over its current size.

The 2.2 million sq. ft. figure for additional retail space does not include the addition of many smaller retail strip malls scattered throughout the City, estimated to add another 800,000 sq. ft. to the City's retail inventory.

As current trends indicate, Calgary's economy will have to continue its rapid improvement if the City's retail sector is to maintain its expansionary mode.

Edmonton Commercial Market Outlook
Rate of growth hinges on continued recovery of resource sector

Edmonton's commercial real estate market is in a state of transition. While some sectors are experiencing moderate growth, others have yet to rebound from historically low levels of activity caused by energy-related instability in late 1986 and early 1987.

Looking to 1988, it is anticipated that renewed activity in the energy and pulp and paper sectors should favorably impact the local economy. In turn, this will assist the general health of the commercial real estate market.

In the longer term, it is hoped that the Federal Government's recently announced Western Diversification Program will spawn economic opportunities in Edmonton. Under the proposed program, to be administered from Edmonton, the Federal Government plans to spend $1.2 billion over five years to reduce Western Canada's dependence on resource and agricultural markets.

The Royal LePage Survey Team recognizes that Edmonton's economic revitalization still is fragile and may be arrested should oil prices drop significantly or interest rates substantially rise. Barring these circumstances, Royal LePage anticipates a continuation of the current recovery of Edmonton's commercial real estate markets.

□ *Office Leasing.* During most of 1987, the office leasing market remained sluggish, operating at historically low levels of activity. While leasing activity strengthened in the latter half of the year, only minimal absorption is expected by December, 1987. Concurrently, no office space will be introduced to the market. As a result, the overall office vacancy at the end of 1987 is forecast to be approximately 19.6 per cent, while central core vacancy will be in excess of 18 per cent.

In 1988, one office tower, the Federal Government's Canada Place, will be completed. While the Government plans to occupy the majority of the 875,000 sq. ft. building, indications are that some space will be placed on the market.

It is projected that office leasing activity by other levels of Government will be marginal in 1988. It should be noted, however, that the Provincial Government has preleased 400,000 sq. ft. of office space in a downtown project being developed by Olympia & York Developments Limited. Construction is expected to begin in 1988. with a scheduled completion in 1990.

Leasing activity in 1988 largely will come from smaller tenants. As total absorption in 1988 is not expected to exceed levels achieved in 1987, an increase in the overall vacancy rate is anticipated.

Private sector users which seek office space in 1988 will continue to benefit from leasing opportunities within Edmonton's relatively static office market.

An examination of current leasing practices reveals a number of key trends.

□ Generally, there appears to be a growing preference for longer term leases, often in excess of 10 years. Tenants perceive that current rates are minimal and they wish to capitalize on this advantage.

□ The use of "staged" or "staggered" rates also is becoming more popular, with minimal rates in the early years of a lease, which escalate over time.

☐ The availability of favorable rental sales and generous incentives in the core also are encouraging some tenants to move downtown from locations in the core periphery.

At year-end 1987, quoted rental rates for core class A space will range from $12-14 per sq. ft. net, with inducement packages ranging from $40-45 per sq. ft. These conditions are not expected to change in 1988.

As in 1987, sublease space will be a significant part of the office market in 1988. The prominence of the sublease market largely is due to a downsizing of space requirements by major tenants. This downsizing has placed a substantial amount of finished core class A space on the market which is available at rental rates which are well below that quoted for newly developed space.

☐ *Industrial.* Following rather sluggish activity in 1987, it is expected that the industrial sales and leasing market will show signs of recovery in 1988.

The majority of leasing activity will be generated from smaller users, seeking 2,500-4,000 sq. ft. small bay units in multi-tenant buildings. These tenants are choosing to upgrade their locations to better industrial areas and higher profile locations. There also is increasing demand for space by larger users, seeking up to 100,000 sq. ft.

Heightened demand by small users and institutions, including those based in Eastern Canada, will create a more active industrial sales market in 1988. As in 1987, small users typically will seek small single-user buildings while institutions will prefer large single-user properties and multi-tenant complexes.

The return of a healthier market should cause rental rates and selling prices to increase. It is anticipated that industrial rental rates, on average, will increase by $0.50 per sq. ft. net, with some higher-end industrial office space increasing by $1 per sq. ft. net. By year-end 1988, rates will range from $2-3 per sq. ft. net for warehouse space and from $2.50-4 for higher end industrial/office space.

Due to the ready availability of all types of industrial space for sale and lease, construction of industrial space was limited in 1987. Demand by tenants for smaller bays dominates in the leasing market. Should demand continue, it is anticipated that shortages of smaller bays may occur in well-located multiple tenancy buildings. As demand increases and supply tightens in 1988, it is likely that more build-to-suit construction will occur. The majority of construction will take place in the northwest and southeast industrial areas.

Renewed construction activity, will create greater demand for serviced industrial land. The supply is adequate, however, and developers should not experience difficulty in acquiring suitable building sites.

☐ *Investment.* An upswing in investment activity occurred in 1987. Providing interest rates remain favorable, this upward trend should continue into 1988. An examination of commercial real estate transactions in 1987 indicates that high rise residential buildings and shopping malls are the

119

prefered investment vehicles.

While smaller investment product is of interest to local investors, many of the larger transactions involve individuals from Ontario and Quebec who are cash rich and perceive that product is underpriced. Offshore investors are beginning to express an interest in the market, but the majority of pension funds and life companies have yet to seek out product.

Generally, buyers are seeking quality product that provides yields of approximately 10 per cent on cash invested. For the most part, purchases are not based on anticipated increases in future rental rates but, rather, on actual income currently in place.

Product that is available usually is released by individuals who wish to sell, by companies which are rationalizing their portfolios or through a bank liquidation or foreclosure.

□ *Retail.* The retail sector continues to be the most active commercial real estate market in Edmonton. Retail projects presently underway include: the 500,000 sq. ft. Eaton Centre — Phase 1; the 84,000 sq. ft. ManuLife Centre; a 400,000 sq. ft. expansion to Kingsway Garden Mall; a 350,000 sq. ft. renovation to The Bay; construction of a 100,000 sq. ft. strip plaza in Sherwood Park; construction of a 450,000 sq. ft. regional shopping mall; a 40,000 sq. ft. expansion of the Edmonton Centre.

Quoted rental rates in the new shopping centres currently range from $20-35 per sq. ft. net. Rental rates for strip mall space is between $12-14 per sq. ft. net. but most malls are fully leased. It is anticipated that rental rates will remain constant in 1988, although the range and type of inducements may alter.

While many economic variables could impact the rate of recovery of Edmonton's commercial real estate market, it is likely that many key sectors will experience positive and continuing growth in 1988.

Vancouver Commercial Market Outlook
A strengthening economy will lead to healthy supply and demand

A resurgence of sales and leasing activity was noted in most sectors of the Vancouver commercial real estate market throughout 1987. In general, the major contributing factor to the current health of the market is strong user and investor confidence based on much improved economic conditions within the Province. One of the key reasons for the strengthening economy is the revitalization of the forestry industry, one of the primary engines of growth.

Ongoing recovery within the general economy, strengthening interest from Pacific Rim investors and expansion by office tenants, should ensure continued health within the commercial real estate market in 1988.

Protracted labor unrest could negatively impact the provincial economy and, subsequently, the commercial real estate market. However, it is hoped that new labor legislation which now is in place will lead to a more stable workforce in 1988.

☐ *Office Leasing.* For the first time in over two years, the overall office vacancy rated posted a significant decline in 1987. This was a consequence of strong leasing activity, together with the limited addition of new inventory in the Downtown and Central Broadway areas.

In 1987, only one Downtown office project — a 96,000 sq. ft. building at 900 Howe Street — was completed. The relocation of several suburban tenants to class A buildings has created healthy leasing activity. By the end of 1987, anticipated absorption of 900,000 sq. ft. is expected to result in an overall office vacancy rate of 15 per cent, down 5 percentage points from December, 1986. Limited office construction, together with sustained demand for space, will ensure that the overall vacancy rate drops even further in 1988.

In Central Broadway, overall office vacancy also is expected to decline. Following a moderate amount of leasing activity, absorption is expected to total 50,000 sq. ft. in 1987. Since total inventory remains unchanged from 1986, overall vacancy stands at 8 per cent, almost two percentage points lower than in the previous year.

Royal LePage researchers note that only two office projects are scheduled to be completed in 1988. Both are located in Central Broadway. The 75,000 sq. ft. MSA/BCE building is almost 75 per cent preleased and healthy interest has been noted for the 46,000 sq. ft. Boxer Holdings project.

Projected absorption of approximately 1 million sq. ft. in 1988 will more than offset additions to office inventory. Consequently, overall office vacancy should drop four percentage points to 11 per cent by the end of 1988.

Since very little "view" space currently is available in new class A Downtown projects, demand has begun to shift to older class A and class B buildings that offer suitable space at competitive rates. There also is a shortage of class A space in Central Broadway.

As the office market returns to a more healthy balance of supply and demand, it is likely that landlords will offer less generous inducements. Quoted rental rates, however, should remain firm in 1988. Downtown class A space will be offered at $15-25 per sq. ft. net, while class A space in Central Broadway will range from $11-16.

☐ *Industrial.* Sales, leasing and development activity gathered momentum in 1987, making the industrial sector one of the strongest components of Vancouver's commercial real estate market.

Growing confidence in the Provincial economy, acceptable interest rates, and sustained leasing and purchasing activity by users and investors were highly conducive to the development of large amounts of speculative space. By the end of 1987, almost 1 million sq. ft. of speculative space will have been added to the industrial inventory. When

121

build-to-suit projects are taken into account, the industrial data base will expand by 1.5 million sq. ft. in 1987.

Demand by service companies, warehousing operations and distributors, however, will result in anticipated absorption of approximately 2 million sq. ft. in 1987. By the end of 1987, only 3.6 per cent of the 96 million sq. ft. of industrial space will be vacant. Overall multi-tenant vacancy is expected to be slightly over 3 per cent, with single-user vacancy at 4 per cent. Looking to 1988, it is likely that vacancy rates in all industrial categories will remain relatively static. Only a small increase in the availability of single-use space is forecast, while available multi-tenant space should continue to hover around 1.7 million sq. ft.

Construction of, and demand for, multi-tenant space will continue to dominate the industrial market through 1988. Royal LePage researchers note that four major speculative projects are expected to be completed in 1988, adding almost 1 million sq. ft. of multi-tenant space to the market. Additional multi-tenant space may also be introduced as owners of older single-use buildings opt to renovate existing facilities to suit multi-user tenancies. It is suggested that demand in 1988 will be especially strong for 3,000-5,000 sq. ft. bays located within South Vancouver, Burnaby, Surrey, Richmond and Annacis Island. Demand for manufacturing facilities in these five principal markets may result in a shortage of product.

An analysis of movement within industrial parks suggests that many larger bulk users will migrate from the higher cost central areas to outlying areas such as Crestwood Park in Richmond, Willingdon Business Park and Marine Way Industrial Centre in Burnaby, Mayfaire in Coquitlam and Annacis Island.

Improvements to infrastructure in the outlying areas will facilitate demand and encourage development.

Quoted rental rates for warehouse and industrial/office space will range from $4-7 and $6-9 per sq. ft. net, respectively, in 1988. Inducements will remain limited.

□ *Investment.* By the end of the year, it is projected that the value of investment sales will approach $1.5 billion. Royal LePage data suggests that the value of office and high-rise residential buildings will be marginally higher in 1987; however, the greatest year over year increase will occur in the industrial market.

In 1988, it is anticipated that prime commercial real estate will become more expensive and initial returns on investment will dwindle as the availability of investment product tightens. As well, a growing awareness of the limited supply of developable land will result in escalations in land prices. A premium will be obtained for land already zoned for commercial use.

As in 1987, investor interest will focus on premium office, high-rise residential, retail and industrial product. The largest thrust of investment activity will come from Pacific Rim investors. As well, pension funds and institutions will become more active in the market. Pension funds, for example, increasingly are investing in the industrial market, attracted by the low vacancy factor, improved rents and the relative east of manag-

122

ing industrial properties.

Royal LePage researchers note that pension funds and institutions are aggressively seeking industrial buildings, portfolios and serviced land. Demand for high-rise residential and condominium buildings will continue to be strong. However, owners will be reluctant to part with such product.

□ *Retail.* While a number of major retail developments are expected to come on stream in 1988, it is likely that quoted rental rates will remain firm. This is because most of the retail space under construction is expected to fill an existing vacuum.

In 1987, it became apparent there was a dwindling amount of prime land available for retail development. Prime assembled sites are in strong demand and command high prices. Rezoning applications generally are subject to stringent guidelines.

With limited development opportunities available, there is growing emphasis on retrofitting existing centres. Renovated and remerchandized retail product is being aggressively sought by various participants in the investment community, specifically Asian investors.

On the whole, Vancouver's commercial real estate market should continue to benefit if key resource sectors remain on the path of economic recovery.

Quebec: Economy in constant growth

Due to its strategic location, a 92 000 000 persons potential market is at Quebec's door. Indeed, Quebec's industrial centers are a one hour flight or within one day's truck drive from the Northeastern and North Central United States and five Canadian provinces.

Thirty national and international airlines serve Mirabel and Dorval International airports and multilane highways link the major industrial centers of the province with the 'States' and neighbouring provinces. Quebec's transportation asset is the St-Lawrence River, open all year round with ten ports along its banks, including the Port of Montreal, the most important inland port in North America.

The primary language of Quebec's population is French but Montreal, which contains half of the population, is a large cosmopolitan center and, like such cities all over the world, Quebec business people are bilingual thus facilitating trade relations in North America as well as in Europe, in Africa and in Asia. Quebec's 2 800 000 workers are the best educated in Canada and are renowned as being productive and ingenious.

The Quebec way of life, a meeting of European and North American influence, emphasizes nature: skiing, fishing, sailing and golfing are within an hour's drive from major cities where very creative cultural activities take place: Concerts, ballets, theatre, movies and fine dining . . . !

Quebec is very stable politically and its economy is in constant growth. The average inflation rate for the last five years is around 4% per annum. Quebec's corporate income taxes are the lowest in Canada and this contributes to a dynamic economy. More than thirty national and international banks and other financial institutions provide wide investment and business support. Montreal Stock Exchange, the second most active in Canada, has high vitality.

Quebec has very diversified manufacturing and industrial sectors as well as extensive commercial and tourist activities. These are well supported by a large variety of natural resources and specialized services and facilities.

Abundant electricity, at one of the lowest industrial rates in the world, is another major asset for Quebec. Produced and distributed by Hydro-Quebec, a Government Agency, the kilowatt/hour rate was 2,68$ in 1986 (1 Can. $ = 0,73$ U.S. approximately).

To create and retain jobs, Quebec has put in place a number of investment incentives covering activities like plan establishment, expansion, product or production process innovation, industrial design, exports, skills training/job creation, research and development. Grants, loans or income benefits are some of the financial assistance available.

Quebec reaches out to the world and the province's export trade has reached more than $20 million a year. Sixteen Quebec trade offices spread over five continents contribute to increase exports.

Quebec's industry focus is on technologies to develop gaps in the province's industrial and commercial sectors. Government aids to promote R&D are very attractive: 20% to 40% tax write off on salary devoted to R&D, 50% reimbursement on buying R&D equipment and other assistance for research.

Quebec's strengths in high technology areas are: Transportation Industries, biotechnologies, microelectronics, in telecommunications and software, the plastic transformation industry, aerospace industries and defence products, energy intensive industries (metallurgical and chemical).

In the **transportation industry,** the need is for new vehicle manufacturers with medium and short series production, assembly activities with R&D, vehicle electronics, quality control and productivity.

More a new products development technology than an industrial sector, **biotechnological industries** nevertheless have high potential and more than 360 researchers in the province are working on medical, agricultural, chemical and environmental applications.

Attractive investment opportunities can be found in the **electronics industry:** Production process equipment such as control, operation systems, devicoc, robotics, components, optic/laser (including industrial and medical applications); design centres in microelectronics, artificial intelligence; software is a very large field; Computer-aids for design, editing, manufacturing, engineering and a lot more. For telecommunications: Video disk and video text: Other specialized electronic equipment for aviation equipment and avionics.

Plastic transformation industries are also a large field: Automotive parts, advanced composite materials, frozen food wrapping, to be used in bothmicrowave and traditional ovens, electronic and electrical components, building materials, medical needs products.

魁北克省：經濟穩步成長

魁北克省處地得宜，祇須一小時飛行或一天行車的時間便可暢達人口多達九千二百萬的美國東北部及中部和加拿大的五個省份。航空交通方面，三十間內陸或國際航空公司穿梭　　　　　　　　　　及　　　　　　　　國際機場。陸路方面，高速公路直貫美國及加拿大各城市海路方面，位於聖羅倫斯河的十個港口全年開放，成爲魁省交通的重要環節。

語言方面，滿地可市由於在國際貿易上十分活躍，所以英文十分普遍，但在魁省其他地方，法語則比較普及。魁省其他地方
但在魁省其他地方，法語則比較普及。魁省近三百萬工人皆是訓練優良及生產力極高的。

魁省的生活方式充滿歐美色采，居民崇尚自然─滑雪、垂釣、揚帆、高爾夫球、音樂會、芭蕾舞、劇院、電影及餐館等，應有盡有。

魁省政治穩定，經濟成長可觀，以往五年的通脹率祇是百份之四。魁省的公司稅項是全加最低的，因此，工商發達。全省有超過三十所具規模或國際性的銀行及財務機構，而滿地可的股市交易所更是居全加的次席。

魁省天然資源豐富，實爲其多元化的工商及旅遊業之支柱。全省電力皆由省府的魁北克電力公司供應，價格相宜。

省府爲增加就業機會，特設有很多資助計劃以速進及改善生產、出口、技能訓練和先進技術的研究及發展等。資助計劃包括資金援助、貸款及稅項優惠等。

魁省每年出口達二千餘萬，省府分別在海外十六處地點設有辦事處以加強出口貿易。

魁省的工業力求向新科技發展，而省府對這方面的支持，不可抹煞─員工薪金支出的百份之二十至四十可作爲免稅額。如購買科研設備，更可享有高達百份之五十的政府資助。

魁省的高科技工業計有：運輸、生物工程、微體電子通訊、塑膠加工、航空及國防、能源（如冶金及化工等）。

在運輸業方面，特別運輸工具的生產、裝置及研究皆爲工業的先驅。而在子應用和質量控制方面也應運而生。

魁省在生物工程的發展潛力也是令人鼓舞的，現有研究人員三百六十人分別在醫學、農業、化學及環境衞生的應用方面進行研究，新產品層出不窮。

　　在電子業方面的投資機會也是俯首可拾：生產設備如生產控制及操作系統、機械人及工業或醫療用的光學或激光設備等。微形電子、電腦及航空電子器材的生產，應有盡有。

　　塑膠加工在魁省也是主要工業之一。產品包括汽車零件、包裝材料、電子零件、建築材料及醫療用品等。

CHAPTER 6

Joseph Hui

Bright Future forecast for Montreal

Montreal immigration consultant, accountant and stock broker Joseph Hui says that the city is full of potential for investors in real estate, restaurants, tourism, trade and many other areas of industry and commerce.

He adds that textiles, garments, metal-work, plastic products and gift items are other 'hot areas' of opportunity.

A flight of capital and business occurred during the 1970s during a time of strong emphasis on the French language and special rights for the province.

That time appears to have passed and the depleted and lagging Quebec economy is making up for lost time vigorously assisted by the provincial government particularly in respect of entrepreneurial immigrant investors.

Joseph Hui is chairman of Montreal based Wall Street Enterprises International which specializes in real estate development, finance, securities, the hospitality industry and trade as well as immigration consultancy.

As chairman of Wall Street International Joseph meets at least ten potential immigrants a day and each year spends some months in Canada and others overseas.

He is well qualified both to identify opportunities in Montreal and Quebec and, himself a recent immigrant, to offer advise to others hoping to settle in the territory. The company has offices in Canada, Hong Kong, Taiwan, Malaysia and Australia.

Almost as testimony to the advice he gives others Wall Street International has itself successfully and profitably invested more than C$2 million in property, real estate development, trade, custom jewellery and wholesale and retail outlets in Montreal.

Says Joseph: "I foresee that the future of Montreal will be brighter and brighter."

"Today we can see the price of real estate rising: we can see numerous new buildings being developed and we can see many new immigrants coming to Montreal bringing their capital skills."

"All these developments will make Montreal more attractive to investors and will create new opportunities for economic growth.

Montreal is a city in a province where French Canadians dominate and Hui and his wife, Sheila, learned the French language before going to live there. Having done so he says language difficulties have not arisen.

"I think if anyone is seriously considering coming to live in Quebec they should learn the French language but 70 per cent of the business population are bilingual in French and English so even if immigrants speak only English they will be able to survive. And French and English courses are readily available."

"The Quebec Provincial Government, especially the Department of Immigration, is very helpful to new immigrants including investors and industrialists looking for opportunities.

"They will help not only in Canada but also through their offices in Hong Kong and other overseas posts."

"In Montreal local cultural organizations can also be very helpful in assisting immigrants to settle in to their new country."

"A number of Quebec Government agencies such as the Economic Development Office and Montreal Urban Community supply free advice and assistance to new investors."

Montreal's Asian population is around 65,000 and to make Chinese immigrants feel more at home Hui says that Chinese food and other recreational facilities, including video tapes of Hong Kong television programs are available in the city.

"My advice to new immigrants to Montreal and Quebec is 'settle down first and take a few months to study local markets before making business decisions.' "

Joe Hui

Ma Kwok-wai
"I took a risk on Montreal but I have no regrets"

Mr. Ma Kwok-wai is an investor who came to Canada in 1985 and because of the potential he saw in the province of Quebec he decided to settle in Montreal instead of following in the footsteps of so many of his countrymen to Vancouver or Toronto.

"Montreal is a place full of business prospects. At first I didn't understand the environment and I bought residential properties but now I find that commercial properties yield higher returns. I have also been thinking of buying land to develop myself."

"I decided to come to Montreal because in my opinion the competition in Toronto is too keen. Whatever I could think of doing in Toronto someone will have started before me. But in Montreal there are not more than 60,000 Asian people including non-Chinese and so the competition is not so high."

"You can probably find a job more easily in Toronto than in Montreal but if you go into business the potential is better in Montreal. That's my observation."

"One reason why so few Chinese people have settled in Montreal may be because the Quebec government hasn't promoted the province enough. I have seen promotional material but I found out about the province from friends."

"I was lucky. I worked in a bank in Hong Kong and many of my clients passed me useful information."

"I think everyone in Hong Kong is scared about having to learn French. I knew Montreal had been the largest city in Canada once but I also knew of the problems with the French language and that many companies had left Montreal for Toronto. But I think Montreal has potential and that's why I took the risk."

In business French is not a serious problem but there are only a few English secondary schools in Quebec and if there was a change of policy and more English schools were opened many, many more Hong Kong people would come here. Definitely, if Quebec was officially bilingual it would attract many more investors."

"I studied French in Hong Kong for one year and I can read a little but I think spoken French is very difficult. It hasn't posed too many problems because majority of people in Montreal — 80 per cent — can speak English. If they really can't speak English I can always ask my sons, my neighbours or my employees to interpret for me. And you can always get a lawyer or notary who speaks English to help you. Of course, some lawyers and notaries are Chinese and this solves the problem."

"If you base your business in Montreal; that doesn't mean you can only sell in Montreal; at first maybe you will but after one or two years maybe you'll sell in Toronto or even New York. Montreal is very close to New York. Companies here are even selling to Vancouver."

"Costs are lower here than in Toronto and lower than Vancouver but the markets are here and so is skilled labour."

"I decided to invest in property rather than manufacturing because although wages are relatively low in Montreal in Canada as a whole wage costs are quite high."

"I am a businessman, I want to make profit and I judged that property would make more profit. I have a supermarket, a costume jewellery shop and now I am investing in a restaurant."

"Initially, my profit will come from increased sales through the retail outlets and this depends a lot on giving good service and offering low prices."

"It doesn't matter where you go it's always very difficult to establish a new business — it's no more difficult here than it would be in Hong Kong. It doesn't matter how successful you've been anywhere else it is still difficult to set up a new business and to overcome all the problems. It takes at least two or three years to get to know a new market."

"I have found that Montreal is a very good place for myself and my family. My two children are enrolled at Concordia University and Dawson College respectively."

"My wife is happy and busy. She helps me run the retail business while I am busy with rent collection and property management."

"I started my first business six months after I came here and I hope I will be lucky. We have made a lot of new friends in Montreal and we are all very happy to be living in the city and doing business here. I took a risk but I have no regrets."

Wall Street International Business Consultants —

Immigration and Business Consultants

Wall Street International Business Consultants Ltd. has its Head Office in Hong Kong and is an associate company of Wall Street Enterprises (Holdings) Ltd. of Hong Kong established in 1978.

The Wall Street Group has been involved in real estate, finance, stock market, property management, restaurant and trading etc.

Wall Street International Business Consultants Ltd. has been set up to cope with the growing demand for professional services regarding immigration applications and to offer subsequent services such as advice on investment and business establishment in Canada and Australia.

This company has its head office in Hong Kong and branch offices in Canada, Taiwan, Malaysia, Australia, Philippines, U.S.A. and associates in Korea and Indonesia.

The main services that this company provides are:—

1. To assist immigration applications.
2. To write business proposals for immigration applications.
3. To assist landed immigrants to set up their businesses.
4. To advise on investments and social life affairs, such as to look for schools and also to locate accommodation for their family.

The services provided by this company are unique in that they also provide services after the applicant has landed.

When an applicant arrives in Canada for an exploratory visit, he will be well taken care of from the moment his plane lands at the airport. He will be greeted by Wall Street staff and accompanied by them to the hotel. Then a well planned city tour as well as briefings about the country's economy, political life and social securities are organised for the potential applicants. Meetings are arranged with certain authorities for an applicant to better understand the environment and to be equipped with other relevant information.

Friends in a new country are very important for a new immigrant. Wall Street will arrange new Landed Immigrants to meet other older immigrant friends so that new immigrants will not feel lonely and isolated in a new environment.

Applying for the Canadian medical card and social insurance number, reporting landing to the Immigration Department, as well as registration of schools for the kids are important issues with which Wall Street assists. After that Wall Street staff will assist new immigrants to open bank accounts and to apply for a telephone etc. Most of these services are complimentary and free of charge.

Wall Street has its Far East Head Office in Hong Kong, so that applicants from Hong Kong and Taiwan are well taken care of by the Hong Kong office directly after their exploratory visit to Canada or Australia. Ongoing services after the first interview are also important to ensure that the applicant has the necessary documents and to ensure that these documents are being well prepared for verification during the Canadian Federal Government Interview in Hong Kong.

Wall Street Business Consultants have a different approach for assisting potential immigrants.

There is free advice and free consultation to potential applicants. Wall Street will discuss the case in person with the applicant in order to be familiar with his background and also to assess his chance of success.

The areas to be discussed and assessed include the applicant's background, business experience, family composition, assets and nature of business. The future investment programme and amount of money to be invested will also be discussed.

Wall Street will also assess the chances of success for the applicant's business in Canada. The ability of the family to settle down will also be assessed in order to let the applicant know what difficulties their family will possibly meet after landing.

All these consultations are free of charge and only after all these discussions will Wall Street advise the applicant about their chances of success regarding immigration and investment.

From this point if the applicant has decided to proceed to apply to emigrate then an estimation of consultation fee will be quoted based on the appropriate amount of time to be involved considering the background and nature of business of the applicant.

If the chance of success is dim, then Wall Street will advise the applicant not to proceed in order to save time and money. In other words, if Wall Street accepts the engagement, then the applicant is quite likely to be successful.

Wall Street International Business Consultants Ltd. has offices in many Asian Countries and their consultants speak Cantonese, Mandarin, Chiu Chow dialects, Fokien dialect, Vietnamese, English and French.

Usually the procedure of application would involve Canada and also the domicile country of the applicant, usually Hong Kong (which covers Taiwan), so that services in Hong Kong are also of crucial importance.

In case of application to Australia, Hong Kong office also plays an important role in assisting applicants.

The services of Wall Street Group are unique in that:—
1. They assess the applicant's chance of success free of charge.
2. They organize preliminary interviews for potential applicants free of charge.
3. They never advise applicants to invest in or buy any business before their applications are approved.
4. They take care of clients even after landing.

5. They have offices in many countries and these offices provide all range of business and immigration consultation services to the applicants' convenience.
6. Their principal consultants speak different languages and dialects which enable personal communications without going through an interpreter.

Although Wall Street Business Consultants Ltd. emphasizes assisting entrepreneurial applicants, they also help retirees as well as family reunion applicants.

If you want to know your chance of success, or if you need free consultation about immigration or investment, you may call or write to Wall Street International Business Consultants Ltd. at the following address:—

Wall Street International Business Consultants Ltd.
1255 University Avenue, Suite 1008
Montreal, Quebec H3B 3W6
Tel.: (514) 878-2588
Telex: 055-66271 Wall Street   FAX (514) 866-2388
or: — Far East Head Office:—
Wall Street International Business Consultants Ltd.
Room 1603-4 Car Po Commercial Building
37 Pottinger Street
Central, Hong Kong
Tel.: (5) 420833   FAX (5) 419341
or: — Taiwan
Taichung — Tel.: (04) 222-1200   Fax (04) 222-1599
Kaohsiung — Tel.: (07) 282-4282   Fax (07) 282-0717

Australia, Sydney — Tel.: (02) 211-3677   Fax: (02) 211-3058
Malaysia, Kuala Lumpur — Tel.: (03) 985-3186   Fax: (03) 717-2704
U.S.A., Los Angeles — Tel.: (213) 262-1388   Fax: (213) 262-2667

對蒙特里爾市美好的展望

蒙特里爾市（滿地可）移民顧問、會計師兼證券經紀許錦松先生謂該市的地產業、飲食業、旅遊業、貿易及工商業對於投資者來說甚具潛力。

他補充謂紡織業、製衣業、五金業、塑膠製品業及禮品業亦是投資的好對象。

七十年代的魁北克省偏重法語與及特權，曾促使資金及商家外流。

然而那種情況已成過去。魁北克省政府正積極復興該省的經濟，並協助企業家、投資者移民該省。

　　許錦松先乃以蒙特利爾為基地的"華之傑國際集團"之董事長。該公司專門處理有關地產、財務、證券、旅遊、貿易及移民等事務。

　　華之傑集團在加拿大、香港、台灣、馬來西亞及澳洲均設有辦事處。許先生本身亦已移居蒙特利爾市，熟識該市及魁北省的投資機會，甚具資格作為移民顧問。

　　許先生在新移民當中亦是一個好見證。他領導下的華之傑國際集團已投資了超過二百萬元加幣在蒙特利爾市的地產、貿易、人造首飾、批發與及零售商店上，並有超卓成就。

　　許先生說：「蒙特里爾市的將來會更美好。」

　　「現時地產市值上升，地產商紛紛興建新樓宇，新移民不斷帶同他們的資金及技能來到蒙特利爾市。」

　　「此種種發展令蒙特利爾市更能吸引投資者，亦帶來了經濟的增長。」

　　蒙特里爾市位於以法裔加拿大人佔多數的魁北克省內。許先生和他的夫人移民該市之前已開始學習法語，故他們抵步後沒有語言上的困難。

　　「我認為每一個決心來到魁北克省定居的人仕應該學習法語。不過這裡的商人有七成能操法語及英語，故即使新移民只能講英語，生活亦不會有太大問題。況且，法語及英語課程處處皆是。」

　　「魁北克省政府，特別是移民局，對新到的移民（包括投資者及工業家）給予很大幫忙。他們除了在加拿大協助新移民外，亦通過他們的海外辦事處提供各種服務。蒙特里爾市的文化機構亦很樂意協助新移民。一些魁北克省政府機構如經濟發展局及蒙特里爾市政廳亦給予新投資者免費資料提供援助。」

　　蒙特里爾市的亞裔人口約為六萬五千人。許先生表示諸如中國食品、文娛設施與及香港電視節目的錄影帶等在該市皆有供應，故華籍移民很容易適應那邊的生活。

　　「我對來蒙特里爾市或魁北克省的新移民的忠告是：先安定下來，然後花幾個月的時間觀察本地市場的動向，才再作任何商業投資決定。」

摘錄及翻譯自：
「1987 年投資加拿大指南」，
第144-5頁

WELCOME

Markham, Ontario, Canada welcomes you.

We offer
- —first class real estate
- —a business-like approach to government
- —low taxes
- —headquarters for Canada's leading high technology and service industries
- —excellent transportation & communications
- —beautiful living conditions

In Markham, your future can last a lifetime.
Welcome.

Markham: One day away from 120 million customers

Markham is the most urban of nine municipalities that make up the Region of York. It is on the northern boundary of Canada's largest metropolitan concentration of people — within a day's trucking of 120 million customers and at the centre of 56 per cent of North America's industrial market.

One-third of Canada's purchasing power operates within 50 miles of this Ontario municipality and it is closer to the bulk of the U.S. market than either Florida, Texas or California.

Markham is a must-see location for any Pacific Rim investor seeking opportunities to start up, relocate or expand operations in the commercial heartland of Ontario, Canada's most prosperous and populous province.

Many international leaders in the high technology, financial service and advanced manufacturing sectors of the economy have based their Canadian operations in Markham already. They include: IBM Canada, Apple Canada, American Express Canada, Allstate Insurance Companies of Canada, Crowntek, Olivetti Canada, Hyundai Auto Canada, and A.C. Nielsen Company of Canada.

For them and many other firms large and small, it is the right place to be because the quality and stability of both corporate and private life in Markham is undeniable.

The growth of Markham has been phenomenal among Ontario municipalities. Ours is a prosperous community that cherishes its pioneer roots as well as its future prospects. Urban energy and rural vigour combine here to produce enviable and exceptionable working and living conditions.

Since 1971, Markham's population has grown from 36,700 to more than 120,000 in 1987. The rate of job creation has been even more rapid from 11,000 to more than 50,000. This unprecedented modern migration has led our planners to project a population of 175,000 and industrial employment for 100,000 by the year 2000.

It has happened because development in Markham has been diversified and cost-efficient. Industries locating here tell us they appreciate the stability that flows from balanced growth and consistently low municipal taxes because it eliminates uncertainty from their long-term planning.

Councillors elected by Markham residents set out more than 15 years ago to be business-like and today's Council continues to operate that way. Its ground rules are simple. Municipal services like water, power, sewers and roads must be in place in advance of new development and they must be paid for in ways that do not burden investors and individuals with unwarranted long-term debt or tax increases.

In statistical terms, Markham's industrial/commercial value since 1971 has increased fifteen-fold to more than $3 billion, while residential value has increased more than five-fold to over $4.5 billion, at a pace of 2,000 new homes per year. As a result, the balance of residential to commercial assessment has shifted favourably from a ratio of 81:19 to 71:29 from 1971 to 1987. This has been accomplished while reducing per capita municipal debt from $190 to $47, the lowest per capita debt in the region.

Revenue Canada regularly surveys 100 Canadian communities with tax-paying populations of at least 17,500. Its 1980-85 reports reveal that Markham residents enjoyed the highest average income per capita in Canada in four of the years between 1978 and 1983; the other two years Markham ranked second highest.

Markham has industrial parks operating on more than 1,800 acres of fully serviced land. Another 2,000 acres of serviced land are available, as is a smaller amount of unserviced land. A welcome new trend in Markham's growth as a stable, diversified economy is the development of a commercial core for the business community. In 1986-87, the Seltzer Corporation, Inducon and President's Choice announced three projects that in total will create almost three million square feet of office tower space at Highway 404 and 7 — the kind of space that investors seeking head office space require.

Markham's links with the Far East were strengthened in 1987 by a number of corporate moves. Hyundai decided to locate its $30 million Ontario Auto Parts Distribution Centre here. The Korean automaking giant decided to join the ranks of advanced manufacturers, including Mitsubishi, who have based Canadian operations here for two key reasons: Markham's low tax rate and prime location. Other new arrivals included Toshiba Canada and Kubota Tractor.

Markham's location is prime for any business moving goods or services. It understands that a company's competitive edge depends on its ability to deliver products to the customer's satisfaction.

Three commercial airports are less than 30 minutes away: Pearson International, Canada's largest passenger and freight terminal; the Toronto Island Airport, offering commuter flights to Ottawa, Montreal, other Ontario cities and cities in the southeast United States; and Markham's own Toronto/Buttonville International Airport. Toronto/Buttonville specializes in corporate and private air traffic. More than 300 aircraft are based here, making it Canada's largest privately operated airport.

Rail, water and road transportation corridors are world-class as well. The nation's rail freight carriers, Canadian National and Canadian Pacific, own lines in Markham and one of their main marshalling yards lies along the municipality's southeastern border. Between Markham and Metropolitan Toronto is the 12-lane expressway, Highway 401, the lynch-pin of the coast-to-coast highway system linking Ontario to the major metropolitan markets of North America. New York and Chicago, for example are less than 550 miles by road from Markham. Meanwhile, fleets of ocean-going and fresh-water tankers ply the Great Lakes waterway system, linked by the St. Lawrence Seaway with Atlantic shipping lanes and via the Illinois Waterway and Mississippi River with the Gulf of Mexico.

Statistics aside, the special something that Markham offers new businesses and new residents is a sense of well-being. There's a gentle roll to the land. The air is fresh, the streams clear, the houses neat, the schoolyards full, the farms productive. Neighbours and local businesses naturally and easily display concern for each other's well-being. For the environment and our history as well, and our roots go back to the 1790s.

Markham's corporate leaders, as well as its Council and residents all welcome inquiries about the quality of life in our community and the opportunities it offers. As a first step to seeing what Markham offers, Pacific Rim investors are invited to contact for more information:

Mr. Alex Barton
Treasurer and Industrial Commissioner
Town of Markham
8911 Woodbine Avenue
Markham, Ontario
CANADA
L3R 1A1

Telephone: (416) 477-7000.

麥咸市：咫尺之遙、居民一億二千萬

位於多倫多以北的麥咸市乃約克區九個市域中最旺的一個。離市中心方圓一天行車的範圍內就有人口一億二千萬，以其極強的購買力，代表了北美半數以上的工業產品市場，正是極盡地利之宜。

投資者如計劃在加發展，麥咸市實爲不容忽視的好地點。因麥市的居住及工商業環境俱佳，所以很多國際性企業皆設總部於此—如 **IBM** 、蘋果電腦、美國運通、**Allstate** 保險、**Crowntek** 、好利獲得、**Hyundai** 及 **A.C. Nielson** 等。

麥咸市的人口由一九七一年的三萬七千人增加至一九八七年的十二萬人。同期的就業人數就由一萬一千人增至五萬人。預料在公元二千年，麥市將有居民十七萬五千人，而就業人數則可達十萬。

麥市近年的發展可謂多元化及經濟效率可觀。麥市的工商業樓宇總值在一九八七年約爲三十億元，比一九七一年增加了十五倍，而住宅樓宇總值則爲四十五億元，增加了五倍。現在每年約有二千間住屋落成。由於市府每年開支可由不斷增長的工商業所分擔，所以麥市的赤字乃全加市府中最低的。

根據加拿大稅局定期作出的報告顯示，在一九七八年至一九八三年間其中四年麥市居民的平均收入爲全加之冠，而有兩年則居次位。

麥咸市有已發展的土地一千八百畝爲工業所用，另有已發展的土地二千畝可作工業用途，再加上未發展的土地，預料可令麥市的工商發展，更趨穩定及發達。在一九八六年至八七年間，**Seltzer Corporation** 、**Inducon** 及 **President's Choice** 所宣佈的三項位於407及第七公路的發展計劃，可爲工商業帶來面積總達三百萬方呎的大小寫字樓單位。

麥市與遠東區的關係也甚爲密切。 **Hyundai** 耗資三千萬的汽車零件廠將座落於麥市。其他遠東的跨國公司，如 **Mitsubishi Toshiba** 及 **Kubota Tractor** 等都受麥市的地點及低稅收所吸引。

離麥市半小時車程分別有機場三個：加拿大最大的皮雅遜國際機場 ；來往渥太華、滿地可及鄰近安省及美國西南部的多倫多島機場 ；及加拿大最大的私人空運機場— **Toronto-Buttonville** 機場—停泊有爲數三百的私人飛機。

麥市的鐵路、水路及公路交通皆達世界水平。加拿大的兩間鐵路公司（ **CN** 及 **CP** ）在麥市東南皆有主要的起卸站。十二線行車的401公路把麥市與大多市互相連接，而由麥市往紐約或芝加哥祇是五百哩左右的路程。

海路方面，大湖泊區的水路由聖羅倫水道伸展至大西洋航線，再接伊利諾斯州水道及密西西比河直通墨西哥灣。

　　麥咸市的歷史可源自一七九〇年代，居民一向守望相助，融洽共處。再者，市容整潔、空氣清新、學校設備完善，正是家居的理想選擇。

　　麥市的工商界人仕、市議員及居民皆歡迎閣下垂詢一切有關麥市事宜。請與

聯絡為荷。謹此致意！

Mr. Alex Barton
Treasurer and Industrial Commissioner
Town of Markham
894 Woodbine Avenue
Markham, Ontario
Canada L3R 1A1

Telephone: (416) 477-7000

CHAPTER 7

Frank Chau

Toronto: city of perpetual growth; opportunities in almost every field

Hong Kong born Frank Chau, a Toronto resident for 22 years and president of Goldyear Realty of Toronto, says that Toronto is favoured by immigrants of Chinese origin because it is Canada's premier commercial centre and also because of the city's cosmopolitan character.

"Historically, the first Canadian city investors of immigrants from Asia look at is Vancouver because it is the first port of arrival from the Far East, the scenery is beautiful and for people from Hong Kong the conditions in Vancouver are similar - with the exception of rain."

However, a lot of immigrants who have settled in or visited Vancouver soon find out that business activity is not as strong as in other major cities and industries are mainly resource. Life is slow, easy and more suited to retirement; the local purchasing power is not as strong as in a city like Toronto."

"Montreal has been historically plagued by politcal issues and language issues and for those who don't speak French it is a problem - in Toronto (and Vancouver) we have significant growth in the Chinese population but in Montreal very little and the reason is that Chinese people are not used to the language there."

Calgary and Edmonton were at one time very prosperous but the fall in oil prices has dragged the two cities down to their lowest levels of economic performance for some years."

"Toronto is a city with no political problems and very stable; it is the most heavily populated city in Canada; it is Canada's most major financial centre and close to Montreal, New York, Boston and Chicago; there are multiple industries offering a wide variety of jobs; purchasing power is strong and life is faster than in smaller towns and cities and, on average, the population is young and energetic."

"The environment offers a lot of opportunity for young entrepreneurs and people who live in Toronto and feel free to do what they like and nowadays need fear no discrimination at all."

"Anybody who wants to work can make a good living in the city of Toronto."

"In a lot of fields I don't think competition is that strong and you can go in and penetrate different markets and make a lot of money."

"In Toronto, if you get it right, there is always a chance of getting into business for yourself. In Hong Kong it's different because everywhere you look there's fierce competition and you have to do everything real right to make money."

"Opportunities exist in Toronto in practically every area - except restaurants because this is very competitive - ranging from industry through construction work to arts and crafts."

"Toronto is a perpetually growing market and this is the reason for the city's success. A lot of people have been coming in during the past few years, not just rich people, but people in the medium income range, who work hard and who are really the backbone of the Hong Kong and southeast Asian economy."

"Some of them go back but most of them stay because even though the weather here is cold they like the business environment."

"They see the opportunities to do business and they like it."

"They might consider going to some other province of Canada but I think it's very obvious that population size, which, in turn, expresses the demand for goods and services is here in Toronto - we have over three million people in greater Toronto alone and the figures go on increasing, maybe up to four or five million by the end of the century."

"Most of the new immigrants from southeast Asia will want to come here and people here already that I have been in contact with are doing good business and making money."

"The number of Chinese people in Toronto now is over 250,000 and around C$2 billion a year is being invested - half of it in real estate."

"In real estate the opportunities for investors are in income properties such as strip shopping plazas, apartment blocks, office buildings, hotels etc., although the most popular are the strip plazas and shopping centres - when lack of merchandise occurs a lot of people are going into development. Also a lot of people are buying sidewalk retail stores."

"The scale of an immigrant's investment will depend on what business he or she goes into but to start a family business, such as a variety store, may need about C$50,000, a restaurant, C$150,000 and any manufacturing industry at least C$100,000 just to get started."

Jake Liem
In Toronto you can succeed in virtually any business

Toronto based trader and investor, Jake Liem, says that the Canadian economy is healthy because of the fundamental political and social stability of the country. "There are many business opportunities here. Take, for instance Toronto. In adition to the normal level of business activity every year tens of thousands of immigrants come in and that makes the economy grow and grow. But inflation is minimal and the currency is stable."

"The free trade agreement with the United States is going to create many more opportunities. In the long run it is very good for Canada because it challenges us to work more productively and competitively."

"If you are not an investor but nevertheless hope to make some money it's very easy to find a job in a city like Toronto, especially if you have re-educated yourself in Canada."

"I took a masters degree in Austria and another in Czechoslovakia but when I came to Canada I started again from the bottom, re-took a master's degree and qualified as a Chartered Management Accountant. If you want to work in a professional field you have to acquire Canadian qualifications."

"If you want to invest, Canada offers a very good climate for investment. Because of the high annual level of immigration there is always a shortage of infrastructure, goods and services."

"If you are putting money into manufacturing you have to know what you are doing but if you don't want to have the responsibility of management then you can always buy mutual funds where the money is invested carefully in a range of enterprises."

"In Toronto the opportunities are so great you can be successful at virtually anything you decide to do. If you go to a smaller city everything is cheap but everything is also very slow, including the business."

"It's not difficult to understand Canadian laws and procedures if you decide to start a business. In any case you can always hire a lawyer or an accountant who can tell you what you don't know."

"The key to success is understanding what you are doing. If you are in the garment industry in Hong Kong, manufacturing processes in Toronto will be similar. Or maybe you will know better because you bring a new technique or be able to cut costs."

"The level of taxation here is very, very bearable. It is not high compared with other countries. The government gives many, many advantages to small business to help them survive. But you have to have a professional accountant who knows about taxes. Many people just go to any accountant but you can't do that. Not every accountant knows about taxation. Some do, some don't. You must go to an accountant who knows about tax.''

Chinese people are warmly welcomed here. Chinese people are well respected by Canadians. They work hard and they bring money.

Frank Hsu
Toronto is the hub, the biggest and best city in all Canada

Frank Hsu operates the famous Young Lok Restaurant in Toronto's downtown prestigious Village-by-the-Grange, a metropolitan dinnery which without losing its unique warmth and character has grown like Topsy and will again soon.

From the point of view of his personal business interests and way of life there is no other city in Canada where he'd rather live.

He says: "Toronto has been booming for the past three or four years and generally the economy in Toronto is always better than elsewhere in the country."

"Toronto is Canada's banking and financial centre, Toronto and southern Ontario is its manufacturing centre producing a major portion of the country's gross national product. Toronto is also a social centre and a centre for culture, fashion, recreation and the retail trades."

"Although I am a businessman I am also in the restaurant business and when you open a restaurant you want to choose a location which is a hub of activity; that's why I chose Toronto."

"The opportunities for business are here in Toronto. The business climate is similar to Hong Kong in the sense of having a fast pace. If you go to a small city somewhere you won't be used to it and you'll find it boring."

"Toronto is the hub. A city like Hamilton is only minutes drive away and probably good for manufacturing. But if you're looking at service industries then Toronto is the place because you have to be close to the best market."

"Labour is more expensive in Toronto than elsewhere but the quality could be better. You get what you pay for. In other smaller towns and cities you find assembly line type workers but I think that in Toronto you get the more skilled people. It may be cheaper in a city like Hamilton but if you don't have the right people it's no good being there. It depends what your needs are."

"If you come to Toronto you're paying a higher price but if you know what you really want and if you can justify paying more there's no problem."

"A lot of people don't understand the differentials. They come to Toronto and start a factory. They don't understand they could reduce the rent by 50% just by driving 40 minutes to the south west."

"Toronto has a good image among Chinese people. They always comment that it's a clean city with ample amenities. The education is of a high standard and the sports facilities are excellent. With a population of 2.2 million it's a good size city — the largest in Canada. The next is Montreal but most people pick Toronto because they fear that if they can't speak French they won't do well in Quebec. Vancouver is really too small."

"When Chinese people come to Canada, besides business, they are naturally looking for a good place to live with an acceptable climate and Toronto stands out from the rest. It is probably the best all round city in North America."

"When they think about what business they'll have a restaurant is probably the first thing that comes to their minds because they don't need any qualifications. Or they may buy a Harvey's or Swiss Chalet franchise but these are not things that I would jump into until I had found out how to operate here. Some of these businesses are successful, some are not."

"I know somebody who bought a doughnut shop that was doing okay before they took over. But once they took over they didn't know how to manage; they didn't even know how to smile at the customers so they were just losing business."

"People really have to ask themselves: Will I like the business? Will I smile at the customers? Will I be able to develop the business or just open it and sit there waiting for customers?"

"Once the business has gone down and you have found out you don't like doing it anyway than you can lose your investment because nobody wants to buy it."

"In the restaurant business you have to be very careful. I think a lot of people have come here and opened restaurants purely for the sake of immigrating and then after a short while they flip the restaurant. Actually most of them lose money."

"New immigrants should not get into the restaurant business by themselves. If you find the right partner then the restaurant business is good. But, usually they don't like to take partners."

"If you're not experienced, the problem in operating a restaurant is management. Managing a restaurant is a very complex business. You're looking at real-time ordering, manufacturing and billing, by which I mean taking orders from customers, preparing the food in the kitchen, satisfying the customer and charging. It all sounds very simple but if you have a major restaurant and you don't have a good system everything will get bogged down."

"The quality of service is very important. You're dealing with customers and some of them are very difficult."

"When it comes to food everyone has a different concept of what's good food. The owner may feel he's given customers the best food on the menu but they may still complain."

"You have to know how to provide consistent service, how to deal with the customer and also how to consistently provide what the customers regard as good food."

"Also the restaurant business is very dynamic and very difficult to control. It's labour intensive and the cost of getting chefs and cooks is very high. You have to control labour costs, food costs, the quality of the food, the level of the service — so many things. Most people don't have the skills to do this."

"For a small restaurant with less than 50 seats you can manage but if you have anything over 100 seats most people go down because of the management problem."

"There are always too many restaurants in any city. Many people think they have a good idea for a restaurant so they open one. But they are not creating a new market; they are merely fragmenting the existing one. So over time some restaurants naturally have to go. Every day there are restaurants opening and restaurants closing. If you're not creative and if you don't control your business you are going to be among those which close."

"To open a Chinese restaurant now is getting a lot tougher because although all operators have the dream of catering to everybody many of them end up just serving Chinese people so the market is not the maximum."

"One problem for new immigrants coming here as investors is that they don't have too much time to do the research. The best idea is to come to Canada and see opportunities first hand, look around for a year until you know the environment and get to know what you are doing."

"Sometimes you can talk to more experienced people like consultants or lawyers to cut the learning curve down to a minimum."

"Whether you're an immigrant or not there are always people ready to take you for a ride. You have to be careful but the choice is yours. It's the same in Hong Kong."

"If you don't talk to people and you rush into a project then you may suffer. If you talk to people, check into things, be cautious and make the right move then nobody can take you for a ride."

"It takes time to become assimilated in the new environment, to make the connections, to check people out, to get a feel. Sometimes books from reputable publishers can give you a lot of insights. Talk to other immigrants and ask them how they're doing. They can help you too."

"I would say that an immigrant who plans to invest should choose a field here with which he is familiar."

"For example, if you were in the textile industry in Hong Kong then you should be looking at the textile industry in Toronto. Try to do what you're good at yourself."

"If you have experience manufacturing can be a good choice. Managing a factory in Hong Kong or here should be much the same. And you'll probably know the market very well because of sales you've made from Hong Kong."

"With the free trade agreement with the United States, definitely the opportunities for manufacturing investment are very good. If you have saleable products now you have access to the whole North American market. That's even a better base than Hong Kong and other countries in the Far East."

"When immigrants first come here, of course, it's difficult because they don't have their own circle of contacts; you have to establish the links and that takes time."

"That's why initially I don't think new immigrants should venture into anything big but should move very cautiously."

"Ideally, if you have to invest to get into Canada, it should be in a business that you don't have to manage directly. Then you can afford to wait for a few years while you get to know the place and find out where are the real opportunities."

"There are investment funds in which if you purchase a specified amount of shares this qualifies you for immigration to Canada. This sort of scheme is ideal. You just pay your money and you don't have to worry about anything."

"You can come here, check things out yourself and then make your investment for the long term."

"Governments try to be helpful to new immigrants but I know people who have gone into the wrong investments and ended up with financial difficulties. So you have to be careful. On the other hand we have many success stories where people come from Hong Kong, go into partnership with local people, bring in new management expertise and capital and turn a company around.,"

"Before you know the country well if you want to invest you should be looking into real estate because this type of investment doesn't need a lot of management skill."

"You still have to have a good agent for you to find a good property. Also there is a risk involved. You really have to know what you're buying. A lot of people who buy commercial property find they have negative cash flow and then their money is just draining away. When they first look at a proposal it looks good but later they may find out there are problems. You need time to check. Of course, if you make the right purchase it's a good investment and you can hang onto it."

"Real estate is one segment that is really booming; although the market has slowed down now prices have doubled within the last four years."

"Today prices are steady; you can still sell a property for what you paid for it; inflation in Canada runs at about 4.5% a year and property prices are still rising faster than that so if you invest you're not going to lose money."

"Inflation is higher in Toronto, of course, because there are more people coming here than going to other parts of Canada. Many of them are immigrants with money to spend."

"A lot of things here are cheaper than in Hong Kong but the tax is probably higher. There again, you get what you pay for; there are good schools, garbage collection, the streets are cleaned, an efficient police force, national defence. . . . If you have a knowledgeable accountant there are many ways of minimizing the impact of tax."

"For me Toronto is the best city in Canada and if you know what you're doing success is very possible."

So you're picky, picky, picky. In Mississauga that's no problem!

In the Toronto area, Mississauga has a most varied and attractive combination of business locations including more than 50 business parks, office and industrial buildings available for lease or sale, low taxes, and much more. And Pearson International Airport is located right in Mississauga – very convenient.

So go ahead, be "Picky" – no need to compromise here.

Find out more. Call Gord Johnstone, Mississauga's Business Development Officer.

(416) 279-7600

Mississauga
Share the excitement

Welcome to Mississauga, Ontario, Canada

Mississauga, population 380,000, is Canada's ninth largest city and part of the greater Toronto region with a total population of about 3.5 million. A major part of Canada's electronic, telecommunications, food processing, metal, plastics and wood fabricating industries, pharmaceutical and chemical industries are located in or within a one hour drive of Mississauga. Almost all of Canada's automotive industry is located within 80 km of Mississauga. Major Ford and AMC plants are located or are now under construction in communities that border Mississauga; General Motors and the new Honda and Toyota plants now under construction, are less than 80 km away and easily accessible by major highways. Auto parts manufacturers are discovering that Mississauga is an ideal central location from which to supply all these companies with their stringent demands for just-in-time deliveries.

The convenience of the international airport located in Mississauga, the fact that downtown Toronto, Canada's financial capital, is only 25 minutes away and the fact that the Mayor, the City Council and staff have gone out of their way to make overseas business people feel at home here, adds up to a combination of factors they couldn't resist.

GROWTH

Mississauga has experienced very rapid population growth, averaging 5.3% over the past decade. Industrial and commercial growth has been even more impressive. 1985 saw industrial and commercial construction permits issued for a total value of $268.6 million, a new record for Mississauga and second only to the City of Toronto in all of Canada. The rate of industrial/commercial expansion in 1986 is running at an even more rapid rate. This is not surprising given Mississauga's location advantages and the fact that taxes in Mississauga are among the lowest in Canada, and we still have hundreds of hectares set aside for new industrial/commercial growth.

TRANSPORTATION

One of the major reasons why multi-national companies find Mississauga so attractive is the fact that Pearson International Airport which serves the greater Toronto region is located right in Mississauga, not more than 15 minutes from any business location. A major freeway system connects Mississauga with Metropolitan Toronto and other parts of Canada and with the USA border. There are three freeways running through Mississauga and a fourth running north and south on our eastern boundary. As well, both of Canada's major railways serve Mississauga's industries with rail serviced land and intermodal facilities. Nearby, the Port of Toronto provides ocean shipping via the St. Lawrence Seaway for nine months of the year.

CLIMATE

Our four distinct seasons, with temperatures moderated by Lake Ontario one of the world's larges lakes, provide for a stimulating and comfortable living environment. While snowfall and cold weather in Mississauga are quite sparse (average temperature in January is -6.7°C), winter sports are abundantly available in hilly country 100 km to the north. When snow does fall in Mississauga the roads are quickly cleared from curb to curb by an efficient fleet of city vehicles equipped for snow removal. Time loss because of weather conditions is an extremely rare occurrance in Mississauga. Mississauga is not prone to climatic extremes such as tornadoes or floods. Summers are warm and pleasant with a high average temperature of 20.6°C in July.

LIFESTYLE

Canadians place a high value on home and family life. For that reason, Mississauga has an abundance of beautiful homes ranging from rental and condominium apartments, to row housing to large executive fully detached houses, many in wooded areas. Private and municipally-owned facilities are available for all types of racquet sports. Minor league baseball and soccer are very popular here and sailing on Lake Ontario has become a major recreation. As a matter of fact, the world's largest fresh water marina is located in Mississauga.

Mississauga residents are served by two major state-of-the-art hospitals, and a full time professional fire department. The Peel Regional Police Force which serves Mississauga is considered to be one of the best equipped and best trained in North America. Mississauga has a very low crime rate and our streets are safe and clean.

With over 300 restaurants covering a wide range of food styles, plus night clubs, live theatre and cinemas, Mississauga residents are well entertained.

EDUCATION

Mississauga boasts a major campus of the University of Toronto, and three campuses of Sheridan College of Applied Arts and Technology. Within easy commuting distance are seven major universities including the University of Waterloo, Canada's top-rated university in computer science.

For complete information contact the Economic Development Office at the City of Mississauga, 300 City Centre Dr., Mississauga, Ontario, Canada L5B 3C1 (416) 896-5016.

安省的密沙西加市歡迎你

人口三十八萬的密沙西加市是加拿大第九大城市，亦是人口總數達三百五十萬的大多市及其衛星城市體系中的最大城市之一。因此，加拿大絕大部份的電子、電訊、金屬、塑膠、藥物、化工、及食品製造業等都位於密市，而加國九成以上的汽車工業更是座落於密市方圓八十公里內，例如福特、通用、美國車廠及正在興建中的本田及豐田車廠等都位於此，而密市亦因此成爲汽車零件商的批發中心。

由於密市歡迎外來投資，加上國際機場位於密市，及其與多倫多市中心（加拿大的經濟中樞）相鄰的關係，所以密市能成功地吸納大量投資。

城市增長率

十年來密市的人口增長率平均爲5.3%，而工商業增長率則更驚人。根據一九八五年所發出的工商業樓宇建築許可證數字顯示，全年興建樓宇總值達二億六千八百六十萬元的高峰，繼多倫多本市之後而居全加次席。密市仍有數百公頃的地被劃爲工商業發展區。鑑於密市在位置上及稅率上所佔的優勢，它的工商業增長率將會更進一步。

交通

密市的交通網，除了位於北面的皮爾遜國際機場及橫過密市的兩條主要鐵路外，還有四條超級公路把密市與多倫多市及加拿大各大城市和美國邊境連貫。此外，附近的多倫多海港及聖羅倫斯運河更可提供完善的海運服務。

氣候

這裏一年四季分明，而且由於接近安大略湖（北美五大湖泊之一）的關係，所以氣候較爲溫和。正月的平均溫度爲攝氏零下6.7度，而七月則爲攝氏20.6度。

生活方式

密市有大量不同款式的屋宇可供選擇，由栢文，排屋以至獨立洋房等，應有盡有。

各類球類運動在這裏都很受歡迎，如棒球及足球等。而在安大略湖中輕舟駕帆，則是居民的一個主要消遣。世界最大的淡水遊艇灣港就位於密市。

密市有兩間設備先進的醫院，而其皮爾區警察隊素被譽爲北美最好的警察隊之一，所以密市市容整潔，治安良好。

教育

除了超過三百間不同類型的食肆外，市內還有劇院、夜總會、電影院，以供居民作各種文娛活動。

密市設有舒爾頓工事學院校園三座，且多倫多大學的依托碧古校園亦位於密市。

Make the great Scarborough comparison!

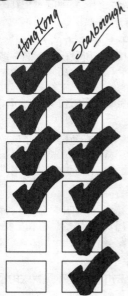

CULTURE

WEALTH

AFFLUENCE

ECONOMIC
SUCCESS

NEW BUSINESS
OPPORTUNITY

SPACE TO GROW

The time to plan for your future is now. The city of the future is *Scarborough*. Scarborough and the Metropolitan Toronto area are home to Canada's largest Chinese population group. Scarborough is Canada's growth centre offering:
- An abundance of prime land
- Access to major Canadian, U.S. and world markets
- Quality housing, education, medical facilities
- A superb quality of life

Make your move to Scarborough — city of the future. For more information, contact:
Frank Miele, B.E.S., EcD., Executive Director
Economic Development Department
City of Scarborough
150 Borough Drive
Scarborough, Ontario, Canada
M1P 4N7.

CITY OF SCARBOROUGH · CANADA

154

Scarborough, City of the Future

Scarborough has all the essential elements to help a successful business compete and grow: an abundant, skilled labour pool; easy access to markets and supplies; an efficient transportation network and a good working and leisure environment.

As one of Canada's fastest-growing cities, it offers a well-developed industrial base and the most available industrial land in Metro Toronto — Canada's major market area.

Scarborough has an excellent network of roads, highways and transit service and is developing its own downtown "Scarborough City Centre" with offices for 40,000.

And it has the attitude and climate which attracts and encourages commercial and manufacturing development.

Major international and domestic companies have invested in Scarborough and are pleased with their choice.

POPULATION

Year	Scarborough (1)	% Change	Metropolitan Toronto (2)	% Change
1085	478,000	1.7	2,163,290	1.5
1984	470,000	1.7	2,131,942	-0.3
1983	462,000	1.8	2,137,960	-0.1
1982	454,000	1.6	2,140,347	0.3
1981	447,000		2,133,001	

LABOUR FORCE

Scarborough labour force is a major component in the Toronto area labour force. The local labour force has been growing rapidly reflecting the substantial increase in population over the years. Scarborough is now the third largest municipality in the Toronto area and has a good chance of becoming the second largest over the next 10 years.

Labour Force Details

Scarborough Labour Force (estimates	(000)	1985
Labour Force		290
Employed		272
Unemployed		18
Participation Rate		76
Unemployment Rate		6

Toronto Area Labour Force	(000)	1985
Labour Force		1,790
Employed		1,669

Unemployed   121
Participation Rate 71.2
Unemployment Rate 6.8

Labour Force Growth

Toronto Area Labour Force (000)

1975	1,420
1985	1,790

% change 1975 to 1985   26

Scarborough Labour Force (000)

1975	179
1985	290

% change 1975 to 1985   62

Scarborough labour force increased by over 62% in the period of 1975-1985 which is more than double the increase for the Toronto area labour force. Now and in the future the local labour force, combined with the Toronto area labour force, provide the potential employers with the biggest labour pool in all of Canada.

MANUFACTURING STRUCTURE:
Scarborough Manufacturing Employment by Major Group — 1985

Food and Beverage	3,279
Rubber & Plastics	2,118
Leather	253
Textile	549
Clothing	780
Wood Industries	1,277
Furniture & Fixtures	921
Paper & Allied Industries	3,157
Printing, Publishing & Allied Industries	3,810
Primary Metal	540
Metal Fabricating	8,405
Machinery	4,955
Electrical Products	6,523
Non-Metallic Mineral	1,397
Chemical & Chemical Products	4,186
Petroleum	358
Transportation Equipment	3,104
Measuring, Analysis Machinery and Electronic	651
Miscellaneous Industries	1,628
TOTAL	47,891

OFFICE DEVELOPMENT

Scarborough's major office centres are located in close proximity to major highways and are served by public transit. Adequate parking facilities are provided at all office locations. Currently, Scarborough has 381,000 sq. m. (4.1 million sq. ft.) of office space in office building with competitive leasing cost. Proposed buildings in the City Centre will increase office space by nearly 223,000 sq. m. (2.4 million sq. ft.).

BUILDING PERMITS

	Total Value Millions of Dollars	% Change
1985	483.5	+ 63
1984	296.0	–39
1983	487.4	+ 99
1982	243.9	–16
1981	289.7	

OFFICE SPACE IN OFFICE BUILDINGS

	Millions of Sq. ft.	% Change
1985	4.10	0
1984	4.10	+ 43
1983	2.87	+ 22
1982	2.36	+ 6
1981	2.22	

TRANSPORTATION

Scarborough is served extensively by all major forms of transportation. By road — direct access to the 401, part of Ontario's major highway system; by rail — both of Canada's national railways (CN & CP) have main lines servicing the city; by air — there is quick and easy access to Pearson (Toronto) International Airport and to the Toronto Island Commuter Airport; and by water — Scarborough is situated on the shores of Lake Ontario, part of the St. Lawrence Seaway shipping system. The Scarborough RT (Rapid Transit) provides a transit connection between the Metro Toronto Subway System and the Scarborough City Centre with five stations located on the line. The RT system can accommodate up to 20,000 passengers per hour in each direction.

CONSTRUCTION
(in million dollars — 1985)

Total Value	483
Industrial	53
Commercial	90
Institutional	23

Residential	315
Other Construction	2

INCOME (1981 CENSUS)

Average Income for all families	$29,615
Average Individual Income	13,647
Average Income — Males	17,891
Average Income — Females	9,197
Personal Disposable Income per Capita	12,693*

(*figure for Metropolitan Toronto to which Scarborough figures are known to be similar)

Scarborough is solidly middle income with a small high income class. Incomes in the area are approximately 15% higher than the national average.

INDUSTRIAL LAND

There are close to 900 ha (2,200 total acres) of undeveloped industrial land available in the city. Locations are also available in existing facilities on single industry sites and in industrial plazas. Scarborough is the only city in Metropolitan Toronto which has such a wide range of industrial sites available.

UTILITIES

Scarborough has an abundant supply of energy for all needs. Consumers Gas, linked by pipeline to Canada's extensive reserves of natural gas, are able to supply a virtually unlimited supply of this resource to its customers inexpensively, (about 17.5¢ (U.S.)/m³ as of August 1, 1984).

Ontario Hydro provides hydro electric power to the area. They are fully capable of filling all types of industrial needs and are able to do so at rates which are among the lowest in the world. Some comparative hydro rates: (average industrial and commercial use, U.S.¢/kwH, August, 1985); Italy 5.65¢; Germany 6.56¢; United States 6.36¢; Belgium 5.55¢; Netherlands 6.53¢; Australia 4.76¢; France 4.82¢; CANADA 3.22¢.

Canada as a whole also has ample domestic supplies of oil and coal with potential to be self-sufficient in these resources. The costs of these forms of energy are also low in world standards. (for fuel oil about 26.5¢ U.S./litre or 1 dollar U.S. for a gallon U.S.)

MEDICAL SERVICES

Four hospitals with 2,363 beds are capable of meeting most of the medical needs of Scarborough residents. For highly specialized medical needs, Toronto's world renowned medical centres ae located just minutes away from most Scarborough residents. Preventative needs are met by 430 doctors and 220 dentists which are registered in the city. The Ontario

Health Insurance Plan (O.H.I.P.) provides universal access to medical services for all residents. The Scarborough Board of Health also has free medical clinics, nursing, nutrition and dental services available for residents.

BANKS/FINANCE/INSURANCE

All types of financial and insurance services are available in Scarborough. Banks, trust companies, credit unions, financial advisors, mortgage and lending institutions are found throughout the city. Some of Canada's major banks have established special commercial banking units in the city to better serve local industrial banking needs. There is also a wide range of insurance and appraisal services available. One of North America's largest insurance companies has established its Canadian Headquarters in Scarborough.

未來的城市仕嘉堡

仕嘉堡市是加拿大發展最快的城市之一，其交通之方便，各類發展用地之多，市場及原料之充裕及勞工之訓練有素，再加上其在工商環境上的配合，足以使仕嘉堡市的發展，一日千里，而在市中心的四萬所寫字樓便是仕嘉堡成功的最佳例子。

人口統計

年份	人口	仕 嘉 堡 市 增長率	大 多 市 人口	增長率
1985	478,000	1.7%	2,163,290	1.5%
1984	470,000	1.7%	2,131,942	− 0.3%
1983	462,000	1.8%	2,137,960	− 0.1%
1982	454,000	1.6%	2,140,347	0.3%
1981	447,000		2,133,001	

人力增長

仕嘉堡因人口迅速增長關係，所以人力供應便倍增，自一九七五年以來，增長率已逾六成之高，而在就業方面，則以金屬製品、電器、化工、印刷、出版、飲食等行業的就業額為高。

商業樓宇

仕嘉堡現有各類商業樓宇四百一十萬平方呎，而計劃在市中心會堂附近興建的商厦總面積則達二百四十萬平方呎。市內所有商業區的寫字樓皆車位充足及交通方便，而很多商業中心都座落在401公路兩旁。

樓宇施工許可證

年份	總值（百萬元計）	增長率
1985	483.5	+ 63%
1984	296.0	− 39%
1983	487.4	+ 99%

1982	243.9	– 16%
1981	289.7	

寫字樓樓面總面積

年份	面積(百萬平方呎)	增長率
1985	4.10	0
1984	4.10	+ 43
1983	2.87	+ 22
1982	2.36	+ 6
1981	2.22	

交通

仕嘉堡的交通極為方便。首先，道路網與橫貫全加的401公路直接貫通，CN與CP的鐵路網可直達市內，航空交通則有鄰近的多倫多皮雅遜國際機場及多倫多島小型機場。水路方面，仕嘉堡南端的安大略湖乃聖羅倫斯水道運輸系統的一部份。還有由市府大樓途經五站而與大多市地鐵相連接的快車服務 (Rapid Transit)。快車每小時載客量可達二萬人次，為乘客帶來不少方便。

一九八五年的建築工程（百萬元計）

總值	483
工業類	53
商業類	90
社區組織	23
住宅	315
其他	2

收入（按一九八一年統計資料）

平均家庭年入	$ 29,615
平均個人收入	13,647
平均收入—男性	17.891
平均收入—女性	9.197
平均個人可供消費收入	12,693 *

（＊此乃大多市數字，但與仕嘉堡市相若）。

仕嘉堡市大多為中等家庭，但亦有一部份為高收入家庭，而平均收入則高出全國數字達15%。

工業用地

全地共有二千二百畝正待發展的工業用地，再加上現成的工業地及鋪位，使仕嘉堡成為大多市最多不同工業用地供應的地方。

水電供應

市內能源供應充足，而且收費相宜。煤氣公司在全市均有地底輸氣管將天然氣直接輸送至各用戶。電力公司(Ontario Hydro)有足夠電源可供市內各用戶之需,而電費可算是全球最低的地方之一。再加上加拿大豐富的石油與煤礦資源,一般能源價格因此而大大降低。

醫療服務

仕嘉堡的四所醫院共有病床二千三百餘,足夠應付在這方面的需求。而數所世界知名的專科醫療中心則位於多市內,咫尺可達。全市共有醫生四百三十人,牙醫二百二十人,居民皆可參加與安大略省健康保險計劃(O.H.I.P.),而仕嘉堡衞生局還爲居民免費的診所、護理、飲食營養及牙科等服務。

銀行/財務/保險

很多不同的銀行、財務及保險機構在市內皆設有辦事處。居民可在市內解決日常銀行往來、樓戶按揭、商業信貸、各類保險及一切與家居或工商業有關的財政上問題。而北美洲其中最大之一間保險公司更設其總部於市內。

Burlington, Ontario, Canada

Diversified Industrial Growth

Thirty years ago, Burlington was a small lakeshore town closely associated with agriculture and food processing. Population 6,000. Today, it ranks as one of Canada's most progressive industrial cities, with a population approaching 120,000.

The major reason for this dramatic growth? A Burlington location offers competitive economic advantages and an appealing lifestyle that consistently attract industrial and commercial investment. People like Burlington, they want to live here and work here.

Although metals fabrication, electrical and electronic components, chemicals, plastics and food processing are considered Burlington's major manufacturing categories, our highly developed base includes a broad spectrum of diversified industrial and commercial interests. In recent years, a growing number of scientific and high technology corporations has found Burlington an ideal location.

High-tech centres develop because high-tech companies have common needs. Access to research facilities is one of the most important.

Canada's most sophisticated corporate, university and government research facilities and talent are within a 30 mile radius of Burlington. They include Sheridan Park Research Centre, Stelco Research Centre, McMaster University, University of Guelph, The University of Toronto, The University of Waterloo, Mohawk College, Sheridan College, The Ontario Research Foundation and Canada Centre for Inland Waters.

Burlington is also situated in Canada's industrial heartland. And basic industries, while not producers of high-tech, are users of many high-tech products and services.

Burlington is close to everything

The City of Burlington is situated on 72 square miles of gently rolling land. Eight miles of Lake Ontario and Burlington Bay shoreline form the southern boundary. The Niagara Escarpment cuts diagonally across the primarily agricultural countryside to the north east.

Burlington is an integral part of the Golden Horseshoe, a highly industrialized area that swings around the head of the lake, from Oshawa to Niagara Falls. Hamilton, a diversified manufacturing centre, is to the west. Toronto, the business and financial capital of Canada, is to the east.

With one quarter of Canada's population living, and buying, within 100 miles, Burlington is right in the heart of our country's richest market. Forty-five percent of Canadian manufacturing shipments are made within this same radius.

People

Burlington's lifestyle has traditionally attracted a broad cross section of skilled and unskilled people from the highly concentrated metro area. They want to live here; in the cleaner atmosphere of our suburban environment.

Many are professionals and skilled technologists. And because many work outside of our area, they provide a potential pool for any new industry locating here.

Research Facilities

Canada's most sophisticated group of corporate, university and government research facilities and talent are in or within thirty miles of Burlington. They include Sheridan Park Research Centre, Stelco Research Centre, McMaster University, The University of Toronto, Mohawk College, Sheridan College, The Ontario Research Foundation and Canada Centre for Inland Waters.

Transportation Highways

The Queen Elizabeth Way (QEW), the main transportation artery serving Canada's industrial corridor, and offering connections to the U.S., runs directly through five miles of Burlington's more heavily populated area. Parallel service roads to the north and south, and five interchanges provide efficient access for both trucks and passenger cars from any part of the city.

A system of north-south routes forms a grid from the QEW to Highway 401 north of the city. The 401 is a direct link to Windsor and Detroit in the west, and Montreal and the Province of Quebec in the east. Highway 403 provides four lane access to Brantford in the west and intersects the 401 close to the Lester B. Pearson International Airport.

Forty Class "A" truck transport companies and four terminals serve the city.

Rail

A complete range of freight and express rail services, providing access to Canada and the U.S., is available from Canadian National and Canadian Pacific Railways.

The Government of Ontario (GO) Transit System offers a modern passenger commuter service between Toronto and Burlington.

Water

Both Hamilton and Toronto are major ports in the St. Lawrence Seaway system. Both have excellent harbours that are well serviced by rail and truck transport, and include modern materials handling equipment, and customs facilities.

Air

Lester B. Pearson International Airport is 35 miles from the centre of Burlington. Hamilton Airport, located in Mount Hope, is twenty miles away. Both airports provide cargo and passenger services. Smaller airports in Burlington, Guelph and at Toronto Island offer some limited freight, passenger and charter services.

Burlington Industrial Sites

Burlington offers the investor a wide choice of industrial sites. All land is fully serviced. Prices range from $70,000 to $110,000 per acre, depending on location and parcel size. These are well below the cost of adjacent metro sites.

The city-owned Centennial Business Park is ideally located on the south side of the QEW corridor. Other sites, including existing industrial parks, have been privately developed by well established industrial and commercial developers and contractors.

Several multiple-unit and free standing industrial buildings offer space for immediate occupancy.

Office space is available in many of the award-winning business parks located along the QEW corridor.

Housing

Burlington offers quality housing of every type and price range. As you would expect in a primarily suburban area, 60% of Burlington's housing is single detached. Housing prices, reflecting lower land costs, are substantially less than comparable neighbouring areas. Apartments account for close to 25% of total households with the remainder made up of town houses and duplexes.

Education

Burlington has a total of 50 primary and secondary schools, both public and separate. As well, a full program of adult education courses are offered throughout the city and in neighbouring municipalities.

McMaster University, The University of Toronto, The University of Guelph, The University of Waterloo, Mohawk College and sheridan College are within commuting distance.

A modern library with four branches serves the city.

Health Services

The Joseph Brant Memorial Hospital, a 500-bed major facility, serves the community. Specialized medical services are also available at McMaster Medical Centre and in Toronto.

There are 112 doctors and 52 dentists covering virtually every speciality practising in Burlington. A full public health program providing nursing related services is available to city residents.

安省布靈頓市：生活方式吸引、經濟條件可觀

工業多元化發展

三十年前布靈頓還是一個人口六千的湖邊小埠，但現今已是加拿大主要工業城市之一，人口達十二萬衆。其發展迅速的主要原因乃工商業競爭條件可觀、生活方式吸引、所以人皆嚮往。樹立於布靈頓的工業包括五金鑄造、電器、電子、化工、塑膠及食品製造業等。而近年更有多間高科技廠商選擇布靈頓爲理想地點，爲其他工商業提供高質原料及產品。

高科技中心的發展是因各高科技企業皆有共同的須求、而科研設備便是其之一。而加拿大企業、大學及政府等機構最先進的科研設備皆可在布靈頓方圓三十哩找到，其中計有舒爾頓研究中心、施特高研究中心、麥馬士打大學、惠富大學、多倫多大學、滑鐵盧大學、馬克理工學院、舒爾頓學院、安大略研究中心及加拿大內陸水道研究中心等。

布靈頓地點適中

布靈頓面積七十二平方哩，八哩長的安大略湖畔及布靈頓灣畔沿於南，尼加拉瓜斜跨郊野農田直貫西北。布靈頓乃安省工業地帶‘金馬蹄’的一主要環節，‘金馬蹄’自安大略湖邊彎入，由奧沙華申展至尼加拉瓜大瀑布，咸美頓市位於其西，而多倫多市則處於其東。加拿大四份之一人口及四成半之工業產品皆源於市中心方圓百哩內。

資源

一般工業原料在布靈頓市方圓五十哩內皆有供應，如鄰近咸美頓市的鋼材出產能量就幾達全加八成，而數間主要鋼業公司皆有辦事處設在市內。電力、天然氣及用水供應充足而價格合理，用水價格更是低於鄰近地區。

居民

布靈頓市的清新市郊環境一向都爲市各階層人仕所嚮往，其中不乏專業及技術人材。所以在僱用員工方面，可以迎双而解。

交通

貫通工業地帶的要道依利莎伯女皇公路把布靈頓與其他安省及美國城市相連接，再加上公路南北兩旁的主道及和五處行車交替點，交通異常方便。

在依利莎伯女皇公路以北乃橫貫加拿大的401公路，由布靈頓經401公路西行可達溫莎市及美國底特律市，東行則可直達滿地可。在布靈頓以西有403公路交切401於皮雅遜國際機場附近。固現有四十間甲級貨運公司往來於市內的四個主要匯集點。

除CN及CP主要鐵路網外，布靈頓還有雙軌快車直達多倫多。鄰近的威美頓及多倫多港口分別爲布靈頓所用。空路方面，離布靈頓三十哩爲皮爾遜國際機場，二十哩外爲威美頓望山機場，再加上在市內和惠富及多倫多島等小型機場，空路客貨兩運得以暢通無阻。

工業用地

布靈頓有大量工業用地以滿足不同工業的須求，而其地價也較鄰近地區爲低，視乎面積及地點而定，一般價格由每英畝七萬元至十一萬元不等。市政府的百年商業中心位於依利莎伯皇后公路之南，而其他工商用地皮樓宇多由著名的私人發展商興建。

住屋

布靈頓因地價相宜，以致屋價比鄰近地區爲低，而各式住屋皆有供應，但以獨立屋及柏文較爲普遍。

教育

布靈頓有公立、私立、中小學共50間，市立圖書館四所，鄰近高等學府計有麥馬士打大學、多倫大學、富大學、滑鐵盧大學、馬克理工學院及舒爾頓學院等，市內外皆有多項成人課程以供居民進修。

醫療衛生

市內若瑟柏蘭紀念醫院有床位五百，另市內有醫生過百、牙醫五十餘人，再加上各級醫護人員以確保居民可得到最完善的醫療衛生服務。居民更可選擇前往麥馬士打醫療中心或往多倫多接受專科服務。

娛樂

布靈頓不乏多姿多采的體育及文娛活動，有適台青年的冰上曲棍球、壘球、攬球、足球、游泳及其他手工藝小組等。市內有公園及草坪七十餘處，佔地共七百畝，可供作單車、游泳、滑雪、跑步、漫步等各項活動。省立的邦狄公園更是四季活動如一。另外市內的公個溜冰場，七個高爾夫球場，青年會，文化中心等設備爲市民提供了不少方便。喜歡水上活動的更上前往安大略湖及布靈頓灣一舒身心。

購物

布靈頓的商店林林種種，由精品店至大小的超級市場，應有盡有，其中三十二個購物中心分佈市內，爲居民帶來不少日常購物的方便。

消遣

住在布靈頓不愁沒有消遣的好去處，精美食肆，交響樂團及劇院等皆可增進閣下生活的情趣。如閣下對球類有興趣的話，更可到多倫多觀看足球，冰棍球及壘球等比賽。

✔COMPARE

The City of Waterloo for innovation, technology and your future.

If you find a better investment location with...

- ✔ Two major universities
- ✔ Highly skilled labour pool
- ✔ Many advanced Technology Industries
- ✔ Good transportation routes
- ✔ Strong service sector with 6 insurance company headquarters
- ✔ Superior life style and cultural ammenities

- ✔ Extensive innovation/research/technology capabilities
- ✔ Availability of serviced land
- ✔ Diversified economic base
- ✔ Plus the entrepreneurial spirit with a city council/staff that gives you priority attention

then you must consider investing in that location.

There is a right place, a right time and a right alternative.

CITY OF
Waterloo
ONTARIO

For information and assistance contact: Gerry O'Neil, Commissioner of Business Development, City of Waterloo, City Hall, Waterloo City Centre, 100 Regina Street South, P.O. Box 337, Waterloo, Ontario N2J 4A8 (519) 747-8707.

This is Waterloo
Ontario, Canada

Introduction

Waterloo is proud of its reputation for hard work and craftsmanship: these are values which are every bit as important today as in the past. Companies locating in Waterloo will find an excellent labour pool, as well as a data base in existing high-technology industry.

The City is still growing. New housing and industrial developments spread outward, while downtown programs promise an even more successful future for the City's commercial areas.

So come and join us. You are welcome!

In the heart of southern Ontario, Waterloo has the best of both worlds. Surrounded by green farmland and fresh air, the city is a modern, vigorous business and industrial community. Small enough to enjoy the best lifestyle, yet close to all the amenities of the large metropolitan centres.

Living and working here is a pleasure. With the best in transportation, education and recreation, the City has something for everyone. And, we have plenty of excellent housing and land.

Growth

In the recent decade the population of the City grew by 50% with current population at 67,000. It is fully expected that before the end of the century the population will grow to 100,000 or more.

Current and Future Expectations

In spite of international and national economic uncertainties, financial restraints and unemployment in some areas, the City of Waterloo continues to demonstrate an economic health and growth that is somewhat unique and envied by other municipalities in Canada. The 1986 results are complete, Waterloo's economic indicators, including value of all building permits, set yet another record. The growth will continue.

The City's Plan, currently under review, includes sufficient land for population and industrial growth to accommodate the continued very favourable anticipated growth trends over the next 25 years. Through long range planning, deficiencies are identified and actions put in place to permit remedies and approvals in an expeditious manner.

Waterloo's labour quality is higher and unexcelled at all levels from unskilled to Ph.D. . . . productivity and motivation are high . . . turnover and absenteeism are low . . . labour/management relations are excellent . . . Waterloo offers operating economies with lower land costs, lower taxes, lower wage rates, lower construction costs, and a dedicated work force.

Workforce

The total labour force in the Region of Waterloo area of draw is approximately 140,000 and public transportation service is available.

The labour force, with a high level of experienced employees, is considered to be one of the most industrious in the country. This stems from the well diversified industrial base.

Such high tech products as computers, electronics systems, video display terminals, circuit boards, radar systems, electrical equipment, manufacturing systems, etc. are produced in Waterloo.

A Place to Live

They come, They see, They stay — The way of living helps spark the growth of Waterloo. Analysts continually examine the economic factors and usually come up with the simple conclusion "People just like to live in Waterloo."

Excellent Housing at lower cost

Cost of an average two storey house with 3 or 4 bedrooms is about 30% less than a comparable house in Metropolitan Toronto. Rental rates on average are also about 30-35% less.

Neighbourhoods

The Waterloo area has residential neighbourhoods to fit all price categories. There are many well planned residential areas that encompass extensive greenbelts and parks, recreation centres, schools and other amenities.

To accommodate growth, the City has approved plans to ensure an adequate supply of lots in all areas of the City. With this planned supply of building lots to meet or exceed demand, there will be continual pressure against abnormal price increases.

Schooling

All residential areas of the City are either within walking distance or via public transportation to elementary and secondary schools.

With the **University of Waterloo** and **Wilfrid Laurier University** near the centre of the City students can complete their entire education within the City.

Conestoga College of Applied Arts and Technology is within the public transportation system and the main campus is 7 miles away. The College also has a campus in Waterloo.

Business Base

The business base for the City of Waterloo is made up of some 1,200 businesses of all kinds; manufacturing, retail, professional, service and educational.

171

Because there is no dominant industry, such as automotive, steel, textile, etc. there is no dominant union activity. There has been minimal strike activity in the City. In the area, there is a good supply of high-quality, well-motivated and trainable production labour.

The caliber of the workforce in the area plus the availability of "education brainpower" makes Waterloo an ideal location for high-technology facilities that can be equalled by few places in Canada. The City of Waterloo and the Region of Waterloo has numerous small and medium sized manufacturers supplying the high tech industries in Canada and the U.S.A.

Although it is difficult to name a product not made in the area, the following are some that are made in the City of Waterloo.
— Computer & laser instruments
— Electronic Communication terminals
— Radar equipment
— Switchboards & circuit boards
— Electronic panels
— Transformers
— Radar equipment
— Televisions
— Micro processors
— Navigational aids
— Electric starters
— Control panels
— Electric power equipment
— Thermoplastic parts
— Injection molding
— Indicator lights
— And many metal, wood, textile, beverage, food and other products.

The engine that drives the local economy is manufacturing. The fuel that drives the engine is the excellent supply of an educated and dedicated workforce. The heart of the manufacturing sector is the high percentage of businesses engaged in high and advanced technology. This will continue to be the growth sector for the city. Innovation and technology is your invitation to success in the City of Waterloo.

滑鐵盧市在此爲你簡介

引言

滑鐵盧市今天的成就乃其努力耕耘的成果。因此,滑市常以此引以爲榮。滑市的勞工訓練有素,高科技發展迅速。滑市現乃不斷發展。建築業與工商業並駕齊居,把城市不停向外擴展。而市中心商業區的發展更是一日千里。本市歡迎閣下前來發展。

172

滑市位於安省南部的中心區域，四周綠田廣闊，空氣清新。市內工商業發達，集小城生活的情趣與大都市的繁盛於一身。滑市擁有上佳的交通、教育與康樂設施及屋宇、土地等，所以居民生活舒適。

人口增長

滑市現有人口六萬七千，十年來的增長率達50%。預料在本世紀末人口將達十萬人以上。

發展趨勢

雖然國際及加國本土的經濟仍受多方面的限制，滑市却可穩步發展。一九八六年經濟成長驚人，今年發展料可持續。市府的整體城市發展計劃中已預有足夠土地以應人口及工商業未來二十五年的增長，而一切有礙長遠發展的因素已受密切註視及加以適當處理。

勞工

滑市擁有卓越的人力資源，由一般員工而至具有博士學歷的專業人仕皆可在滑市招聘。除此之外，滑市可說是一個生產力強、罷工率低、勞資關係良好，地價、稅率、工資及建築成本皆宜的城市。

滑市的就業人數有十四萬。由於滑市工業發達，所以很多都被不同的高科技企業僱用，其中包括電腦、電子、電路板、雷達系統、電器及生產系統等工業。

理想居處

很多人到過滑市的最後都在此定居。因此，滑市本身的吸引力可謂其發展的原動力。滑市有不同種類及價格的樓房以迎合居民不同的需求，在滑市一般有三至四睡房複式屋宇的售價平均低於多倫多30%，而租金則較多市低出30%至35%。市政府更有計劃地確保土地供應充足，以使樓價不致大幅上揚。一般住宅區皆有完善的社區設施，如公園、康樂中心及學校等。

學校

所有住宅區或其鄰近地區皆有中小學校。市內有著名的滑鐵盧大學及偉弗羅禮亞大學。Conestoga理工學院的校園離滑市祗有七哩，但其在市內也設有校舍以方便居民就讀。

工商業

滑市共有大小不同工商機構一千二百所，其中包括工業生產、零售、專業人仕、服務及教育等不同行業。因為工業多元化，所以很多工會活動也被分化，罷工行動因此鮮有發生。再者，滑市就業人仕的質素高踞全加前列，而中小型工業則供應區內及美國各地主要製造業在原料上的需求，所以產品質高類廣。以下列出數類滑市的產品：電腦及激光激器、電子通訊設備、雷達設備、電視機、電腦微型配件、各類大小電機產品、工業包裝、五金、紡織、食品等。

173

London: A special combination lures investors

There is a special combination of requirements that encourages a business to locate and thrive in a given city.

Certainly, the formula calls for a sound economy, good services, reliable transportation connections and abundant labour.

But one of the critical components is the cooperation of the municipal government — its active willingness to assist growth.

London, Ontario, prides itself on just this kind of track record.

London, the Forest City, with 60,000 trees lining its streets and thousands more in its 2,300 acres of parkland, can offer business unrivalled opportunities.

From a geographic standpoint alone London, with a population now nearing 300,000, offers a strategic window-seat on the cross roads of North American developments.

And more than 500,000 non-Londoners live within 45 minutes driving of the city limits making London a financial, educational, industrial and commercial centre in the region.

With easy access to the city are all the continent's key manufacturing and distribution centres. Six major highways — including Ontario's Highway 401 — link London with key metropolitan centres. Two Canadian railways plus two U.S. lines supply excellent rail services. Four commercial airlines provide vital air routes from an airport just seven miles from downtown.

Located half way between Chicago and New York, London is about two hours driving time from Toronto, Detroit and Buffalo. And Cleveland is just a short 30 minute hop away by daily, scheduled, direct airline flights.

London's ideal size — eleventh largest city in Canada — and position, between North America's culturally rich northeast and the industrial furnace of the midwest, have contributed to the development of a distinctive cosmopolitan flavour.

Stability is the hallmark of London's robust economic environment. The roller coaster troughs and peaks of the North American economy have a limited impact upon the city.

London's economy is built upon a fully diversified industrial and commercial base which smoothes out the more extreme effects of economic cycles.

The local economy is aided by the abundance of favourably serviced industrial sites, commercial space and a balanced labour force.

Over 1,500 acres of municipal and privately owned industrial land is currently available for development in the city which already boasts in-

175

dustrial parks at Westminster, Wilton Grove and Pond Mills. The new Trafalgar Industrial Park includes 400 acres of land for light, medium and heavy industry.

City officials maintain a complete listing of industrial buildings and industrial malls and even for small industries there is a wide selection.

Firms choosing to locate in London are pleased with the skilled and well educated work force — the product of high average levels of educational attainment at Fanshawe Community College and the University of Western Ontario. It's also a product of existing industries that draw upon a diverse work force — blue collar, trained professionals, clerical and managerial.

Fanshawe College in London, Ontario helps local manufacturers to be competitive in world markets by training people in the latest manufacturing methods. Graduates from full-time college study include engineering technologists and technicians; certified tradesmen; and skilled production workers. Depending upon the graduation level, courses will vary in length from eight weeks to three years. All courses are developed by industry for industry, and from the School of Technology alone they graduate over 1,500 people per year.

For families new to London, Fanshawe offers English language training. Individualized help is offered in mathematics to prepare entry for skilled training programs. Newcomers are encouraged to participate in our comprehensive night school and part-time program which offers literally hundreds of opportunities to become involved in lcoal community activities.

London boasts an outstandingly low rate of management-labour disputes and the productivity and flexibility of the workforce is proven.

Average real wages are substantial yet the city offers a relatively low cost of living, particularly housing costs.

On a per capita basis Londoners have more than 6% more disposable income than the average Canadian and the buying power of Londoners has pushed the retail sector to 14% above the national average.

The result is one of the highest per capita allotments of retail shopping space in North America, a vital city core, and some 20 suburban retail shopping complexes, among which are the largest between Toronto and Winnipeg. These shopping complexes serve upwards of 800,000 people within the London retail trading zone.

Some of the best examples of the fertile economic environment in London are the international companies with roots in the city. Firms that have expanded to the point where they have household recognition throughout Canada, and, in some cases, markets overseas and in the United States.

The list of local firms contributing to the national and international marketplace is lengthy. These firms have chosen London as the location of their businesses because of its up-beat economy, active lifestyle and the maintenance of family values.

The view of the future is bright. London seems to be in line for continued economic, cultural and technological expansion.

One of the most encouraging areas is in medical research and health related industry. Pioneering breakthroughs in medical research and health services have made London a world-regarded healing centre. The city possesses some of the world's most advanced medical facilities and leading researchers and doctors.

A leading medical school, four teaching hospitals with renowned research facilities, two specialized research institute and two schools of nursing are all part of the mix that places London squarely in the forefront of medical developments.

The University of Western Ontario's research laboratories are responsible for major scientific and technological advances each year. Its sciences, computer science and electrical engineering departments are open to approaches from business.

These facilities and various support services, are available to industry for contract research and joint ventures. Among these facilities is the boundary layer wind tunnel that has undertaken wind engineer studies on many of the world's tallest structures including the Hong Kong bank.

"London's economic base will continue to be varied with the added strength of a technologically advanced manufacturing base that is stronger in comparison to other major Ontario communities.

"London will become one of the pre-eminent research and science communities in a broad spectrum of topics with specific developments in health, education and agriculture.

"Londoners' lifestyles and satisfaction will be enhanced by a growing cultural and leisure sector without sacrificing any one of the city's present amenities."

Because of London's proximity to major U.S. markets economists are predicting that the city will benefit greatly from promised closer economic cooperation between Canada and its southern neighbour.

A combination of high levels of education, relatively low unemployment and a thriving economy has made for a distinctive atmosphere and highly civilized family lifestyle that has become London's reputation.

Within London, one finds most of the amenities a large city has to offer. However, because of steady, even paced growth the Forest City has avoided the social and economic problems generally associated with larger cities. High rates of serious crime and oppressive municipal debts are foreign to London. Snarled traffic tie-ups are unusual along the city's tree lined streets and boulevards.

Londoners also profit from superior resort areas close at hand. In less than an hour, one can drive to delightful, sandy beaches, provincial parks, and boating marinas on Lake Huron, Lake Erie and Lake St. Clair. However, one needn't leave the city to enjoy clean, fresh air, verdant greenbelts and parklands.

倫敦市：投資者嚮往之地

倫敦市位於北美的樞杻地帶，市內人口三十萬，但市周則有人口五十萬，使倫敦市自成爲一個財經，教育及工商業中心。

倫敦市交通方便，４０１公路，鐵路及機場等把倫敦市和北美各大城市貫通一駕車二小時可達多倫多、底特律或布法羅。

倫敦市乃加拿大的第十一大城市，工業根基穩固，經濟欣欣向榮。市內有超過一千五百畝的工業用地正待發展，市府還有市內各工業單位的資料以供廠商應用。

倫敦市的工人教育水平甚高，而勞資關係亦十分良好。市內的西安大略大學乃加拿大知名學府之一。工人一般的收入比全國平均數字高出百分之六，而消費水平則高出百份之十六。

市內的大企業多不勝數，所以倫敦市的經濟前景極佳。

倫敦市在醫學研究方面素負盛名，市內有多位世界知名的醫生及學者。西安大略大學的醫學院有四所附屬醫院及兩所護士學院。除此之外，西安大略大學在自然科學、電腦、電機工程及科技研究上的成就皆可與有關的工商業機構共享，這包括應用於香港匯豐銀行大廈結構測量上的風速計儀器。

最近Woods Gordon 有關倫敦市的經濟報告指出：「倫敦市的經濟發展將會與其快速的科技發展並駕齊車。」

「倫敦市將成爲一個傑出的醫療、教育及農業科研中心。」

「倫敦市的居民會繼續享有現在的康樂及文化生活。」

倫敦市因鄰近美國的關係，所以在踏足美國市場上佔盡地利。因此，倫敦市的就業率高，治安良好。

離倫敦市不遠有多處著名的郊遊勝地，如Lake Huron 、Lake Erie 及Lake St. Clair 等。

最後，倫敦市無論在工商業及生活的條件上，皆有其勝人之處。

The South Bruce region: Headed to the future.

Introduction

Think of the United States, the world's most lucrative market, then think of Ontario, Canada's largest province with access to over 120,000,000 consumers. In the middle is the South Bruce region, one of the most progressive communities of its kind.

Toronto is the largest city in Canada and an important market for the South Bruce region. Ten of the top U.S. metropolitan markets are within one day's trucking. These markets include New York, Chicago, Detroit, Boston, Philadelphia, Buffalo, Cleveland, Pittsburg, St. Louis, Minneapolis and Newark.

Strategically situated, the South Bruce region is located on the eastern shore of Lake Huron, one of the world's largest bodies of fresh water.

The area is made up of ten municipalities including the towns of Southampton, Port Elgin and Kincardine, the villages of Paisley, Tiverton and Ripley and the townships of Saugeen, Bruce, Kincardine and Huron.

With a population of 27,000 the determination of the region to develop and grow is attracting many new businesses.

Transportation

Major highways link the area with Toronto, Hamilton, London, Kitchener, Guelph and many other urban centres in prosperous Southern Ontario. They also provide easy access to the U.S. market. Three airports are located in the area and Toronto's Lester B. Pearson International Airport is only about a two hour's drive away. Deep water seaway ports are located at Goderich, Owen Sound and Collingwood.

A Place to Visit and Settle

In terms of business, the residents of South Bruce region are an hour or so away from the throbbing, billion dollar market of Southern Ontario and the Northern United States but when it comes to pleasure they are on the brink of the beautiful and varied Canadian outdoors.

There are clean, white beaches and green forests which offer virtually every kind of outdoor recreation.

Tourism is a major sector of the South Bruce region's economy. Over 220,000 visitors spend more than C$135 each summer. The strength of the tourist industry is based on the natural features of the area — especially the miles of sandy beaches accompanied by clean, relatively warm, shallow waters ideal for swimming.

The unspoiled shoreline provides excellent opportunities for hiking, camping, fishing, sailing, swimming and sailboarding. The terrain of the area is ideal for cross-country skiing or snowmobiling.

Industrial Opportunities
The Bruce Energy Centre

The Bruce Energy Centre presents a unique and exciting opportunity for companies to take advantage of an economical, reliable and secure supply of steam and electricity.

The Energy Centre is an industrial and agricultural park covered with medium pressure steam from the adjacent Bruce Nuclear Power Development (BNPD).

The Bruce Energy Centre offers the following advantages over conventional industrial parks:

- Steam prices will be up to 65% less than steam from conventional fossil fuelled sources. Depending on individual energy requirements, this could mean as much as a 30% increase in gross margin.
- By eliminating the need to build steam generating equipment, a company saves on initial capital outlays.
- Firm prices will be negotiated to meet specific energy requirements in long-term contracts.
- Electrical rates that are 1/3 of Ontario's already low rates.
- The Centre will enjoy outstanding reliability and security of energy supply.

Other Opportunities

In addition to the Bruce Energy Centre there are two new industrial parks in the South Bruce region with industrial land available for development.

Land is available at the 45 acre Port Elgin Business Park at between C$3,500 and C$9,000 per acre and at the 25 acre Kincardine Business Park for about C$5,000 per acre. Services are presently up to each respective site and lots will be serviced to meet requirements.

There are also a number of businesses for purchase in the South Bruce region, each offering opportunity for investment.

Additionally, there is a multi-storey industrial building in Southampton that is in the process of being converted into an industrial mall. The building was originally constructed and most recently used as a furniture manufacturing company. There is also a similar building located in Port Elgin offering 36,000 sq. ft. of industrial space. The building is fully serviced with water, sewage, electricity and telecommunications.

Existing Businesses

A diverse list of companies have already chosen the South Bruce region as their business home. Business activity and manufacturing output includes: Yachts, wood products, kitchen cabinets, cap and shirt crests, beef and pork slaughtering and processing, brooms and brushes, plastic film, tomatoes, cheese, fish processing, clay drainage pipes, snow blowers and farm equipment, radio equipment and business telephone systems, custom machinery, animal feeds, awnings and contract sewing and stitching, arms distribution, meat processing, pre-cast concrete tanks, tile, patio and sidewalk slabs and specialized wood turnings, concrete, stone ground flour, greenhouse vegetables, fertilizer blending, structural steel and steel fabricating and machining.

Labour Force

Approximately 20% of the work force is in primary and manufacturing industry, 15% in trade and finance, 38% in transportation, communications, and utilities and majority of the remainder in community business or public administration. There is an abundant labour force made up of skilled, non-unionized workers available for employment, including an untapped female labour market.

Agriculture

Agriculture is a major contributor to the economic base of the South Bruce region. There are 830 farms complemented by 160,000 acres of farmland — 74% under crops, 23% under pasture. Bruce County has the highest concentration of cattle in the province of Ontario. Pigs, sheep and chickens are also raised in large numbers.

Schooling, Health Care and Recreation

Whether it is schooling for the young, medicine for the sick or nourishment for the mind, the South Bruce region and surrounding areas are well endowed with the educational institutions, hospitals and health care centres, libraries and churches that a family community prizes.

Entertainment includes concerts, films, dances and performances by local or visiting drama and musical groups.

Local recreation facilities are unrivalled. Modern community centres feature ice rinks, Olympic size swimming pools, and public auditoriums. Squash/racquetball courts, spa facilities, fitness programs and weight training clinics are offered by modern recreation clubs in the area.

Shopping is a combination of picturesque, traditional, small-town businesses and modern shopping malls. In the primary retail centres of Kincardine, Port Elgin, and Southampton there are more than 600 shops employing over 300 people.

Conclusion

The South Bruce region is headed to the future. You probably are too. The South Bruce Lakeshore Economic Development Corporation is here to help introduce you and your business to the South Bruce Region of Ontario. We are here to help develop business opportunities and to

182

locate and mobilize the financial, physical and human resources needed to succeed. We're ready to hear from you anytime.

南布斯市：美好的明天

南布斯湖畔位於休倫湖東岸布斯市的西南端，面積九百五十平方公哩，離北美的大城市如紐約、芝加哥、波士頓、斯堡及聖路易等只是一天行車的路程。市內人口二萬六千，平均家庭收入每年二萬四千元。

南布斯交通極為方便，從高速公路可直達多倫多、咸美頓、倫敦、、基徹納及惠富等。多處海港及多倫多皮雅遜國際機塲皆只離南布斯一小時的路程。

南布斯湖色醉人、生活舒適。但離商業中心則只是咫尺之地。旅遊業乃南布斯的主要行業之一，每年約有遊客二十二萬人，消費額高達一億三千餘萬。

在能源方面，南布斯有一所超級的核子發電廠。除能吸引遊客外，還可為該市帶來就業機會。核電廠以東有六百畝地現正在發展為工業邨。位於南布斯的工業皆因能源價格相宜而受惠。

除以上的工業邨外，南布斯還有一處四十五畝及一處二十五畝的工業邨，地價則在每畝三千五百元至九千之間。離南布斯不遠還有一所樓面面積十四萬方呎的先進工業廠房。

有很多廠商都在南布斯設廠，產品多樣化，包括遊艇、廚櫃、各式食品、肥田料及鋼廠等。另外，南布斯有農塲八百餘個，農產品豐盛。

南布斯不乏中小學、圖書館及教堂等。市內有四間報館、四所電台及兩間電視台。而在娛樂及戶外活動及購物方面亦多姿多采。

南布斯湖畔經濟發展局（ＬＥＡＤ）歡迎閣下前來投資，請隨時與我們聯絡。

CHAPTER 8

Federal and provincial economic outlook

Continued growth 'till decade end

Extracted from the 'econoscope' by kind permission of The Royal Bank of Canada.

Although the recent stock market decline certainly clouds the economic outlook for Canada and the provinces, we continue to believe that recession is unlikely. In the wake of the stock market collapse, the co-ordinated and positive response of the major central banks to increase the levels of liquidity and lower interest rates provides some reassurance that a serious recession can be avoided. However, uncertainty about how fiscal deficits, particularly in the United States, will be managed is clearly a negative factor.

Our economic outlook for Canada and the provinces prepared before the stock market crash outlined our view that these economies in general were facing a period of weaker growth. Although that forecast did not anticipate a recession, it was our view that most of the risk to the outlook was on the downside. The stock market crash has not greatly altered that fundamental outlook. But, some elements of the forecast clearly have changed. We see three primary impacts that will reduce demand in the economy.

First, lower stock prices will clearly reduce personal wealth and, as a result, will almost certainly exert a drag on consumer spending. However, the strength of this reaction may not be major as equity holdings make up only about one-quarter of all household financial assets. Our earlier forecasts had anticipated that consumer spending would slow significantly next year as households try to rebuild savings and improve balance sheets. This reaction will undoubtedly be somewhat greater than originally anticipated but could well be within the parameters we had earlier expected.

Second, investment spending by firms is also likely to be somewhat slower than we had expected mainly because of reduced opportunity for equity financing as well as the announced programs of many corporations to use internally generated funds to repurchase their equity.

Third, the stock market has an important influence on consumer and business confidence. Sharply lower stock prices could shift the spending and savings decisions of households and businesses, including those which have not directly been affected by the stock market fall or are only marginally affected, towards a more cautious spending and saving posture.

The response of the monetary authorities may offset much of these negative consequences. Clearly, less momentum in the economy will lower inflationary pressures and has already permitted an easing in the level of interest rates. This will offset much of the negative impact of lower equity prices on consumer and business spending. Recent official statements and actions would suggest that major central banks recognize their responsibilities in this regard and are prepared to meet them.

However, there is a major risk in the fiscal policy area. If the U.S. government finds it impossible to make credible progress in reducing its fiscal deficit, then a further sharp market correction with significant negative consequences for the economy would be a very real risk. At present, we are assuming that such progress will be made.

On balance, we continue to call for continued, but slower, growth for Canada and the provinces for next year and quite possibly in 1989. At this stage, we feel that appropriate economic policies in Canada and abroad should be able to steer the world economy away from recession.

Moderate growth in Atlantic Canada

Our earlier forecast of real growth for Atlantic Canada's economy in 1987 appears to be generally on track. The region's resource sectors (mainly fishing, forestry and agriculture) and their related industries are performing well and should continue to do so for the remainder of this year and into 1988. One area of surprising strength in the Atlantic region's economy has been the trade sector. Thanks mainly to a fairly brisk pace of consumer spending, this sector's contribution to the region's growth will probably be stronger than earlier anticipated. On balance, we project the region's economy to grow by 2.7% in real terms for this year as a whole. In the absence of a significant pick-up in the depressed pace of exploration and development activities, we continue to project a very moderate pace of overall growth, just above the 2% mark, for Atlantic Canada during the next two years.

Newfoundland

A stronger-than-anticipated trade sector, thanks to brisk consumer spending so far this year, has led us to increase our 1987 forecast of real growth for Newfoundland to 2.5% from the 2.2% we had earlier projected. For the same reason, we now expect employment growth to come in at close to 2% for 1987 as a whole and the province's unemployment rate to average near the 19% mark. With a virtually dormant offshore sector, Newfoundland's economy should continue to grow at a modest pace of 2% per annum in real terms during the next two years.

In 1987, Newfoundland has seen substantial improvement in its job market, with employment rising and unemployment falling sharply. Due to a pick-up in the pace of job creation during the second and third quarters, employment in Newfoundland rose on average by 1.8% during the first 10 months compared to the same period in 1986. This was equivalent to more than 3,000 additional jobs. These jobs were mostly accounted for by the trade sector and, to some extent, by the construction sector. Meanwhile, with an essentially flat labour force, Newfoundland's unemployment rate has shown a downward trend, falling to 17.1% in October compared to its January level of 20.4%. For 1987 as a whole, however, Newfoundland's unemployment rate will probably average just under 19%

A soft area in Newfoundland's economy this year has been manufacturing. This sector's value of shipments rose by only 0.8% during the first eight months compared to the same period in 1986. Weak shipments growth was the result of sharply lower sales of food products (mainly fish) which offset good gains in pulp and paper products sales. Based on these trends, it appears that growth in the value of Newfoundland's manufacturing shipments for 1987 as a whole will likely be between 1% to 2% compared to the very strong 20% growth last year.

Retail sales have also shown solid growth. In August, the province's retail sales advanced by a strong monthly 2.8%, faster than any other province except for Saskatchewan and Alberta. For the January-August period, retail sales grew by a brisk 9.4% compared to the same period a year ago, faster than the 8.9% national average. Based on the data for the first eight months and an expected retrenchment in consumer spending during the second half of the year, we are now projecting 8% growth for retail sales in Newfoundland for 1987 as a whole.

Demand for housing and house building activity in the province have not shown the same buoyancy as the labour market and consumer spending. This can partly be attributed to home buyers' feelings of uncertainty about the province's medium to longer term economic prospects. In August, urban housing starts fell by a sharp 2.8% from the previous month. Urban housing starts were also lower, by more than 6%, during the January-August period compared to the same interval in 1986. Based on these figures, we continue to call for virtually flat housing starts in Newfoundland for 1987 as a whole.

The year-over-year inflation rate, measured by the change in the St. John's all-items consumer price index, stood at a moderate 3.2% in October, noticeably below the national average. For 1987 as a whole, the inflation rate should come in at close to 3%.

The recently approved Newfoundland Stock Savings Plan is scheduled for implementation next spring. The plan, which offers tax credit for the purchase of shares in eligible companies operating mainly in Newfoundland, is expected to boost the level of capital spending and economic activity in the province.

Favourable conditions benefit Prince Edward Island

Our earlier forecast for Prince Edward Island's economy for 1987 re-

187

mains on target. The Island's economy has benefitted from favourable conditions in the fishing, agriculture and tourism sectors so far this year. As a result, we continue to project a real growth rate of 3% for the Island's economy in 1987, followed by somewhat slower growth in the next two years in line with a more sluggish economic environment in the rest of North America.

Measured by the rate of growth in the value of shipments, the manufacturing sector in Prince Edward Island has put in the best performance among the provinces so far this year. The province's manufacturing shipments jumped by a strong 9.6% during the first eight months compared to the same period in 1986, close to five times as fast as the national average. Higher sales in the food industry have been mainly responsible for this strong showing.

Consumer spending during the first eight months was also quite robust relative to the rest of the country. This was no doubt a reflection of improved farm incomes, resulting from higher sales of potatoes, as well as increased revenues from sales of fish and fish products. For the January-August period, retail sales were up by nearly 10% compared to their level during the same period last year. This compares quite favourably with the all-Canada average of less than 9% for the same period. Consumer spending in the province should remain strong during the remainder of this year and, as a result, we continue to forecast a 8% growth in the Island's retail sales for this year as a whole.

Job creation has been weaker than we had anticipated earlier. Despite a nearly 2% monthly jump in October, the Island's employment figures show an overall increase of only 0.4% in jobs during the first 10 months compared to the same period in 1986. Meanwhile, slightly faster growth in the labour force has prevented the Island's unemployment rate from falling significantly. In October, the unemployment rate stood at 12.7%, down from its January level of 14.6%. Our earlier forecast of the average unemployment rate at just above 13% for 1987, however, remains on target.

As anticipated, the province is experiencing a fairly quiet housing market this year. In August, the latest month for which data are available, urban housing starts on the Island dropped by nearly 53% from the previous month. Cumulative urban starts were also weak for the January-August period as they showed a decline of more than 6% compared to the same period last year. With the current pace of residential construction activity, we continue to call for a lower level of housing starts (about 1,000 units) in the province for 1987 as a whole compared to 1986.

The year-over-year inflation rate, as measured by the change in the combined Charlottetown/Summerside all-items consumer price index, stood at 4.1% in October. This rate was slightly below the national inflation rate of 4.3% mainly because of more moderate increases in food, housing and clothing costs. For 1987 as a whole, we are projecting an inflation rate of 3.4% for the Island.

188

The P.E.I. government's opposition to the proposed free trade agreement with the United States is, in our view, a disappointing development. The Island's export-dependent economy can only benefit from free trade with the United States. Prospects of protectionist measures against exports of fish and agricultural products to the United States, in the absence of a free trade agreement, most likely will convince Islanders to support the proposed free trade agreement.

The construction of a fixed link between Prince Edward Island and the mainland is very close to becoming reality. In fact, the federal government has indicated that it is accepting proposals from the private sector for the project. From the interest shown by a number of Canadian and foreign companies, it appears that this project can be self-financed, requiring no cash outlays by the federal government. The cost of the project is estimated at close to $1 billion and is expected to have the potential to directly generate more than 5,000 new jobs in the Atlantic region during its construction. On a longer term basis, Prince Edward Island's economy will be the prime beneficiary of this project as it will improve market accessibility for the existing and potential business on the Island. This will no doubt lead to an improved standard of living and prosperity for Islanders in the years to come.

Low petrol sales still haunt Nova Scotia

Data for the first 10 months paint a positive picture for Nova Scotia's economy. Healthy consumer spending as well as a continued good performance by the resource-based industries (fishery, forestry and agriculture) should give the province a real growth rate of 2% for 1987. Employment growth for the year as a whole will probably come in at 1.5% with the province's unemployment rate averaging about 13%. During the next two years, and until there is a recovery in the offshore sector, the province is expected to grow at a steady annual rate of 2% in real terms.

Nova Scotia's manufacturing sector saw the value of its shipments decline by 2.5% during the first eight months compared to the same period in 1986. The decline was almost totally the result of lower sales of refined petroleum products which more than offset higher sales in the food and beverages and forest products industries. From these figures, it appears that Nova Scotia's manufacturing sector is heading for its second consecutive year of lower shipments.

Unlike manufacturing shipments, retail sales in Nova Scotia have been quite healthy so far this year, thanks to strong consumer confidence resulting from a steady pace of activity in the province's resource sector, particularly fishing and forestry, and a falling unemployment rate. During the first eight months, the province's retail sales advanced by more than 8%. This was slightly below the national average because of a fairly slow start earlier in the year. With an expected levelling off in consumer spending during the remainder of the year, retail sales in Nova Scotia will probably register a growth rate of about 7% for 1987 as a whole, somewhat higher than our earlier forecast.

In the labour market, employment grew by a respectable 1.7% during the first 10 months of this year compared to the same period last year. Good growth in jobs in combination with relatively sluggish growth in the labour force have pushed down the province's unemployment rate noticeably in recent months, with the unemployment rate standing at 11% in october, the lowest in the Atlantic region and well below January's level of 14.3%. Based on these figures, Nova Scotia should see its employment grow by about 1.5% for this year as a whole and its jobless rate average about 13%. As in the rest of the Atlantic region, housing construction in Nova Scotia has been generally weak. The province's cumulative urban housing starts for the January-August period of this year were about 9% lower than during the same interval in 1986. This was in sharp contrast with the nearly 38% jump in urban starts at the national level during the same period. In the light of the latest residential construction figures, our earlier housing starts forecast of 7,000 units for 1987 remains on target.

The year-over-year inflation rate, measured by the change in the Halifax all-items consumer price index, stood at a moderate 3.1% in October, well below the 4.3% national average. The relatively more moderate inflation rate in Nova Scotia reflects small increases in food, housing and transportation costs. For 1987 as a whole, Nova Scotia's inflation rate should average about 4%.

Litton Systems Canada Ltd. will receive about $300 million worth of orders for missile launchers and radar components from Oerlikon Aerospace Ltd. of Quebec related to the recent $2.5 billion contract to supply the U.S. Army with air defence and anti-tank systems. A large portion of Litton's orders will be filled beginning next year from the company's Halifax plant which is currently under construction. This project is estimated to create more than 300 direct jobs in the Halifax area.

New Brunswick outperforming other Atlantic provinces

Our earlier forecast of New Brunswick's economy is still on track. At an annual growth rate of just above 3%, New Brunswick is expected to outperform the rest of the Atlantic provinces on the strength of its manufacturing and mining sectors as well as fairly strong growth in non-residential capital spending. Despite strong employment growth (in excess of 3%), the province's unemployment rate will probably remain near the 13.5% mark on average for 1987. For the 1988-89 period, we continue to project slower growth in New Brunswick's real output in line with a more sluggish economic climate in the rest of North America.

The performance of New Brunswick's manufacturing sector so far this year has been strong compared to the rest of the country. Mostly as a result of higher sales in the food and paper and allied products industries, manufacturing shipments rose by nearly 4% during the first eigh months compared to the same period in 1986, almost twice as fast as the national average. At this rate, New Brunswick's manufacturing shipments for all of 1987 should register a growth rate very close to last year's 4.3%.

New Brunswick's job creation record so far this year has been outstanding. During the first 10 months the level of employment was up by a strong 3.4% (amounting to more than 9,000 new jobs) from the same period last year. Most of these jobs were created in the trade and services sectors. However, despite solid employment growth, the province's unemployment rate has not declined much since the beginning of the year because of rapid expansion in the labour force. New Brunswick's unemployment rate in October stood at 13.7%, marginally lower than 13.9% in January. Judging from these figures, our earlier labour market projections for 1987 appear to be reasonable.

The fairly strong pace of consumer spending during the first seven months was no doubt a reflection of the province's healthy job market. Retail sales registered growth of nearly 8% during the January-August period compared to the same interval in 1986. Based on this trend, we now project the province's retail sales to increase by about 7% for 1987 as a whole, faster than our earlier forecast, but still slightly slower than the national average.

As in other parts of the region, the housing market in New Brunswick has been very quiet. In August, urban housing starts fell by 30% from the previous month. The downtrend in starts was also evident for the entire January-August period when housing starts showed a decline of more than 9% compared to the same interval in 1986. Given these trends, we continue to call for little or no growth in total housing starts during 1987 as a whole.

The year-over-year inflation rate, as measured by the change in the Saint John all-items consumer price index, stood at 4.3% in September, the same as the national average. Our earlier forecast of inflation for 1987 has now been changed to 3.4%.

Saint John Shipbuilding of New Brunswick is expected to be chosen by the federal government to be the prime contractor for the second set of six new frigates for the Navy. The securing of this contract, with an estimated value of $3.5 billion, will no doubt contribute significantly to the long-term growth of the province.

Quebec experiences strong growth

Our earlier forecast of Quebec's economy for 1987 remains on track. Non-residential capital spending in the province remains strong, while housing construction and consumer spending have yet to ease. As a result, we continue to project a strong real growth rate of about 4.5% for Quebec in 1987. During the next two years, Quebec will probably experience a noticeable growth slowdown because of an anticipated fall-off in consumer and business spending, as well as a less active housing market.

Consumer spending in Quebec continues to forge ahead at a very healthy pace. Retail sales jumped by a strong 11.6% during the first eight months of this year compared to the same period last year. Consumer spending should show a cyclical slowdown during the remainder of the year due to exhaustion of pent-up demand. Therefore, we continue to project an overall growth of 8.5% (in current dollars) in the province's retail sales for 1987 as a whole.

In another strong area, manufacturing shipments in Quebec have also been growing at a relatively healthy pace this year. During the first eight months, shipments of manufactured goods rose by 6.2%, much faster than the national average of about 2.4%. Strong sales in the machinery, food and beverages, paper and allied products and construction-related industries have been mainly responsible for the manufacturing sector's strong performance.

Quebec's labour market is also having a very strong year. Employment growth during the first 10 months was a respectable 3.4%, much faster than the national average of 2.5%. So far this year, Quebec' economy has generated nearly 100,000 new jobs. However, a rapidly expanding labour force has not permitted the province's jobless rate to drop substantially. In October, this rate stood at 9.8% compared to 10.7% in October of 1986. Based on these figures, our earlier forecasts of employment growth and the unemployment rate seem to be reasonable.

In spite of some slowing down in residential construction activity in recent months, housing starts are headed for a record year in 1987. During the first eight months, urban housing starts jumped by 40% compared to the same interval in 1986. Based on this trend, we now project that total housing starts will amount to about 67,000 units for 1987, very close to the record-high level of nearly 69,000 units reached back in 1976.

The year-over-year inflation rate, measured by the change in Montreal's all-items consumer price index, stood at 4.5% in October. This was slightly higher than the national rate of 4.3% for the same period. For 1987 as a whole. we are projecting an inflation rate of 5.1%.

Quebec's aerospace industry is one of the major beneficiaries of the recent $2.5 billion contract to supply the U.S. Army with 60 air defence and anti-tank systems. Oerlikon Aerospace Inc. of Quebec will get about $950 million worth of work in this project through its parent, Oerlikon-Buhrle Holding Ltd., a leading member of the consortium that was awarded the contract. The project is scheduled to be completed by 1992. During this period, Oerlikon will spend about $80 million on plant expansion and equipment directly related to this project and will add 250 employees to its 400-member work force. An additional 200 jobs will be created next year when the company begins to increase the size of its complex in St. Jean-sur-Richelieu.

Consumer spending boosts Ontario economy

Despite a very sluggish performance in the manufacturing sector, Ontario's economy continues to advance at a healthy pace. The buoyancy in the province's economy this year is mainly attributable to brisk consumer and business spending as well as a high level of residential construction activity. Under these conditions, we continue to call for a real rate of growth of 4% in the province's economy for 1987 as a whole. For the next two years, however, we are projecting the province's economy to grow much more slowly as consumer spending in North America cools off and housing construction settles down at a lower level.

Manufacturing has been a very weak spot in Ontario's economy so far this year, mainly because of sharply lower sales in the dominant transportation equipment industry. Total manufacturing shipments rose by less than one percent during the first eight months compared to the same period last year, much more sluggish than the 2.4% national average. Based on these figures, we continue to call for little or no contribution from the manufacturing sector to overall growth in Ontario's economy this year.

In sharp contrast to the manufacturing sector, Ontario's trade sector appears to be very strong. One indicator supporting this view this is the pace of consumer spending which continues to be brisk. For instance, retail sales in the province have registered a growth rate of more than 10% during the first eight months, noticeably faster than the national average of less than 9%. With an eventual slowdown in the pace of consumer spending during the remainder of the year, as pent-up demand diminishes, our earlier forecast of retail sales growth of 8% for 1987 as a whole appears to be reasonable.

Ontario's labour market performance has also been very respectable. Employment in the province showed an increase of about 3% (amounting to 168,000 new jobs) during the first 10 months. Meanwhile, the province's jobless rate has been on a steady downward trend, falling to 5.7% in October, its lowest level since 1974. These figures are generally in line with our earlier forecast of labour market conditions in Ontario for 1987.

The anticipated slowdown in Ontario's housing market appears to be underway. After peaking in June, urban housing starts dropped noticeably during the July-August period. Despite this, urban housing starts for the January-August period were still nearly 50% higher than during the same period in 1986. Although we expect a further slowing in housing construction during the rest of this year, the province should, nevertheless, finish 1987 with total housing starts of close to 100,000 units, the highest level since 1973, and more than 20% higher than in 1986.

The year-over-year inflation rate, as measured by the change in the Toronto all-items consumer price index, stood at 5.3% in October, one full percentage point higher than the national inflation rate. Sharply higher housing and transportation costs have been mainly responsible for the relatively high inflation rate in Ontario so far this year. Our earlier inflation forecast of about 5% for 1987 has now been raised to 5.8%.

Lacklustre performance by Manitoba

The overall pace of activity in Manitoba has been very lacklustre so far this year. The province's economic performance has been hampered by slow growth in its manufacturing sector and unfavourable conditions in the agricultural sector. The main source of growth in Manitoba this year has been the construction sector and related industries, spurred by the continuing work on the Limestone hydro project. Under these circumstances, our earlier forecast of 2.8% real growth for Manitoba in 1987 still looks reasonable. During the next two years, Manitoba should resume above-average growth performance, growing at an annual rate of close to 3%, as its manufacturing sector strengthens and grain prices bottom out.

Manufacturing shipments in Manitoba have shown very little growth (0.5%) so far this year mainly because of weakness in the food and machinery industries. Lower sales in these industries in recent months have offset increased shipments in the construction-related industries. As a result, total manufacturing shipments rose by only 0.5% during the first eight months compared to the same period last year. Nationally, manufacturing shipments grew by 2.4% during the same period.

In the labour market, Manitoba's performance has also been quite modest. Employment in the province grew on average by only 1.1% (5,000 persons) during the first 10 months, significantly slower than the national average. Meanwhile, a similar growth rate in the labour force did not allow the province's unemployment rate to fall substantially. In fact, Manitoba's jobless rate has been rising since the middle of this year. In October, the unemployment rate in the province stood at 8.2%, more than one percentage point higher than in the same month last year. Despite this most recent trend, we are still projecting Manitoba's unemployment rate to be lower on average this year than in 1986 at 7.5% versus 7.7% as indicated in our earlier forecast.

Another weak area in Manitoba's economy is consumer spending. This is a reflection of overall weakness in the economy as well as higher sales taxes introduced in the province's 1987 budget. Retail sales grew by only 4.5% during the first eight months compared to the same interval in 1986, significantly slower than the 8.9% national average. We do not expect much improvement in consumer outlays during the rest of the year because of still fairly weak consumer confidence in the province. Our earlier forecast of 4.5% growth in retail sales for 1987 remains on target.

Demand for housing this year has been depressed by lower farm incomes, higher personal taxes and general weakness in the economy. Despite these negative factors, urban housing starts showed a modest increase of about 9% during the first eight months. However, taking into account likely weakness in construction activity in rural areas, due to falling farm incomes, we do not expect the province's total housing starts for 1987 as a whole to show a noticeable improvement over last year. In our view, total housing starts in 1987 will probably be virtually flat as the 8,000 unit level.

The year-over-year inflation rate, as measured by the change in the Winnipeg all-items consumer price index, stood at 3.1% in October, well below the national inflation rate of 4.3% in that month. Small increases of North America, our views on the other two areas are essentially unchanged. Despite downside risks resulting from sluggish demand growth, high inventory levels, and recent OPEC overproduction, oil prices stand a reasonable chance of remaining near or rising moderately above current levels. Meanwhile, grain prices continue to be low and are likely to remain so.

We continue to call for a recovery in Alberta's economy during the second half of this year and through 1988. Next year, under the assumptions of no recession in North America and steady oil prices, Alberta's economy should be able to shake off the lingering effects of the 1986 recession, registering good overall growth and falling unemployment. With improved conditions in the oil patch, the increased activity associated with the Calgary Winter Olympics could serve as a catalyst for a strong pick-up in consumer spending next year, a trend that would be in contrast to the rest of the country.

Looking out to 1989, the province's economic and business outlook is even more encouraging as we expect grain prices to bottom out in 1988 and the pace of activity in the oil patch to remain on a steady upward course. Under these circumstances, Alberta could well outperform the all-Canada average in terms of overall growth in 1989.

Manufacturing in Alberta is dominated by the food and beverages and petroleum products industries. A very respectable performance by the former so far this year has been more than offset by very weak conditions in the latter. As a result, total manufacturing shipments dropped by nearly 4% during the first eight months, with sharply lower sales in the machinery industry also contributing to this decline. Given these trends, Alberta will probably finish this year with a modest decline in its manufacturing shipments for the second consecutive year.

Consumer spending in Alberta has been very sluggish due to weak consumer confidence resulting from uncertain economic conditions, particularly earlier in the year. The apparent stability in oil prices and improved prospects for the oil patch have, however, boosted consumer confidence in recent months and retail sales in Alberta have lately shown some strength. In August, for instance; retail sales rose by a very strong 5.1% compared to the previous month. Despite this, and due to weaknesses earlier in the year, retail sales rose by only 2.3% during the first eight months as a whole. With healthy consumer confidence currently prevailing in the province, we expect further strengthening of consumer spending during the rest of 1987. As a result, we continue to project the province's retail sales to grow by about 4% for the year as a whole.

Housing construction activity has strengthened considerably in recent months in response to improved prospects for the oil and gas industry. Urban housing starts in the province rose by nearly 3% during the first eight months compared to the same period last year. Given this trend, we are now projecting total housing starts in Alberta for all of this year to come in at just under 10,000 units, up about 15% from last year.

In the labour market, Alberta's performance has not been impressive. Employment during the first 10 months was virtually flat compared to the same period last year. For the year as a whole, Alberta should show a very modest 0.5% growth in it employment, amounting to about 5,000 new jobs. The province's unemployment rate, which dropped sharply to 8.7% in October mostly because of a decline in the labour force, should average just under 10% for 1987 as a whole.

The year-over-year inflation rate, as measured by the change in the combined Edmonton/Calgary all-item consumer price index, stood at just over 4% almost the same as the national inflation rate. For this year as a whole, our earlier inflation forecast of 3.4% for Alberta appears to be on target.

Growth bolstered in British Columbia

British Columbia's economic performance in 1987 has been bolstered by a modest recovery in the mining sector, resulting from improved metals prices, including gold and silver, and from continued growth in the forest products industry. These positive factors in combination with a booming housing market and fairly buoyant trade and services sectors have permitted the province to avoid a post-Expo '86 hangover. We now project British Columbia's economy to grow by 3.5% in real terms this year, a full percent faster than our earlier forecast of 2.5%.

During the next two years, British Columbia's economy is expected to grow more slowly than in the 1986-87 period, reflecting the effects of slower growth in the United States and the rest of Canada on the province's exports to these markets. However, with the anticipated continuation of recovery in the mining sector and good growth in the pulp and paper segment of the forest products industry, the economic slowdown in British Columbia is likely to be much less severe than in the rest of Canada. As a result, we expect the province's economy to expand at a rate slightly faster than the national average during the 1988-89 interval.

Led by the forest products industries, British Columbia's manufacturing sector has significantly outperformed its counterparts in the rest of the country so far this year. Total manufacturing shipments in the provinces rose by a fairly strong 7% during the first eight months, nearly three times faster than shipments growth at the national level.

Consumer spending has also been quite brisk. Consumers have been responding to improvement in the province's economic performance and in its immediate prospects. As a result, retail sales rose by a healthy 8.5% during the first eight months of this year compared to the same period last year. With economic fundamentals remaining favourable, retail sales should continue to perform well during the rest of the year. Our earlier forecast of 8.5% growth for British Columbia's retail sales for this year as a whole looks quite reasonable.

One of the strongest areas in British Columbia's economy this year has been residential construction activity. An improving economic climate in food, transportation and housing costs were mainly responsible for the relatively moderate inflation rate in the province. For 1987 as a whole, Manitoba's inflation rate should come in at about 4.3%, slightly below the national average, and more moderate than our earlier forecast of 4.5%

Agriculture holds back Saskatchewan

Saskatchewan's short-term economic performance will continue to be dampened by unfavourable conditions in the province's agricultural sector and uncertain prospects for potash and uranium mining, resulting from increased protectionism in the United States. We are now projecting Saskatchewan's economy to grow by 1.5% in real terms in 1987. Improving conditions in the oil patch and continued growth in the manufacturing sector are expected to be the main sources of growth during the next two years. With an expected real rate of growth of 2% a year, Saskatchewan will likely continue to underperform the rest of the country in the next two years.

As a result of fairly strong sales in the food and beverages and construction-related industries, Saskatchewan's manufacturing shipments rose by a modest 2% during the first eight months of this year compared to the same period a year ago. The province also showed a modest increase of 4.2% in its retail sales during the same period. Meanwhile, urban housing starts registered a 3.3% year-over-year growth rate during the January-August period.

In the labour market, Saskatchewan's performance has been less encouraging. Employment remained virtually flat during the first 10 months. A shrinking labour force during the same period, however, prevented the province's unemployment rate from moving up. In October, the latest month for which data are available, Saskatchewan's jobless rate stood at 7.3%, marginally lower than the 7.5% in October of last year. We expect Saskatchewan to finish 1987 with flat employment and a slight decline in its labour force. As a result, the unemployment rate should average 7.7%, close to last year's average.

The year-over-year inflation rate, as measured by the change in the combined Saskatoon/Regina all-items consumer price index, stood at 5.3% in October. This was one full percentage point higher than Canada's inflation rate, reflecting mostly higher health care costs resulting from the significant reduction in the provincial government's subsidies for prescription drugs. For 1987 as a whole, inflation in Saskatchewan should come in at about 5%, somewhat higher than our earlier forecast.

Alberta economy set to recover

Our earlier forecast of Alberta's economy was based on several key factors: weaker growth in the rest of North America, essentially stable oil prices and continued depressed grain prices. While the recent stock market crash could amplify the anticipated growth slowdown in the rest and rising consumer confidence have been mainly responsible for a surge in housing starts. Urban housing starts showed an increase of more than 40% during the first eight months of this year compared to the same period in 1986. As a result of this stronger-than-anticipated residential construction activity, we are now projecting the province's total housing starts for 1987 as a whole to increase by more than 23% to 25,000 units, their highest level since 1981, and much stronger than our earlier forecast of 22,000 units.

In the labour market, employment grew by 1.8% on average during the first 10 months, the same as the labour force growth. In the most recent months, however, employment of this period, outpaced the labour force. This led to a noticeable decline in the unemployment rate from about 13% during the first half of the year to 11.4% in October. Based on labour market data so far this year, we are now raising our earlier forecast of employment and labour force growth for 1987 from about 1% to 2%. However, our earlier forecast of the average unemployment rate of 12.7% for the year still looks reasonable and we are now forecasting 12.2%.

The year-over-year inflation rate, as measured by the change in the Vancouver all-items consumer price index, stood at 3% in October. This was significantly lower than the national rate of 4.3% for the month because of very moderate increases in food, housing, clothing and health care costs in the province. For 1987 as a whole, British Columbia's inflation rate should average 3.5%, lower than our earlier forecast of 4%.

British Columbians are likely to see major changes in their province's socio-economic structure under the current Social Credit government of Mr. Vander Zalm. Premier Vander Zalm has announced a decentralization plan consisting of the establishment of eight development regions within the province. Each region would be assigned a cabinet minister, a parliamentary assistant and a $1 million start-up budget. In cooperation with local governments, the regional administration would assume responsibility for the coordination of economic development and provincial services.

Premier Vander Zalm has also announced his government's much-touted privatization plan called "Opportunities B.C." This initiative would involve the sell-off of about $3 billion worth of Crown assets and government services. The money raised is expected to be used to pay down the government's outstanding debt.

In our view, both plans should enhance the operational efficiency of the government and the role of the private sector in the British Columbia economy. If managed well, these initiatives would make the province's economy more dynamic.

On another positive note, a stronger-than-expected economy so far this year has improved the province's fiscal position. The latest fiscal figures indicate that the province's deficit for the first six months came in at $351 million, significantly lower than the expected $606 million. The reduction was due to both higher revenues and lower government spending in certain areas. These figures suggest that the government's projected annual deficit of $875 million for this fiscal year can be easily met.

Subsequent to the imposition of a 15% tax on softwood lumber exports to the United States, only two provinces, Quebec and British Columbia, have introduced increases in stumpage fees eventually to replace the export tax. While Quebec's objective is to use stumpage increases to come up with a higher fee structure that will meet the conditions of the agreement with the United States, the B.C. government's plan goes beyond the replacement of the export tax. The B.C. program, which came into effect in October, will require the private sector to assume the additional cost of reforestation and silviculture over and above stumpage fee increases. Government revenues are expected to rise from $580 million a year, including $350 million in export taxes transferred from the federal government, to $680 million. However, if reforestation costs are taken into account, the final cost to the industry could be close to $800 million. The imposition of this extra cost burden on B.C. producers comes at a time when the consensus among forecasters calls for steep declines in housing starts over the short-run, implying an erosion in profitability for lumber producers.

The prospects for the multi-billion dollar Quintette coal mine and the several thousand jobs associated with it do not look promising. The mine's Japanese customers/shareholders are insisting on renegotiating their long-term contract under which they are committed to buy about five million tonnes of metallurgical coal a year at the price of $96 per tonne. By refusing to take delivery of their coal, Japanese buyers are trying to force down the contractual price of $96 per tonne for Quintette coal to the international market price of less than $60. With operating costs of about $80 per tonne, Quintette cannot accept the Japanese demand without incurring huge financial losses. Unless the Japanese budge from their position, the future of the Quintette project is in jeopardy. This would be a serious blow to British Columbia's economy.

Royal Trust and you . . .
"A partnership for success"

Whether you have decided to invest in Canada, move to Canada, or both, Royal Trust can help you better than any other financial institution.

We want to help you prosper, because as you prosper, so does Royal Trust. We call it a "partnership for success".

Royal Trust is your passport to a global financial network, offering an unparalleled range of quality services to help arrange your move or investment. More important, we can give you good old fashioned advice; like how to enjoy a 5 year holiday from Canadian tax when moving to Canada, or the right investment mix for your specific needs.

Ahead of you lie investment decisions and major challenges. With almost a century of experience to draw from, we will share with you the knowledge we have acquired through helping others like you.

More Than A Bank

Royal Trust, founded in 1899, is among Canada's most conservatively capitalized and prudently leveraged major financial institutions. Under Canadian law, a trust company is able to offer services comparable to those of chartered banks. But, in addition, a trust company has broader powers to advise clients and administer and manage investments on their behalf.

Led by energetic management, Royal Trust has become known for its innovative services, international focus and quality advice.

Adding to its own strength, Royal Trust is part of the Trilon Financial Corporation group. Trilon is a network of major Canadian corporations, including:

• Royal LePage, Canada's largest real estate broker selling both residential and commercial property.

• Triathlon Leasing. The country's largest vehicle leasing and fleet management company, Triathlon also leases furnishings and equipment.

• London Life, leading the individual life insurance market in Canada.

• Wellington Insurance, the largest shareholder-owned general insurance company in Canada.

• Canada Systems Group, Canada's largest supplier of computer-based information systems.

Your Passport To A World of Financial Services

Through Royal Trust, you have a passport to a world of financial services, all through the convenience of a single Account Manager.

Our range of services for individuals, small businesses, and large corporations includes:

PRE-IMMIGRATION SERVICES

- pre-immigration advice and tax planning
- Approved."Investor" category investments
- Transfer of investments
- Opening bank accounts
- Help in finding a home
- Mortgage arrangement
- Full insurance services

BANKING SERVICES

- Personal and business accounts
- Lending and credit, including personal mortgages
- Corporate lending
- Corporate finance
- Real estate finance

ASSET MANAGEMENT

- Global portfolio management
- Unit trusts
- Certificates of deposit
- Offshore trusts
- Pension and institutional management

TRUST & ADVISORY SERVICES

- Asset protection
- Tax planning
- Personal financial Planning
- Executor and trustee services
- Corporate trust
- Global custody

Our tax planning and investment advisory services are best suited to those individuals or businesses with at least Cdn. $250,000 of capital to invest.

Royal Trust is Your Best Choice: Call Us Now!

If you were selecting a financial institution to manage your everyday needs, Royal Trust would be an excellent choice. But, for the sophistication of a move or international investment, Royal Trust is your **best** choice.

For a confidential discussion about the opportunities that await you, contact the Royal Trust office nearest you. We look forward to working with you.

投資加拿大？移居加拿大？
皇家信托及閣下成功之籲。

皇家信托公司在財務方面已有近百年的歷史，其國際性服務網可爲閣下服務：

個人服務

- 移民前投資顧問服務
- 新居民五年免稅計劃
- 國際投資資料
- 銀行服務及信貸
- 房地產及信托服務
- 客戶經理爲閣下處理一切

商業服務

- 商業貸款
- 企業財務
- 地產發展及投資
- 廠房設備及汽車租賃計劃
- 各類信托服務
- 公司秘書服務
- 一切工商業服務

無論閣下想投資或移居加拿大，皇家信托皆可爲您提供最皆服務。如想獲知詳情，請與以下皇家信托分行聯絡：

香港—東京—新加坡—倫敦—蘇黎世—澤西— Isle of Man
—荷蘭—克曼羣島—加拿大各分行

香港：

Ms. Amy Shum
Manager, Private Banking
Royal Trust
32nd Floor
One Exchange Square
8 Connaught Place
Hong Kong

Tel: 5-8478666
Telex: 64877 RTAL HX
Fax: 5-8450346

加拿大：

Mr. Jeffrey Halpern, C.A.
Director, Personal Financial Planning
Royal Trust
P.O. Box 7500
Station A
Toronto, Ontario
Canada M5W 1P9

Tel: (416) 864-7000
Telex: 06524306
Fax: (416) 864-9021

皇家信托與您……"最皆拍檔"

無論閣下是想投資或移居加拿大,皇家信托皆希望可爲閣下服務,與您共同成長。我們爲閣下提供的各項服務,如五年免稅及投資組合等,旣穩固,又實際。我們積累了近百年的經驗正是閣下信心的最皆保證。

不祇銀行咁簡單

皇家信托公司早在一八九九年成立,現在已發展成爲一間旣健全又穩固的財務機構。在加拿大,信托公司的服務可與銀行分庭抗禮。除此之外,信托公司在投資及資詢性服務方面更趨多元化。

由於皇家信托在組織及管理上力求盡善盡美,所以無論其在國際性及多元化服務方面,早已信譽超著。

皇家信托除其本身實力雄厚外,它還是加拿大 **Trilon Financial Corp** 的屬下公司之一。 **Trilon** 其他的企業成員計有:

- **Royal LePage** ——加拿大最具規模的地產公司。
- **Triathlon Leasing** ——加拿大最大的車輛、工商業設備及傢俬租賃公司。
- **London Life** ——具規模的人壽保險公司。
- **Wellington Insurance** ——全加最大的上市保險公司,業務多元化。
- **Canada Systems Group** ——加拿大最大的電腦資料系統供應商。

皇家服務,爲您大開方便之門

皇家信托爲私人和大小企業所提供的服務包括:

移民前各項服務

- 移民前資詢及稅務策劃
- 「投資者」移民計劃
- 資金調動
- 開戶
- 置業
- 物業按揭
- 各類保險

銀行服務

- 私人及商業戶口
- 各類信貸及按揭
- 商業財務及貸款
- 地產貸款及資金參與計劃

資產管理

- 全球性資金管理
- 單元信托
- 存款証
- 海外信托
- 退休金計劃

信托及資詢

- 資產保值
- 稅務策劃
- 私人財政策劃
- 執行人及托管人服務
- 公司信托
- 全球性托管

我們的稅務及投資資詢服務特爲投資二十五萬元以上的人仕而設。皇家信托實爲閣下的最佳選擇，如想預約面談，請與就近的皇家信托辦事處聯絡，所有資料，一概保密。

Make the right move

Thunder Bay offers more than a business opportunity; it offers a satisfying new lifestyle opportunity:

- An uncrowded, spacious place to live, work and grow
- Excellent education, with top-notch college and university facilities
- World-class recreation, with golf, theatre, skiing, fishing and much, much more.

On the business side you'll find:

- A skilled and ready workforce
- Easy access to United States and Canadian markets
- Abundant, serviced industrial sites

- North America's 20th largest port
- And a very pro-business environment.

This is only a small part of the Thunder Bay story.

To have us show you more, call (807) 623-4060 or Telex 073-4175 (TBEDC THB) or write:

Dick Charbonneau or Richard Pohler Thunder Bay Economic Development Corporation Suite 203-B. 620 Victoria Avenue East Thunder Bay, Ontario Canada   P7C 1A9

Discover a bright future in Thunder Bay, Ontario, Canada Discover a better choice

When you think about your future, why not look for the Thunder Bay advantage? Our friendly City in the heart of Canada has welcomed new Canadians for more than a century. For our size, we have the largest variety of cultures in all of Canada; more than one percent of our citizens are of Chinese descent. If you are looking for a less-crowded place, discover a better choice in Thunder Bay.

Look for the centre

Thunder Bay is in the centre of North America, 800 miles west of Toronto, 350 miles north of Minneapolis and 700 miles northwest of Chicago. Because our City is located on the shore of Lake Superior; our busy harbour is open directly to the Atlantic Ocean at Montreal, with shipping through the St. Lawrence Seaway for most of the year. All of Canada's major highways and railways connect Thunder Bay to the entire country and to the United States, less than forty miles away. Our international airport provides service by most major air carriers.

A good home for your family

What could be better for children than plenty of space to play and grow? In Thunder Bay, most families own houses with large yards. Our average home is 1,200 square feet; the usual yard or lot is 5,000 square feet; together, the cost of a good family home is only $100,000 (Canadian), much less than in most North American cities.

In Thunder Bay, our low property taxes are only $1,200 (Canadian) per year for the average home. This tax pays for most public services, all elementary and high school operations, and many recreational facilities. Discover the warmth of family living in a friendly City that wants to make you feel at home.

The good life

Our part of Canada offers some of the best recreational opportunities in North America. Our new concert hall, Canada's largest indoor swimming facility, golfing, curling, hockey, baseball, the best ski-hills in central Canada, sailing, fishing, hunting, museums, art galleries, a fine symphony orchestra.

All facilities are open to everyone; most are located only a short drive or walk from home. When it's time to relax, discover the good life in

207

Thunder Bay.

Ready for the future

Every parent wants a fine education for his or her children. Thunder Bay has one of the most modern school systems in Canada (including our own part-time Chinese school). We also have a Technical College (3,000 students) and a highly-respected University (4,000 students). With technology changing every day, learning the skills of the future is important today.

Let's talk business

In Thunder Bay, we want and need your manufacturing investment and your business skills and experience. And we'll work hard to find the right opportunity for you and help you make it a great success. Already we have three very successful manufacturing plants established by Hong Kong investors. In our community you and your business will be important.

Moving to Canada

Many people think of Canada as a wonderful place to live and do business. And our government now offers an attractive immigration preference for businesses and investors. Our Corporation works closely with the Commission for Canada and the Ontario Government. Our support, experience and contacts can help you through the paperwork quickly.

You're welcome

Our EDC will help you explore the many opportunities for business investment, free-of-charge and without obligation. All of our discussions will remain strictly confidential. We want you to succeed!

在根德埠找尋您美好的明天

　　根德埠早在百多年前已歡迎移民到此定居。至今，根德埠的居民有很多是源自世界各地的，而其中華人則佔超過百份一。如您是想找一個較寧靜的地方以建立您的將來，爲甚麼不考慮根德埠呢！

地點適中

　　根德埠位於北美的中心地帶，在多倫多的西面約八百哩，明尼亞布列市北面約三百五十哩及芝加哥西北面約七百哩。正因根德埠是座落於大湖區，所以一年四季船舶可經聖羅倫斯水道及滿地可直出大西洋。還有，主要的陸路及航空交通通皆可經根德埠前往加拿大及美國各地。

理想居所

　　有甚麼可比使孩子們有更多舒暢身心的機會來得重要呢？在根德埠，平均的房子有一千二百方呎，地段則五千方呎，但價錢祇是十萬元左右，比加拿大其他的地方相宜得多。

　　根德埠平均的地稅每年爲一千二百元左右，而地稅則是用於一切社區設施、學校及康樂設備等。根德埠確是您安居樂業的好地方。

生活健康

　　根德埠擁有北美最佳的康樂設備，如音樂會堂、全加最大的室內游池、高爾夫球場、溜石、冰上曲棍球、棒球、全加最佳的滑雪勝地、遊艇、釣魚、搜獵、博物館、美術館及交響樂等。而以上的康樂活動皆位於極方便地點，以供市民享用。

計劃明天

　　爲人父母者皆想其子女可接受優良的教育。根德埠設有先進的教育制度，其中包括一所中文學校。我們還有一所可容三千學生的理工學院及四千學生的大學。現今科技日新月異，教育的重要實不容忽視。

言歸正傳

　　我們極須要您的從商經驗及投資，我們定會竭盡所能以助您生意的成長。現在在根德埠定居的三戶香港移民便是成功的最佳例子。對根德埠來說，您們是極受歡迎的。

來加安居

加拿大確是一個令人嚮往的地方。透過我們與加拿大領事館及安大略省政府的密切關係，您的申請移民過程定會加倍順利。

歡迎您們

我們的經濟發展委員會可提供免費投資資詢服務，一切資詢，盡皆保密。謹此預祝閣下的理想得以實現！

CHAPTER 9

C.L. Cheung

Winnipeg offers excellent base for companies starting small but with plans to grow

Friends and contacts are important when you move to a new country so it was quite reasonable for C.L. Cheung to open his infant sleepers and accessories factory in Winnipeg where lived the good friend who had been responsible for his coming to Canada in the first place.

"When I first came to Winnipeg in 1972 I never thought about opening my own business and one thing I knew was that the people were nice and friendly and because Winnipeg is a small city they were very helpful too."

After one year, in 1973, he moved to Montreal where he stayed for five years.

"In Montreal I worked in the knitting division of a company where I met some Italian friends who, although they knew the garment business very well, were not familiar with the ways in which I worked and I didn't know what they did so in 1977 we were able to join together to start an infantwear business."

But every year while the Cheung family lived in Montreal his friend from Winnipeg kept contact so that when the time came when he began to think about setting up a business on his own what more natural thing to do than to enlist the support of this long time friend.

"He had been in business for himself for many decades and I felt he could help us out with all the aspects of setting up a new factory and he did making all the arrangements for me to obtain 6500 square feet of space and get the machinery. He really helped us out a lot. At the beginning he even brought in some of our first small orders."

So in 1979, fed up with the emphasis on the French language in Quebec to the exclusion of English, he sold his interest in the Montreal firm to his Italian partners and headed west.

"When we first started our orders were only local, for example Saan Stores. There was another big company but it went bankrupt three years ago and we lost a lot of money; there are a few wholesalers but they buy once in a blue moon and not in big quantities — it's not enough to keep going."

"In Vancouver we have a little bit of advantage compared with Toronto because we are so much nearer but again there are only a few companies like Fields's and Woodwards Stores; it's still a small market."

"Most of the head offices of the national companies like the Bay or Eaton's have their head offices in Toronto or Montreal so that where you have to go to get orders. That's why I say that it's hard to do business in

Winnipeg."

"Today, now that I realize some of the problems in Winnipeg I would say to newcomers that they would possibly be better in Toronto. At that time we had no experience about Toronto, the Canadian marketplace or its population."

"Now we know that more than 50 per cent of Canada's population lives in Ontario and Quebec and business depends on population; unfortunately, in Winnipeg there are not enough people; you've got to rely on Toronto and Montreal."

"I decided to go into baby sleepwear because it's something everyone must buy as a number one requirement. You don't have to buy a lot of clothes for yourself or your wife but you must buy for a baby. And a baby grows so fast that you have to buy and keep buying."

"The profit margin is not much on baby sleepwear, not like on ladies fashion clothes, but it is a bread and butter item because it is a necessity."

"Because I had never had a business of my own my first thought was never mind the profit so long as I could do something that was steady and would keep growing. Once we were on the right track we could always do something else."

"If new immigrants come to a city like Winnipeg they should be looking for steady growth not spectacular growth and they should not expect to sell too much."

"I may be a bit old fashioned because I believe this is the best way to start a business anywhere. If you come to a new country where you have no friends or relatives to consult with or ask questions the best thing is to go for a steady business. Don't try to make lots of money overnight. Establish your roots first and after that you can do whatever you want but first you have to get to know the people, the place, the surroundings — everything."

"Although Winnipeg is small if new immigrants start a small company, say, a family size business or perhaps a little bit bigger with between five to 15 employees you can't lose because there are lots of independent stores here and if you make something and you go to these stores if the price and the quality are right they will buy from you, they will at least give you a try. The big guys won't even look at you."

"If you want to sell to the chain stores you've got to go to Toronto or Montreal and when you get there they look at you and ask you how many people you have at your factory and if you say only five people they'll ask 'Are you sure you can deliver?' "

"If you start your business here locally it may be small but it will be O.K. and once you've made some progress you certainly sell to the big chains in Toronto or Montreal."

"Whatever product you decided to make in a city like Winnipeg you've got to keep in mind that the buying power is in Quebec and Ontario."

"The main reason new immigrants choose to come to Winnipeg is that although they have expertise they probably don't have lots of capital and if I apply to Ontario to start a business with, say, C$50,000 that's not a sufficient amount for officials of the Ontario Government to even consider and Montreal or Quebec may be the same although because of the French language problem not too many people go there and therefore they may look at you."

"Winnipeg is looking for businessmen to start a business here; they want more people to come to Winnipeg but in fact most go to Toronto and the only way to get people to come here is by not looking for the big companies, the big investors. They can expect somebody with knowhow and prospects to come here, start a business and grow bigger and bigger. That is the main reason people want to come here."

"Don't get me wrong. Of course the government would like to see big investors here. I'm pretty sure the Government of Manitoba will be willing to give the bigger investors a lot of benefits to encourage them to come here and settle down."

"Definitely government is making a big effort to encourage new immigrants to come here and set up businesses to help reduce unemployment."

"Those smaller investors who choose Winnipeg I guarantee they will like it here. Winnipeg is one of the friendliest cities in Canada; government officials are very helpful and it is easy to get permissions. You can start small and when you grow bigger you can open sales offices in Toronto or Montreal."

"Although opening a sales office in Ontario or Quebec will increase overheads I think a business will be able to afford it because the cost of doing business here is less than in the East. For example, rents are a lot cheaper, the cost of hydro is considered the lowest in Canada and there are no labour problems."

"All the facilities are here to do business; it's cheaper to operate a business here than in the east; some people worry about shipping charges but I have found out from experience that because of the way freight charges are structured in Canada it's cheaper to ship from Toronto to Winnipeg than within the province of Quebec! You can do anything you want but, remember, the big markets are in the east."

ST. THOMAS

"A Good Place to Live, Work and do Business"

PROFILE: Located only two hours from Toronto, Ontario; Detroit
Michigan, U.S.A. and Buffalo, New York, U.S.A.
POPULATION: The County of Elgin population is 69,284
The City of St. Thomas is 29,000
LOCATION: 10 minutes from Ford Assembly Plant; 45 minutes
from GM Suzuki Plant; 90 minutes from Toyota Plant;
750' above sea level
AREA: 4,560

AVERAGE TEMPERATURE - Summer 25.3 degrees C.
- Winter   2.0 degrees C.
AVERAGE RAINFALL: 725 mm per year
AVERAGE SNOWFALL: 209 cm per year

The City boasts a large and diversified industrial manufacturing base and
a rich diversified agricultural base in the County.

OPPORTUNITIES: "Many are often overlooked"

Mr. Ming Wong has lived in Vancouver, B.C. since 1971. In 1985, he
purchased a commercial and apartment complex (121 units) in St.
Thomas, Ontario and is now proceeding with the second phase consisting
of 138 apartment units and additional commercial space. These are some
of his quotes:
"The Chinese community in a city like St. Thomas is small and at first
you feel a real stranger but Canadians are all very friendly and the 15
years I have spent in Canada have all been very pleasant ones — I have
never faced any discrimination.
Hong Kong has a high profile in Canada at the moment because of
1997 and Canadians think that a lot of Hong Kong people will come with
investment funds and they are looking outwards to welcome this foreign
capital.
In the past St. Thomas may not have been too outward looking but
today they welcome foreign investors and will do everything they can to
help.
The city government is very co-operative and they will help with
regulations, with the bureaucratic paper work, with problem solving; in
fact do everything to make the way smooth for the investor."
My experience is that just about everything in Canada is cheaper than
in Hong Kong and if something could be produced in St. Thomas and

214

shipped to the United States because of the shorter distance to the U.S. market it could be very beneficial.

Places like St. Thomas and Canada's smaller centres generally tend to be overlooked by investors because they don't know about them and not enough information is readily available.

Of course, Canada's smaller towns have only recently started to show an interest in Asia so perhaps what we need is more information from their side and more effort by people from the Far East to make themselves known in these towns and cities.''

聖湯馬仕市：被受忽略的投資好地方

由香港移民來加的Ming Wong（黃先生）體會到聖湯馬仕乃地產及多類投資的理想地方。他說：'加拿大既能給與人民自由，又能以立法方式使社會得以協調。'

黃先生是在英國及美國接受高等教育，自一九七一年由港來加後便在溫哥華定居及從事地產投資。由於一九八一年溫哥華的地產市道過熱，黃先生便開始密切註視溫哥華以外的投資機會，他對多倫多及倫敦市的地生市道皆素研究。但最後黃先生選擇了聖湯馬仕市。

聖湯馬仕的住宅單位求過於供。黃氏稱：'聖湯馬仕有甚多富裕及退休人仕定居，所以對高級柏文的需要甚欣。如明天閣下建柏文單位二百，相信一星期內便可如數租出可。'以下是一連串黃氏就投資之於聖湯馬仕市的見解：

'很多居民都到鄰近的倫敦市購物，如聖湯馬仕能多建同類形的購物地點，居民也一樣會在市內購物。'

'無可否認，聖湯馬仕是須要投資者在市內興建購物地點。'

'市政府也積極發展工業，但鑑於港人對本地工人及政府的措施皆認識不深，所以工業投資的吸引力大打折扣。'

'香港在輕工業方面的根基穩固，如政府能給與香港工業界的人仕提供在聖湯馬仕投資的資料，相信投資者定能在此發掘到投資的機會。'

'雖聖湯馬仕的華人多，但當地居民的和善態度定會另外籍人仕有家居愉快之感。'

'香港一地常爲加人所樂道，所以香港的投資者在加極受歡迎。'

'以往聖湯馬仕對外資的熱枕不高，但如今則採取甚積極的態度。'

'市政府對投資者皆採合作態度，爲投資者大開方便之門。'

'本人認為加拿大的物價一般較香港為相宜。因此，如在聖湯馬仕設廠生產，取其地利而外銷美國，相信一定有利可圖。'

'在加一般較小的城市都易被投資者所忽略，聖湯馬仕便是其中的一個，此乃投資者對它們認識不多之故。'

'加拿大較小的城市對遠東發生興趣乃近期之事，如雙方能在現時級此能在多方面交換意見，相信對日後的發展必能大有裨益。'

ST.THOMAS

is located in the Centre of Elgin County!

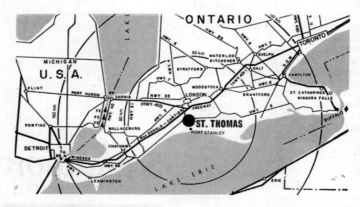

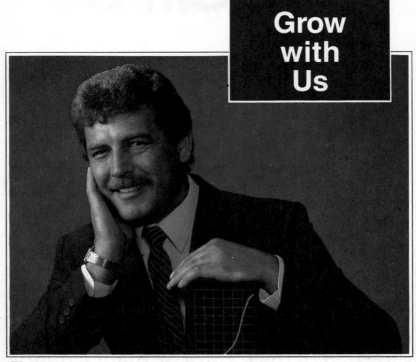

Saskatoon: A future as enjoyable as the present

Introduction:

Growing population, diversifying economic base, and a strong redevelopment program have created an environment of great potential. Saskatoon is a city with a future.

It is also a city that cares about the present. A great deal of attention is placed on maintaining the quality of life, from careful integration of commercial and recreational landspace to community programs and services. Saskatoon is planning carefully so that the future will be as enjoyable as the present.

Location:

Situated in the geographic centre of Canada, in the province of Saskatchewan, Saskatoon provides major airlines, railways and highways to key world distribution points and provides efficient access to an ever-expanding U.S. market. For travellers, Saskatoon is less than three hours by air from Vancouver, and only two hours from the beautiful Rocky Mountains.

Growth:

As the fastest growing city in Canada, Saskatoon's population increased by a dramatic 13.5% during the last six years. Today its population stands at just over 200,000, making it a city roughly the same size as Zhanjiang. Important to note, from an economic viewpoint, is the city's trading area population. Because of surrounding communities, Saskatoon's trading area population is almost 550,000.

Economic Base:

Mining, exploration, engineering, electronics, food processing, machining, and distribution companies are among those who have found a home in Saskatoon. And manufacturing is increasingly important. Mining equipment, farm implements, agricultural monitors, and high-technology communications equipment are among the internationally marketed products currently made in Saskatoon. In fact, Saskatoon is one of the new technology centres of Western Canada, especially in the field of communications, and is the home of Innovation Place, Western Canada's first research park.

World demand will also continue for those resources which

Saskatoon-based companies can supply far into the next century — oil, potash, uranium, gold, and agricultural products.

Finance:

Among the many financial institutions serving Saskatoon's growing business sector are more than a dozen banks, including the Hong Kong Bank and Barclays. In addition, financial institutions, governments and private venture capitalists have identified Saskatoon as a prime area for business investment, both national and international in nature.

Research and Education:

Many Saskatoon companies carry on extensive research and development work, and the Potash Corporation of Saskatchewan has located its R & D facility in the city. The University of Saskatchewan, National Research Council, University Hospital Cancer Clinic, POS Pilot Plant Corporation, and Veterinary Infectious Disease Organization are among the research centres which make their discoveries, facilities, and talents available to industry.

Saskatoon offers the opportunity for an excellent education, from kindergarten to PhD. For youth, school curricula is enhanced by special programs for gifted and handicapped children, skilled coaches in all sports, plus a rich variety of musical and artistic programs. The University of Saskatchewan is located in the city and excels in areas such as medical, agricultural, and high tech training and research. Saskatchewan Institute of Applied Science and Technology (Kelsey Campus) further provides technical training in many disciplines.

Skilled Labour:

Saskatoon enjoys an excellent labour force of skilled full-time and part-time workers in many diversified fields. As well, the city's university, technical institutes, and other education centres offer opportunities for workers to upgrade their skills. Saskatoon puts education to work, too. Compared to other cities where job opportunities have disappeared, Saskatoon leads all of Canada in job creation per capita.

Environment and Lifestyle:

Saskatoon has long been renowned as one of the most beautiful cities in Canada. Care has been taken to create enjoyable living and recreational space in the midst of the city's growing industrialization. A perfect example is the scenic downtown riverside park, through which jogging and cycling paths wind.

The city's cultural environment is also flourishing. One of Canada's finer public art galleries, several museums, commercial galleries, a symphony orchestra, and two professional theatres are well supported, and attracting international talent.

Housing:

Saskatoon offers a wide variety of home styles, from highrise condominiums and apartments to small, modest single dwellings. The city's land bank policy has kept prices reasonable and has prevented artificial land speculations from driving prices up. The city is continually expanding its residential area, with a stable number of 'new home' starts each year, so the choice exists for the buyer or renter to locate in bright new neighbourhoods, or locate in more established, and often beautifully treed, sections of the city. The 1987 average selling price for a three bedroom bungalow (1100 square feet) was $72,000.00 Canadian.

People:

Saskatonians are not content to be spectators. They get involved in the life of the city, organizing and participating in exciting annual events which offer an opportunity to share in the rich multicultural celebration of customs and cuisine. Whenever the city hosts national and international events, the citizens are famous for their spirit and enthusiasm in volunteering their time and energy. This same spirit shines when it comes to fitness and recreation, with six golf courses, sailing and skiing clubs, bowling alleys, racquet clubs, swimming pools, and skating rinks always being busy.

Downtown Redevelopment:

Of special note is the redevelopment program scheduled for the south downtown area. This program, which represents tens of millions of dollars, is the culmination of almost a decade of planning and calls for integrated commercial, residential, cultural and recreational facilities, and will make the riverbank even more accessible to the public. The redevelopment is just starting now, and has created a prime investment environment.

That's Saskatoon — the Success Address

薩斯卡通市

人口增長、經濟簇新發展……使卡市的前景一片遠大光明。卡市對市民生活質素十分重視，所以對工商、住宅及一般康樂用地的發展及配合，不費餘力。

地點適中

卡市位於加拿大中心的薩斯喀徹溫省，往來世界各地及美國的交通，異常方便。從卡市往溫哥華祇須三小時，到洛基山脈則祇是兩小時。

發展迅速

卡市乃加拿大發展最快的城市。過往六年的人口增長高達１３·５％，使人口數字達二十萬的水平，與中國的浙江不相伯仲。除本身人口外，四周城市的人口亦不少，二者合共有人口五十五萬，所以市場活躍。

經濟基石

卡市乃加拿大西部的工業及科技中心，很多礦務、工程、電子、食品、車機及運輸公司皆設於卡市，而產品計有開礦機械、農業機器及通訊器材等皆暢銷世界各地。其他出口如石油、炭酸鉀、鈾、黃金及農業產品也十分重要。

財經體系

在卡市有大小銀行十二間，其中包括香港匯豐及柏克萊銀行，以助投資人仕在卡市發展。

科研及教育

在卡市有很多機構都從事科技的研究工作，如沙省大學、國家研究院及各醫庫機構等。

卡市有極優良的教育體系，由幼稚園至博士課程皆可一一在卡市進修。除此之外，還有特別爲傷殘兒童而設的學校，或爲特別想選修專科的兒童而設的體育、音樂及藝術課程等。而沙省大學及理工學院更是以醫科、農科及工程而馳名。

勞工精鍊

卡市因教育體系健全之故，所以在多方面都可造就出優秀的人材。而很多工人在工作之餘都不斷進修以加強技能的訓練。

生活方式

卡市市容秀麗，爲加拿大最美麗的城市之一。市中心的河畔公園更是跑步及乘脚踏車的好去處。在文娛方面，卡市有藝術館、博物館、商業展覽館、交響音及戲院等。

屋宇樓房

居民在卡市可選擇不同款式的樓房，由高層住宅至覆式獨立屋皆未嘗有缺。而政府的土地政策亦以保持地價平穩爲目的，所以卡市屋價合理。在一九八九年三睡房平房（約千一方呎）的平均價爲七萬二加元。

居民

卡市居民對社區活動皆十分擁躍支持，但凡有社區或國際盛事，市民都極力參與。

市中心發展

政府在市中心南部的重建計劃，耗資千萬，以求使商業、住宅及其他樓宇得以在協調的情況下發展，而河畔一帶也可變爲更方便。重建計劃現正開始，所以帶來了很多投資機會。

This man can show you a unique Canadian opportunity for

Investment

Saskatchewan is known to investors world wide for our dependable and profitable economy, based on natural resources and agriculture. And we have bold, new incentive packages to help you take advantage of our many investment opportunities.

and Trade

Our agriculture, mineral and forestry commodities are what makes Saskatchewan the largest per capita exporter in Canada. Our manufactured goods have earned a reputation for innovative design, dependable construction and cost efficiency — from agricultural implements to high technology.

We've been building our Pacific Rim trading partnerships for 25 years. And we are eager to see continued trade growth. We've established an office in Hong Kong. Our agent, George Hazen, and his staff can put you in touch with Saskatchewan suppliers and Saskatchewan investment opportunities.

Importing, investing, or both — Saskatchewan is a good place to do business. Contact us. Today. We'll give you the facts on Saskatchewan.

I'm interested in trade and investment opportunities.

☐ Send me the publication:
"Choosing Saskatchewan" ☐
"Investment Opportunities" ☐

Name: _____ Title: _____

Company: _____

Address: _____

_____

Phone: _____ Telex: _____

Mail to: Agent for Saskatchewan in Hong Kong
#1902 Two Exchange Square
8 Connaught Place, Central
Hong Kong

Government of Saskatchewan

CANADA 🍁

Saskatchewan

Saskatchewan: Building on its strengths

The pioneering spirit that shaped Saskatchewan more than a hundred years ago is still alive in this province, but today the new pioneers are exploring far beyond the prairie landscape. There's a new atmosphere of excitement in the province, as Saskatchewan people prepare to meet the economic and social challenges they will face as part of the global village during the rest of this century. And just like the pioneers of old, they will work toward the goals of providing their people with a secure political and economic environment as well as a comfortable lifestyle. Business people from throughout the world are invited to participate in Saskatchewan's exciting future.

For those considering relocating to Canada, this chapter will provide details on the people of Saskatchewan and what it's like to live in the province. It will also offer insight into the numerous business opportunities that are available in Saskatchewan.

Saskatchewan's population topped the one million mark just a few years ago, so there's plenty of room for everyone in an area that totals 651,900 km squared. Saskatchewan people have come from many lands, including Hong Kong, China, the Philippines, Korea and Japan. In fact, today there are about 10,000 Asian people living and raising families in this province that they now call "home". Most of Saskatchewan's residents live in the southern half of the province, which has rich agricultural land. About 60 per cent of the people live in the province's 12 cities, while the others live in towns and villages or on farms.

Saskatchewan is large enough for a great variety of restaurants, world-class theatre, symphony orchestras and the fine arts, but small enough for an attractive pace, caring neighbours and pleasant, safe communities. It is an ideal environment in which to raise a family.

Another of Saskatchewan's attractive features is its low cost of living, coupled with one of the highest standards of living in the world. As well, the unemployment rate is consistently among the lowest in Canada, and the province continues to be a leader in the development and implementation of social and health programs. All Saskatchewan residents are fortunate to receive free medical care, while low-cost prescription drugs ensure affordable health care.

Saskatchewan provides a wide range of quality educational programs through its 1,000 schools, 25 vocational institutes, 16 community colleges, four technical institutes and two universities. Hundreds of students from countries throughout the world travel to Saskatchewan each year to study at the universities in Saskatoon and Regina, where the standards of education are high. This past year more than 600 Hong Kong students were enrolled in commerce, business administration, computer science, engineering and other courses at Saskatchewan's universities.

People who are not familiar with Saskatchewan often wonder about its climate and how it affects lifestyles. To set the record straight, we don't spend all of our time bundling up to endure the cold. In fact, Saskatchewan has more days of sunshine every year than you will find almost anywhere else in North America. Our climate is generally dry, but temperatures vary greatly to provide us with four seasons. Spring is moist and green, summer is hot and dry, fall is crisp and bright, and winter is clear and invigorating.

During the winter, homes are centrally heated and the weather does not generally restrict activity in the province. Saskatchewan residents appreciate the changes in climate during the year because of the recreational opportunities each season affords them — swimming, boating, fishing, water skiing, golf and baseball during the spring and summer, with skating, sledding, curling, hockey, downhill and cross-country skiing in fall and winter. Also, the province is extremely fortunate in that it rarely experiences natural disasters such as volcanoes, earthquakes and floods.

First-time visitors to Saskatchewan are astounded by its breathtaking scenery. A Saskatchewan sunset is a sight to behold, as is the landscape that leads one to believe that the horizon stretches to infinity. In this beautiful province, one can visit the northern forests for a wilderness experience, camp in one of hundreds of parks, or just wander into the peaceful, uncrowded countryside. There is so much to enjoy and explore in Saskatchewan's outdoors, and most of it is within 20 minutes of even the largest city.

Besides offering the very best in lifestyles for its residents, Saskatchewan is a most favourable location to do business. Although its population is relatively small, the province holds tremendous business opportunities because it operates in the international marketplace. On a per capita basis, Saskatchewan is the biggest trader in Canada. The province exports almost half of everything it produces, and 25 per cent of all jobs are trade-related.

Saskatchewan's central location in western Canada and North America offers many advantages to businesses, including convenient transportation routes and proximity to the large United States market.

Saskatchewan's economy is dominated by intense resource activity, particularly in agriculture, potash, oil, uranium and forestry. And the pioneering spirit is currently flourishing in the north where several exciting gold discoveries have recently been made.

But Saskatchewan's new pioneers realize that other economic avenues must also be explored, so the province is vigorously pursuing a plan of economic diversification. Thousands of small and medium-sized businesses already flourish, while the service sector continues to expand.

Saskatchewan welcomes further development in both areas, but invites business people to explore the unlimited opportunities that are available in the food processing and manufacturing sectors.

Saskatchewan's massive agricultural base encourages investors to start up or expand food processing operations. There's also room for a variety of manufacturing and service businesses to support the province's internationally recognized dryland agricultural equipment industry.

Investors are also welcome in Saskatchewan's natural resource sector, both in the development of resources and in further processing. For example, there are opportunities for growth in agricultural chemicals and the processing of agricultural products, as well as in the processing of specialty foods. The province also needs manufacturers of machinery and other supplies and services that support the natural resource sector.

Further opportunities for investment can be found in: plastics; health care products, especially hardware, disposables, medications and pharmaceuticals; and in Saskatchewan's growing high technology industry. Close to 150 high tech companies are putting Saskatchewan on the map as a leader in fibre optics, biotechnology, satellite and digital communications, mining robotics and radio telemetry. The province is excited about the expertise and innovations it has already developed and looks forward to more growth in the high tech industry.

The provincial government's pro-business attitude makes international investors feel welcome. People are encouraged to apply their knowledge and skills, along with investment capital, to the business or commercial venture of their choice.

Provincial government consultants help businesses launch projects by providing counselling services, cost-shared feasibility and market study funds, guide site location assistance, and by arranging introductions to business and industry leaders, professional groups, the banking and financial community and government officials.

Individuals and families from countries throughout the world have taken advantage of the investment opportunities in Saskatchewan, and they're enjoying success in small and medium-sized businesses in many communities. There is also evidence of larger foreign investment in Saskatchewan. The Marubeni Corporation of Japan is building a steel fabrication plant in the province, and the Hong Kong Productivity Council is investigating the possibilities for joint ventures between Hong Kong and Saskatchewan companies.

Saskatchewan is building on its strengths, and the province welcomes interested people from around the world to join it in the exploration of its potential and its future. To help Asian business people find out more about Saskatchewan, the provincial government has an office in Hong Kong. The Agent for Saskatchewan, George Hazen, is pleased to offer his assistance and information on the unique opportunities offered by Saskatchewan.

沙斯喀徹溫省：根基實況穩固

沙斯喀徹溫省面積約六十五萬平方公哩，人口百餘萬，其中六成分佈於其南部的十二個大城市。從世界各地來沙省的移民眾多，亞洲區移民則為數逾萬，其中包括香港、中國、菲律賓、南韓及日本等。

沙省的文娛活動多姿多彩，食肆種類，包羅萬有，再加上民風淳樸，正是宜家宜居的好地方。

沙省就業率高，民生豐裕，但物價低廉。此外，沙省的社會福利及醫療健康計劃乃全國的典範，醫療免費、藥物價廉。

沙省設有具規模的大學二所、理工學院四所、社區學院十六所，職業訓練所二十五所及中小學千間。每年皆有無數的留學生從世界各地來沙省的Saskatoon 及 Regina 大學功讀。去年在沙省的香港留學生約有六百名，分別選修工商管理、電腦及工程等科目。

沙省天朗氣清，四季分明。因此，居民可享受各種不同的戶外活動，如游泳、揚帆、垂釣、滑水、哥爾夫球、棒球、溜冰、冰上曲棍球及滑雪等。

很多遊客來到沙省都被其秀麗的大自然景色所吸引。省內公園無數，而離市區祇是咫尺之遙，所以，居民常以郊外露營或遠足為樂。

沙省人口雖少，但工商業發展機會甚多。每年出口佔全省生產總值的半數，所以沙省的平均個人出口為全加最高。出口也為沙省提供了四份之一的就業機會。

沙省位於加拿大西部的中心地帶，生意往來，極之方便。

天然資源乃沙省經濟的命脈，特別是農業、炭酸鉀、石油、鈾礦及林木業等。最近更在數個不同地點發現金礦。

沙省的居民瞭解到經濟多元化的優點，現在數以千計的中小型企業在沙省不斷地成長，而服務性行業也隨之而生。沙省除歡迎你們在以上兩方面發展外，也希望你們能加入食品加工及工業生產的行列。

沙省的豐富農業正是食品加工業的中流砥柱，而其乾田農機工業也極需其他工業及服務性行業的支持。

　　沙省也歡迎投資者參與其天然資源的開採及加工。例如，應用於農業的化學劑、特別農產品加工及有助於天然資源的工商業等。

　　投資者也可考慮其他的投資對象：塑膠、醫療衞生產品、手工具及藥品製造等。沙省現有的百五間高科技公司在光學纖維、生物工程、衞星通訊、開礦機械臂及雷達測遠方面的發展，成就驕人。

　　沙省政府對投資者極為支持，也極鼓勵他們各展所長，在不同的行業發展。省府的商務顧問可為閣下提供資詢、市塲調查、地點選擇及引見各工商界、政府及專業人仕等服務。

　　各地移民在沙省成功的例子不計其數。大型的投資，如日本的 Marubeni Corporation 在沙省的鋼廠及香港生產力促進局現正在研究中的港加公司在沙省合資計劃等便是個中例子。

　　為協助亞洲移民來沙省定居，沙省在香港特設有辦事處，其代表 Mr . George Hazen 樂意為各界提供進一步資料。

Regina: Big city opportunity — small town friendliness

If you value small town warmth and friendliness but are looking for big city opportunity you may want to find out more about the city of Regina.

In the heart of Canada's prairie grain belt, midway between Calgary, Alberta and Winnipeg, Manitoba, Regina is home to 180,000 people.

Regina is the focal point for business, trade and transportation on the vast Canadian prairies and as the capital city of the province of Saskatchewan it acts as a thriving centre for 325,000 people.

It is also a financial centre. Six major banks maintain regional headquarters here. Local venture capital, together with a growing number of off-shore investors, foster new business and business expansion.

The economic outlook is good.

Regina is a manufacturing centre. The Saskatchewan Manufacturing Opportunities Show encourages entrepreneurs to pursue hundreds of new and real possibilities. The city also has a growing base of advanced technology companies.

Ross Industrial Park offers 1,500 acres of serviced land, with 2,000 acres reserved for future expansion.

Regina is a steel centre. The largest mill in North America's west — Ipsco Inc., — produces sheet metal and tubing for international markets.

As a distribution point Regina offers excellent access to Canadian and American markets. By truck, bus, rail or air you'll find a transportation network that moves raw materials, products and people quickly and conveniently.

Pipelines converge on Regina's boundaries. And there's substantial oil and gas exploration and producing wells nearby. A multi million dollar oil upgrader project is underway. This activity means readily available and competitively priced energy supplies. And, related business opportunities.

Rail relocation will release 97 acres of railway land for redevelopment in the heart of the city, offering a new alternative for inner city living. This C$160 million project presents opportunities for investment in redevelopment, as well as opportunities for the manufacture and supply of railway construction materials.

Agriculture is still a strong and stable base. The world's largest wheat co-operative, the Saskatchewan Wheat Pool, headquarters here. Related industries thrive.

A skilled labour force works for you. Regina's education system is first class. There are 106 publicly supported elementary and secondary schools. The University of Regina has 9,500 students enrolled in a broad spectrum of undergraduate and graduate degree programs. Specialized research institutes can assist business and industry. Advanced education is also offered by the Saskatchewan Institute of Applied Arts & Science and Technology.

Regina is served by one French and two English language television stations, cable television, nine radio stations and one daily newspaper.

But life is not all work and no play.

If you choose to live in Regina you'll enjoy splendid shopping; the cultural, sporting and special events fill up a calendar quickly. Recreation facilities and programs are rated among the best in Canada. And cottage life is popular — a 35 minute drive puts you at Regina Beach. The Qu'Appelle Valley chain of lakes is only 50 minutes away.

As soon as you arrive you'll feel welcome. And you'll soon discover the many activities and features contributing to the quality of life here.

Theatre, ballet and the symphony for arts lovers. Golf, curling, Regina Pats and the Saskatchewan Roughriders for sports fans.

And there's Wascana Centre, known as one of the largest and most beautiful urban parks on the continent. The park is home to the Saskatchewan Legislature, the Centre of the Arts, Diefenbaker Homestead, Norman Mackenzie Art Gallery, Museum of Natural History and the Royal Canadian Mounted Police Centennial Museum.

Regina is a city where you can expand your horizons with new hobbies, new interests, good friends.

For you and your visitors quality hotels and motels satisfy your accommodation needs, with an excellent selection of conference and trade fair facilities.

When you become a part of Regina, you join a community with commitment — dedication to a neighbourly atmosphere and to a satisfying, stimulating lifestyle.

For a city with small town warmth and big city sophistication, Regina's the one. Make it Number One on your horizon. Regina — the city with its mind on business and its heart in supporting a quality of life you'll thoroughly enjoy.

You're invited. Come and discover a new future in Regina.

勒賈納：安居樂業

勒賈納位於沙省，人口十八萬，居民友善，工商業前景可觀。

勒市乃是加拿大中部的財經及工業中心。六所銀行的加中總辦事處皆設於市內。工業方面，羅斯工業邨佔地一千五百畝，另有二千畝現正在發展中。北美西部最大的鋼廠Ipsco Inc 便是設於勒市。

勒市在交通及運輸方面亦十分方便，產品可暢達北美各地。勒市的石油工業十分發達，多處的輸油管在勒市的邊沿匯合，另外亦有一個數千萬元的鍊油廠正在興建中。

市內現有九十多畝的火車地段因火車站遷移的關係而改作其他發展用途，工程費用預計達一億六千萬。

勒市的農業十分發達，世界最大的沙省穀物合作社總部則設於市內。

勒市的教育體系是一流的。全市有中小學百餘間，勒賈納大學可容學生九千多人，課程多元化，學生可隨意修讀學士或研究院課程。另外，薩斯喀徹溫理工學院亦有多項專上課程。

勒市有英語電視台兩所及法文台一所、電台九個、省報一份及有線電視等。

勒市的康樂設施是十分完善的，無論是購物、看電影、運動及往湖邊散心皆極其方便。

勒市的Wascana 中心是北美最美麗的市內公園之一，園內有沙省的議會及多間博物館等。

在勒市您及您的朋友可享受一流的酒店及浪漫的景物，請現在就來勒市一遊以親身體驗您的明天。

CHAPTER 10

Jennifer Poon
Calgary offers cost advantages but major markets elsewhere

Calgary! The Houston of Canada and the far north; a city of oil and gas industry skyscrapers reflecting its primary sources of wealth; home of Canada's most famous stampede — a legacy of the ranching days of the nineteenth century when cowboys, cattle and chuck wagons dominated the endless prairies.

An unlikely setting, one might think, for a young entrepreneur in the costume jewellery business!

Jennifer Poon didn't choose Calgary as her business base; her Trinidadian-Chinese parents did back in 1968. But she grew up in the city and received her education there and so, in a sense, Calgary chose her.

At 26 the talented young jewellery designer says her business is, in fact, not anchored in any particular sense to Calgary; it just happens to be where she lives at the moment.

"Whether I lived in the Yukon or New York I would be a jewellery designer", she says without a trace of self-doubt.

"My goal at this point is to manufacture a product that is of a high taste level, of good quality and is not overly priced in the sense that it is accessible to the average woman. Of course, I want to maintain a distinct look and style. What I'm trying to achieve is the fine line between the exclusive designer look and the mass produced costume jewellery type product."

"The materials I use are acrylics, base metals that are gold plated or silver coloured and any type of wooden beads."

"Calgary is economically a good place to live and work because compared to bigger centres like Toronto the rents are cheaper and in general I can keep my over-heads low. Also the tax laws are much better in Alberta than they are in Ontario."

"Because of the cost advantages of doing business in Alberta and the skills in the province, Calgary would be a good place for a base in which somebody new coming in could decide to manufacture something but, of course, the major markets are elsewhere."

"For me the one drawback that it has is that I live and work in the West of Canada but the heart of the fashion industry is in the East."

"I studied jewellery design at the Alberta College of Art in Calgary and after graduating I really didn't have any specific goal and one thing led to another until I just found myself in the fashion industry."

"I was working around town freelancing just to make a living — designing hats and scarves, even windows — so I always maintained this association with fashion. From doing that and meeting differenc people I got into designing costume jewellery."

235

"I had toyed with this idea while I was in school because of the access I had to materials, the variety of materials available and, of course, the lower cost involved compared with the cost of, say, gold which is often not accessible to the average person."

"One day when I was doing a window job I ran into a supplier at a trade show that dealt in beads and different types of jewellery making findings and I placed an order with him and started experimenting with the materials until I got a product that I really felt good about. Then I went door to door to all the local stores in town and one thing led to another and the whole business started going."

"Most of the stores I was dealing with at the time were accessory shops dealing in earrings, bracelets, belts and so on; I dealt with a few women's hair salons that had a service where they did make up but also wardrobe and they would have the jewellery there to cater to the client's complete appearance needs."

"In Calgary there are a lot of independent boutiques that specialize in a certain look or in a certain type of clothing, such as for the career woman or evening ware or perhaps imported clothing."

"That was in September 1984 and by December I couldn't keep up with the demand. At that point I got an agent to sell the jewellery for me so that I could concentrate on making the jewellery."

"The sales representative in Calgary was associated with a distributor in Vancouver who imported a lot of jewellery from the Orient and he saw the line, really liked it and immediately took it across Canada for me. That's how I got so far so quick!"

"Another thing that helped me was that at the time I started out I based my jewellery on the Coco Chanel look which is now a very big look. At that time few people had seen it and it was new and they thought it was great. It was different from anything else in the market and they just jumped on it."

"The oil industry has given Calgary much of its character; you're dealing with a lot of money and there are many social events surrounding the industry. There is a large population of executive or career women in Calgary and these are the women I would cater to. Calgary is definitely not the Wild West!

"Calgary is changing at the moment because of the changed status of the oil industry and the whole attitude of looking elsewhere for another type of industry or business is very apparent in the air — not only in Calgary but throughout the province."

"I think people are just starting to realize that they can't just rely on one industry for their main bread and butter. Certainly there is the potential in Alberta for many different industries to be started particularly in anything to do with technology."

"Per capita Calgary has the most educated people in Canada because for most jobs in the oil industry you have to have a BA or whatever qualification is needed; there is less unskilled labour in Alberta than in many other places."

"I certainly think that new investors would be welcome here now that people are beginning to think about doing things other than oil."

"Venture capital is very easy to come by here, particularly if you need a lot of it. Many companies have set up here who do nothing other than handle venture capital."

"There are some programs available from the government which help you set up your business but really there's not a lot available for someone coming in and starting a business."

"Definitely it is possible to start up a business from nothing; I did it. But if you start with nothing it is very difficult to raise money from banks or even from government institutions set up to help small businesses which cannot get money from the banks. Getting money from government is like selling your soul. You pay a very big price. But it's something you learn to live with."

"Calgary and Alberta are not big enough for me now and hopefully by 1987 when we begin exporting to the United States or wherever else we can the Canadian market as a whole won't be big enough for us. At this point the Canadian market is satisfactory but we do most of our sales in the East."

"Eventually, hopefully within the next year, we shall have to consider a move to Eastern Canada which is the heart of the industry; it's where I have all my manufacturing there and my suppliers are there; most of my sales are there. It seems really silly that I'm here."

"I think there is a benefit to being in the heartland of the fashion industry because the design business is a very high profile one; there are events at which you have to be seen; you have to be visible to top people in the industry.

"Calgary is Calgary. But Toronto is more international and there is more opportunity there to maybe get into New York, go overseas or to do something bigger. Toronto has better connections than Calgary does to the U.S. or to Britain or to the Orient."

"There are very few Western suppliers of the materials I use; there are a couple in Vancouver but virtually everyone else is in Toronto or Montreal, including the biggest so the prices are better and they are much easier to deal with."

CHAPTER 11

Stocks, bonds and funds markets
Opportunities for Asian investors in Canadian securities

By William A. Buik, President
Burns Fry Investment Management Limited
Ten Reasons Why Canada is The Place to Invest:

1. Canada has a stable political and economic climate and Canadian government policy encourages private investment from both domestic and international sources.
2. Canada is a major international trading nation negotiating a free trade agreement with the United States, the world's major marketplace.
3. The Canadian economy produces the fourth highest per capita gross national product in the Western world and its well educated, youthful and productive work force has created one of the highest standards of living in the world.
4. Canada has a superb infra-structure of transportation and communication facilities.
5. Canada is self-sufficient in all forms of energy and has an abundance of natural resources including agricultural products for both export and domestic consumption.
6. Canada's banking and financial system is competitive, active and growing. There are no foreign exchange restrictions for either residents or foreigners and few restrictions on international investors.
7. Canada is endowed with lands as vast as China, the United States or all of Europe with less than one-tenth the population. The quality of life is unmatched anywhere with clean and safe cosmopolitan cities, wide open spaces and a beautiful natural environment.
8. Over the last five years, the Canadian economy, the seventh largest in the industrialized world, has expanded faster than any other industrial nation. Wage costs which were the second highest in the world two years ago are now the tenth highest due to devaluation of the Canadian currency.
9. Canadian securities markets are highly organized, easily accessible and as well regulated as any in the world.
10. Country risk analysts rate Canada as one of the five safest nations in the world today for investors. Canada has enjoyed over one hundred

years of continuous stable democratic government as an independent nation. No wars have been fought on Canadian soil in almost two hundred years.

In summary, an improved business environment, the prospect of free trade with the United States, and a favourable exchange rate provides the climate that should encourage Canadians to realize their immense potential for future economic expansion. With a highly productive work force and rich resource endowment, there is every reason to believe that the Canadian economy will experience strong economic growth over the next decade. As the result, we believe that those investors looking for longer term rewards should be looking to Canadian securities markets now.

Types of Investments Available

Investors in Canadian securities have a wide variety of government and corporate securities from which to choose in a capital market which is one of the world's best developed and best regulated to protect both domestic and international investors.

— **Short Term Securities**

Otherwise known as money market securities, these consist largely of Government of Canada and Provincial treasury bills maturing in three years or less, commercial paper, bankers' acceptances and guaranteed investment certificates issued by trust companies. These are low risk investments which provide individual investors temporary alternatives to longer term investments in bonds and common stocks.

— **The Bond Market**

This market consists of some $325 billion of bonds issued by all levels of government and government agencies and crown corporations as well as private sector corporations. There is a wide variety of maturities and credits available and an active market in new issues with secondary trading providing market liquidity. Interest rates normally provide a rate of return higher than the national inflation rate and since Canada is a capital importer, compare favourably with rates available in the other industrialized countries.

— **The Stock Market**

The $275 billion Canadian equity market ranks as the world's fifth largest with Canadian equities representing about 3% of global market value. Unlike most other developed markets where domestic ownership is typically very high, it is estimated that as much as one-quarter of the Canadian market is owned by foreign investors. Shares of over 1,000 companies are listed on the Toronto Stock Exchange, the most active of Canada's exchanges reflecting the fact that Toronto is Canada's major financial centre. In terms of liquidity the Canadian market also ranks highly. For the first three quarters of 1987, an unusually active period, the dollar trading volume of Canadian exchanges totalled over $100 billion with another $33 billion of Canadian equity business transacted in the United States. This amounted to over $800 million of trading per day.

Although the Canadian market is viewed internationally as a source of liquid world scale cyclical stocks of energy and natural resource companies, the market value of these issues only accounts for half of the total. Indeed, from an investment results perspective it comes as a surprise to most international investors that the non-cyclical half of the Canadian market has generally been the better long term choice.

The Investment Process

International investors have the same access as domestic investors to the facilities of Canadian investment dealers which handle all types of securities, and banks and other financial institutions which deal largely in bonds and money market securities. International investors often employ investment managers or investment counsel to make appropriate investments for them as do many Canadian investors.

Foreign investors are not subject to Canadian withholding tax on interest paid on securities of or guaranteed by the Government of Canada, the Provincial governments or municipalities. The rate of withholding tax on interest and dividends paid by corporations varies according to the tax treaties with individual foreign countries. In no case is the foreign investor subject to Canadian income or capital gains taxes. There are no foreign exchange restrictions on international investors and non-residents have the same protection under the securities laws as do Canadians.

Some Differences Between Asian and Canadian Markets and Investment Approaches

At the risk of making too simple generalizations, there are some differences between Asian and Canadian securities markets which it might be useful for Asian investors to bear in mind.

1. There is a much greater variety of money market bond and stock investments available in Canada than in individual Asian markets. Foreign investors should be sure that they are being properly exposed to the full range of possibilities.
2. With a good flow of information about all types of securities and a wide variety of institutional and individual investors participating, markets are generally less volatile, more open and more closely regulated. As a result, short term speculative returns in quality securities may be lower than in some other markets. However, long term, risk and currency adjusted returns compare favourably with any in the world.
3. Substantial Canadian investors, both institutional and personal, generally are conservative in their approach and long term in their investment horizons.
4. Substantial Canadian investors are likely to employ professional investment management firms to invest for them on a discretionary basis within agreed upon guidelines. Such professional investment management firms are closely regulated by provincial securities com-

missions and their portfolio managers must meet stringent academic and professional requirements.

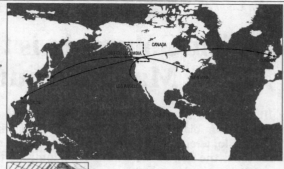

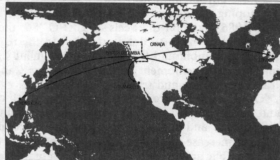

British Columbia is the future. Make it yours!

It comes as a real surprise to many people to learn that although British Columbia is but one of Canada's 10 provinces at almost 1 million square kilometers it occupies 10 per cent of the country's land space, is four times the size of the United Kingdom, 2.5 times the size of Japan, exceeded in size by only 30 countries in the world and at nearly 3 million has a population the size of small nations like New Zealand or Wales.

To the south are the U.S. states of Washington, Idaho and Montana, eastwards, Alberta and the great Canadian prairies and toward the Arctic lie the Northwest Territories, Yukon and Alaska.

Together with eastern Canada these areas and others further south in the U.S. have traditionally offered British Columbia markets for its resource and manufactured goods.

Today, a combination of changed world manufacture and trading patterns plus advances in the technology of transportation by land and by sea have opened an historic gateway for British Columbia into the great developing markets of the Pacific Rim.

In 1986, hard on the heels of EXPO '86, the world class exposition which did so much to draw attention to the region, the government of British Columbia and the federal government signed an agreement promoting the development of the province as Canada's Pacific centre for trade, commerce and travel.

The objectives were to encourage the growth of international banking and other services in Vancouver, to co-ordinate transportation improvements and stimulate new economic activities around transportation, to increase and extend the range of trade related services provided by the public and private sectors and a valuable reservoir of technical and professional expertise and to improve the public and private marketing of tourist destinations and conference facilities.

The Asia Pacific Foundation was set up in Vancouver in 1985 to coordinate the efforts and activities of business, education and government in the advancement of Asia Pacific Affairs and an Asia Pacific Business Institute was established the same year under the aegis of British Columbia's three universities.

As a result of EXPO '86 the commercial capital, Vancouver, boasts new hotels, impressive convention centres, new modes of transportation, highways, bridges, airports, port facilities and railways which not only impressed the millions of visitors to the world fair but are in place for the future.

Visitors are a major source of income for the province. Tourism is the largest employer in British Columbia and in 1986 the industry generated

C$3.2 billion in revenue.

Vancouver is already one of the busiest Pacific coast ports serving more than 3,000 vessels annually from more than 50 countries around the world.

Rail links are supplied by three Canadian and five U.S. companies; Canadian and U.S. airlines offer services throughout Canada and the Americas; trans-Pacific and other international flights touch down at Vancouver International Airport; excellent road links exist everywhere and in a coastal province dominated by the ocean, lakes, rivers and streams local ferry services carry up to six million passengers a year.

In recent years British Columbia's financial community has made great strides in the expansion and diversification of its system.

More than 800 branches of Canada's chartered banks are located throughout the province and the presence of 33 foreign banks demonstrates the key importance now placed by international banking organizations upon this region as a trading zone.

The Vancouver Stock Exchange enjoys an international reputation as the world's major venture capital market. Traditionally dominated by resource industries it is now attracting a rapidly growing number of high technology companies and is positioned to assist investors in virtually every field of enterprise in obtaining the venture capital required for their projects.

The province is emerging at a brisk pace from what has been largely a primary industry economy into an amalgam of primary and secondary industries.

Industry is responding vigourously to escalating consumer demand for computer software items, plastic and ceramic products, more specialized processed foods and other finished commodities, luxury goods and other items of specialized use.

Apparel manufacture is another good example of rapid new expansion into ever more sophisticated areas of the consumer market.

For years British Columbia's main contribution to the fabric and clothing industry was the manufacture of sail cloth and durable fabrics required for tents and rugged work clothing.

The transition to high fashion apparel occurred in part through the design and manufacture of fashionable skiwear proceeding to a wide range of fashionable leisurewear that tapped a large market.

In 1986 alone eight apparel companies went public, taking advantage of the Canadian dollar position in world markets, the proximity of British Columbia to major markets and the availability of ample, skilled labour. One company alone had achieved C$50 million in sales by 1987 and projected sales of C$100 million by the end of the decade.

Business opportunities in British Columbia's consumer goods industries include: High quality apparel, sportswear catering to outdoor lifestyles, sports and recreational equipment, pre-fabricated wooden structures, wooden outdoor furniture, toys, ornaments, chop sticks and other items fashioned from wood, ceramics, especially high quality tableware, items designed from specially prepared fish skin "leathers", costume jewellery and other items fashioned from sea shells and other marine materials, processed food products, consumer computer software and accessories for major leisure industries such as skiing, boating, camping and summer cabin lifestyles.

Among high technology industries British Columbia's electronics industry has increased substantially in recent years demonstrating an annual growth rate of 26% and generating an estimated revenue of C$700 million per annum.

The majority of the electronics firms are small to medium size concentrating on specialized markets, many of them focused on resource based applications within the province. In the process they have developed leading edge expertise.

A wide range of world-class electronics hardware is produced in British Columbia including: industrial controls, data communications systems, microprocessor based control systems, printed circuit boards, robotics, machine vision, instrumentation satellite imaging equipment, medical equipment, engineering and survey equipment and much more. At least 50% of the electronics equipment produced in the province is exported.

While the conventional definition of high technology relates principally to electronics there are many other areas where state of the art technology is a significant factor.

For example, the application of plasma science in the development of new types of ceramics, the evolution of new materials for use in advanced aero-space components and sub assemblies, metallurgical discoveries leading to new alloys, the efficient and economic manufacture of specialty chemicals derived from petroleum resource bases — all this and more is under way in the province with many opportunities still unexplored.

Excellent industry/university interaction at the research and training level, the activities of the B.C. Research Council in working closely with industry and the establishment of industrial parks close to the universities have all spurred and assisted industrial innovation and production.

Agriculture continues to be the fourth largest resource in the province characterized by a wide diversity of pursuits including: dairying, cattle ranching, poultry raising, the cultivation of fruit trees, vegetables, berries, grapes, bulbs, ornamental shrubs and other nursery stock. Combined with this is mixed livestock-crop farming conducted throughout the province.

Business opportunities in agriculture include: fruit processing, beef and swine production, cottage wine industry, fresh and processed vegetables, dairy farming, processed food including biscuits, confections, flour, bakery products and natural foods, bulbs, shrubs, nursery stock, greenhouse culture and processed meats.

Aquaculture is a rapidly emerging aspect of British Columbia's healthy fishing industry. Fishing from the sea is already yielding excellent results even though it is still in its formative stages. Growers with a variety of shellfish and salmon farming techniques are experiencing continued success.

By the year 2000 it is expected that this new British Columbia industry will be worth over C$200 million and directly employ at least 3,500 people.

Consumer goods industries, high technology, tourism, fisheries, forestry, agriculture and mining offer outstanding business prospects and a lifestyle to match.

British Columbia is a multi-cultural province, reflecting the presence of newcomers from many lands who have settled down and enriched the province with their aspirations, personal values and skills. In the large cities there are well-established communities from many parts of Asia and in Vancouver especially, a large Chinese business community.

The standard of living in British Columbia is high by any measure. Fine homes, universities and technical colleges, sports facilities producing athletes of world standard, orchestras, art galleries, theatres and outdoor recreational facilities from snorkelling to skiing where the weather is so temperate that there is no closed season.

British Columbia is the future. Make it yours!

請成爲卑斯省居民的一份子

卑斯省的面積有一百萬平方公哩，佔全加總面積的十份一。相對面積爲英國的四倍，日本的兩倍半，全球祇有三十個國家的面積比卑斯省爲大。人口三百萬，與紐西蘭或威爾斯相若。

美國的華盛頓、愛達荷及蒙塔那州位於卑斯省之南，加拿大的愛伯達省及中部各省在其東，北部則有亞拉斯加等地。而以上各地一向都是卑斯省品外銷的地方。因科技不斷的改進，最近亞太區也成爲卑斯出口市場之一。

在一九八六年，正當世界博覽會在卑斯舉行期間，卑斯省與聯邦政府簽署了一項共同拓展亞太區市場的協議，其目的爲加強卑斯省在國際貿易、財經、旅遊及交通上所扮演的角色。

一九八五年卑斯省成立了一個亞太基金，同時，省內的三所大學也成立了亞太商業研究所，以加強和亞太區在商業，教育及外交上的關係。

旅遊業在卑斯省的地位舉足輕重，在一九八六年單是旅遊業的收入就達三十二億元之鉅。因世界博覽會的關係，卑斯省在旅遊設施上得以大大改善，所以遊客日衆。

每年有船舶三千艘從世界五十多個國家到達溫哥華。航空及鐵路交通皆極其方便。而在渡海輪的載客量方面每年達六百萬人次。

近年卑斯省在財經界的發展令人側目，加拿大的商業銀行在省內共有分行八百間。另外，有三十三間海外銀行在卑斯省皆設有辦事處。而一向以籌集資金而知名的溫哥華交易所，也開始吸引更多的高科技公司在溫哥華上市。

卑斯省的工業現正趨向多元化發展，如電腦，高級消費品及成衣等皆能適應日漸擴大的消費者市場。如在一九八六年就有八間製衣廠在溫哥華上市，而其中一間在一九八七年的營業額竟達五千萬，預料在三兩年間可達一億元。

卑斯省的商業發展機會多不勝數，其中包括高級成衣、體育用品、玩具及人造首飾等。

電子工業在卑斯省也發展神速，近年的增長率達百分之廿六，營業額達七億元。而行內的廠商以中小型居多，產品有五成以上是外銷的。

卑斯省的工業與大學間的關係密切，卑斯的科研發展局更與工商界合作共同發展工業邸以助工業發展。

農業在卑斯省排行天然資源工業的第四位，農產品包羅萬有。在農業上的投資機會包括：蔬果加工、豬牛肉類、餐酒、餅乾、麵粉、糖果及溫室種植等。水產如三文魚飼養及繁植等皆前景可觀，預料在本世紀，水產工業可帶來二億元的收入及容納三千五百工人。

卑斯省乃一個多元文化的社會，各地的移民可在省內自由發展，如華人在卑斯省的商業活動就十分龐大。

卑斯省在生活享受上也十分誘人：優美的居住環境及完善的康樂文娛設施，正好是您創造明天的好開始。

CHAPTER 12

Ting Garcia

Vancouver ideal centre for Pacific Rim oriented financial operations

British Columbia is a land of snow-capped mountains, rain forests, rocky shores and rivers and rich natural resources in the capital of which generations of Chinese immigrants to Canada have chosen to make their lives.

Kagitingan (Ting) Garcia is a money manager based in Vancouver, a city now bidding to become North America's Pacific Rim financial centre.

Garcia and his family have come to have a warm love of Canada and because of the clarity of their vision about what they hoped to achieve he has a firm view of the value of Vancouver as the one city in Canada in which it is preferable for him to locate to conduct his business.

"I came to Canada in 1985 from Portland, Oregon in the United States where I had lived for three years after consistently living in Manila, the capital of the Philippines, where for almost nine years I was co-manager of one of the largest stockbroking/investment/banking firms — JJA Securities Inc."

"I thought my experience in the 'States could have been a lot better in immigration status terms."

"Although, as a result of a substantial investment committment I had made in the 'States on an entrepreneurial basis, I was allowed to stay there indefinitely. I only had Treaty Investor Status and since this could not have matured into permanent resident I didn't have any long term security for myself and my family."

"In choosing the 'States I guess I fell into the natural scheme of things within which the Philippines and the United States have always had close relations partly because we were under the U.S. for 50 years from the turn of the century to the Second World War and partly because there are substantial Filippino communities across the country."

"For the nine years prior to going to live in the 'States I was travelling extensively as part of my international stock broking, financial investment and banking activities and my company had an office in New York.

"My wife and children love America in terms of the facilities, conveniences and products available there and not available in Manila."

"You know the saying that 'the grass is always greener on the other side?' For us the only grass we wanted to be in was the 'States."

"My company had an office in London, England so we were also exposed to Europe but our personal experience was that England and

Scotland tended to be gloomier, lonelier places for us."

"My immigration lawyer in Portland pointed out the fact that Canada had opened its doors vis-a-vis foreign investors prepared to make serious committments in Canada and since I don't have relatives who can sponsor me. I knew investment was the only way I could get into another country."

"I had always viewed Canada as the last frontier but I could clearly recognize the very positive benefits that the country could derive from being next door to the world's most powerful economy — i.e. the U.S."

"Before I came I did a lot of reading to catch up with what Canada is all about and everything that I learned attracted me including the stability of the political and economic situation, the multi-culturalism that's built not only into the system but into the basic fibre of Canadians as well."

"We felt that whatever we were looking for in the 'States we could find here and over the past year since we have been here that conviction has only deepened to the point where I guess there is no return."

"As a matter of fact I was recently informed by some of my business associates that now would be an excellent time to reconsider my position with the stock market in Manila going crazy and on the upswing and with things only likely to get better for the Philippines."

"But my family loves it here; there's no other place that they would rather be and that's the most simple rationale of why I want to stay in Canada."

"Among the OECD (Organization of European Economic Development) countries I note that Canada will be the second fastest growing economy over the next five years, second only to Japan. Of course the study was done before the collapse in oil prices but when I thought about how this would affect Canada my conclusion was that it will be a net blessing because of its depressing affect on inflation and costs."

"For the things that I envision I will want to do in Canada, some of which I have already started to do, Vancouver is the only place for me; I am only really addressing the Pacific Rim."

"There is a new fund management company that we have formed in Vancouver made up of a representative of one of the largest and most conservative securities dealers in Canada, somebody who is one of the most respected and successful private venture capitalists and there's somebody whose the chairman of First Generation Capital Corporation, a China oriented publicly held company. I was recently elected chief executive officer for this fund management group the name of which is the Canadian Maple Leaf Fund Inc."

"Depending on the market it is our intention to heavily market this fund in the Far East as a means of attracting immigrants. The fund is expected to grow quickly to about U.S. $50 million."

"We have to observe certain regulatory government guidelines, basically the venture capital oriented terms of the 'new investor' category of Canada's business immigration program which means job creating, economy stimulating type investments."

"As a group we recognize excellent and secure investment opportunities in established natural resource developments by investing in companies which are expanding their operations."

"Another stream of possibilities would be smaller companies which have excellent, exceptional or clearly defined opportunities in terms of the exportability of their products or increasing market share."

"I have also been asked to join for a publicly held Vancouver company called First Generation Capital Corporation which proposes to administer and manage a China investment fund and, again, because this company is looking towards China being located here in Vancouver is ideal for me."

"First Generation's target is to raise U.S.$240 million to be exclusively invested in the People's Republic of China."

"I am working closely with First Generation's chairman, Dr. Steven Funk, to bring this about and my role is to oversee the overall groundwork and preparation that will allow the company to be launched and start raising the capital."

"From my point of view the fact that Vancouver is the gateway to North America makes it an ideal base for what I want to do."

Horace M.T. Chan
Vancouver: Growing by leaps and bounds

Horace Chan has lived in Vancouver since 1975 and he is now the managing director of Park Georgia Realty. As one of the largest private owned Vancouver based real estate companies with over 300 employees operating in the Vancouver core area alone he naturally has keen insights into opportunities for investment in real estate. But as a businesman he also has valuable insights into the Vancouver and provincial economy as a whole.

"Vancouver has approximately 1.4 million people so compared with Toronto it's not that big and the economy is relatively small compared with southern Ontario. But the economy is not as slow as a lot of people perceive."

"The B.C. economy is based on natural resources like lumber and coal and the majority of the population of the province live within a 50 mile radius of Vancouver."

"When the natural resource sector is down the perception is that the whole economy is down. But, sometimes, when you look at the entire graph of output, of earnings and of exports and imports the Vancouver core is unaffected because people there are engaged in different, non-resource related industries."

"A lot of the resource products from British Columbia are sold into the California market so by locating your business in Vancouver you are much closer to a market people call 'the sixth greatest nation in the world'.

"If you are in the business of lumber or ancillary trades to hydro electric power or any of the other industries in which British Columbia is strong and even leads the country then this proximity to California and other U.S. states is very important and a major reason why you would choose Vancouver as a base."

"Also, if you are selling into the U.S. it's much more beneficial to be based in Canada than directly in the States because the Americans impose income tax on your world wide income whereas in Canada you can declare non-resident status while retaining your citizenship.

"Vancouver is the one and only city on the western rim of Canada. So, as a port, as the western outlet for the whole country, just by virtue of its location it captures a certain amount of business and this generally spreads throughout the local economy."

"People coming from Asia are stimulating the economy here as well as people coming here from other provinces. The underlying health of the British Columbia economy has improved a lot and we are expecting a substantial growth in the coming year."

253

"Victoria is the capital of the province and therefore attracts a lot of government money but it is also the retirement capital of Canada and the purchasing power of this affluent group also helps stimulate the economy."

"Expo '86 was a big step forward for Vancouver, making it known as a world class city. With the advantage of proximity to high growth markets, the benefit of its time zone and an increasingly health underlying economy I can see Vancouver attracting more and more immigrants and becoming a major centre on the Pacific Rim."

"If you look at all the economic activity in the world obviously the Pacific Rim is where the growth is in the next 10-15 years and by virtue of its location Vancouver is really going to play a major part in this growth."

"People call Vancouver the gateway to the Pacific and through any gateway there's traffic passing in and out and that's business which will be good for the economy. Vancouver may also become a financial centre."

"In the future I think the likelihood of heavy industry locating in Vancouver is small but still the city will grow by leaps and bounds because it is the only Pacific Rim city in Canada."

"However, high technology, for example, is quite a leading industry around Vancouver and a lot of firms in the computer software industry have established themselves in such suburbs as Richmond, Burnaby and Coquitlam.

"A lot of these firms in the high tech sector are contracted to firms in the U.S. defence industry yet this is a success story few people really know about."

"Comparatively speaking it is true that Vancouver offers a very limited market but there are opportunities and if you decide to go into some kind of business and you "do it right" you can be successful."

"In Vancouver every business has its ups and downs but if you really know what you are doing then, definitely, there are opportunities."

"Even in the most competitive situations there are still opportunities if they are well researched and undertaken by businesspeople who know what they are doing."

"On the research side if you make a visit to Vancouver and stay two weeks or a month you can easily find all the information you're likely to need to start a business. Within six or nine months after start up you'd pretty well know all about it."

"The population of British Columbia is expanding all the time. I think British Columbia and Ontario are currently the only two provinces in Canada enjoying positive population flow — that is more people are arriving in those provinces than are leaving."

"In the Vancouver area most of the Chinese people move to the core of the city — Vancouver itself, North Vancouver, Richmond, Burnaby and there are relatively fewer living in the outer suburbs."

"The population of the outer suburbs is increasing too but people settling there are coming from Alberta and other Canadian provinces; they are generally not Oriental people.''

"This pattern of settlement helps I think because most of the Oriental people come in with a certain spending power which is soon felt in the economy.''

"People starting businesses in the province will be pleased to know that labour relations have improved a lot during the past few years and, in any case, the new Social Credit government has put in place legislation to curb labour actions affecting the economy.''

"Oriental people like Vancouver because it is on Pacific Coast time which is 16 hours behind Hong Kong or many of the other Pacific Rim countries. When business closes in Vancouver it is just opening in Hong Kong so you can send out your faxes and telexes and expect action even while you relax or sleep.''

"We have mountains, water and everything is so handy. Vancouver is a clean city, a healthy city for children to be brought up in and the crime rate is a lot lower than many other places, especially in the U.S.''

"Canada has a huge land mass and extremes of climate but there are not that many pleasant cities for newcomers to choose from. Vancouver has the only viable location in the west, the weather is mild, there are four seasons and the lifestyle is rich and varied.''

"The door is wide open to investor immigrants in this province and no special industry sectors are preferred just so long as a business proposal is viable.''

"Hong Kong people are well known for their involvement in real estate but this doesn't mean that all their money goes into real estate alone. Chinese people like to own the places where they operate their business — a retail shop of a factory and so investment in real estate may also be an investment in business.''

"Of course, Chinese people are always interested in a good piece of real estate, especially in Vancouver because of the ability of their investment to grow.''

"Vancouver didn't experience the same jump in values as Toronto but if you know what you're doing and where you're buying, purchasing real estate is still one of the safest investments in terms of growth of equity.''

"If you take good small commercial properties with good returns in the C$2 to C$5 million dollar range there's nothing available. Everything that's good has gone and that shows how strong the market is.''

"In terms of security Vancouver and Toronto are parallel and definitely ahead of other Canadian cities.''

"In the residential real estate market, even in suburban areas, prices are increasing and properties get snapped up fairly quickly if the price is reasonable.''

"To investors generally the Government of British Columbia is saying it's rolling out the red carpet for you, trying to improve the investment atmosphere, controlling labour and trying to short cut all the bureaucracy that curtails foreign investment.''

255

"This is a very positive thing because it is making things easier for investors to come in and makes them feel very welcome."

Discovery Foundation

DISCOVERY FOUNDATION is the entrepreneurial arm of British Columbia's science and technology program. As an independent, non-profit society, the Foundation's role is to spearhead joint efforts by industry, government and higher education. The Foundation received its initial funding in 1979 from the British Columbia government with a mandate to stimulate the growth of knowledge-based, advanced technlogy industries for the purpose of diversifying B.C.'s traditionally resource-based economy. Discovery Foundation operates through three principal vehicles:

1) Discovery Parks Incorporated (DPI)

Discovery Parks Incorporated, as the Foundation's operating division, manages the naturally landscaped research parks adjacent to B.C.'s major educational institutions. Each park provides access to the many amenities of the adjacent university or technical institution and is conducive to the creative work of knowledge-based industries.

In keeping with the entrepreneurial spirit of the Discovery concept, DPI is a highly responsive and flexible organization. Multi-tenant facilities, for example, accommodate a wide range of tenants — from small start-up operations requiring turn-key, short-term accommodation, to large companies requiring sophisticated custom-designed laboratories. Private research establishments can either build separate facilities on sites clustered around a central courtyard, or they may locate on their own naturally-landscaped site and maintain their own separate corporate identity.

In addition to the principal Discovery Parks sites adjacent to the University of British Columbia, University of Victoria, Simon Fraser University, and the B.C. Institute of Technology, DPI is establishing specialized facilities around the province. For example, a major aquaculture research centre is being constructed at Nanaimo, on Vancouver Island.

DPI's most important service, however, is bringing people together and creating reality out of ideas.

2) Discovery Enterprises Inc. (DEI)

Discovery Enterprises Inc. provides venture capital and guidance to high-technology enterprises, products and processes in advanced stages of development.

Proposals are considered on the basis of business and technical risk, job creation, relevance to the B.C. economy and pay-back potential. Projects funded are usually limited to those that would be unable to proceed without DEI funding. DEI's investments range from electronics and computer software to biotechnology and robotics, and involve new companies or established companies undergoing expansion or restructuring.

3) B.C. Innovation Office (BCIO)

The B.C. Innovation Office is essentially a counselling and referring service for innovators. The office draws on its broad contacts within the public and private sphere to help individuals and small companies assess the scientific and commercial viability of their particular innovation. Advice is provided on obtaining necessary technical evaluations, business and marketing plans, patents, venture capital and manufacturing capital.

Together, DPI, DEI, and BCIO function as facilitators and as a common ground for government, universities and industry. These communities are thereby enabled to come together and expedite the development and promotion of new technology projects.

British Columbia's positive business climate, together with its strategic location and the beautiful lifestyle it has to offer, makes it a natural environment for advanced technology. Both the federal and provincial governments offer a considerable array of support programs, including grants covering research and development, capital equipment, employee subsidies, and general business and development loans.

On the capital side, Vancouver is increasingly becoming an international banking centre, and, in addition, the Vancouver Stock Exchange is North America's largest market (in volume of trading), for venture capital. A large, well-educated, versatile labour force, a favourable exchange rate, and self-sufficiency in energy supplies also contribute to B.C.'s ideal business environment.

The lifestyle in B.C. attracts talented people from all over the world. They come and stay because its a clean, healthy, vigorous and beautiful environment. Vancouver epitomizes the B.C. lifestyle; with all the style and exuberance of a dynamic westcoast city, but combined with old world civility, sophistication and charm.

Discovery Foundation is creating the entrepreneurial environment in which advanced technology will thrive, by providing park sites, financial assistance, and aiding in the search for technical expertise and marketplace opportunities.

Discovery Foundation has extensive networks in place for the purpose of assisting business people in locating investment opportunities in advanced technologies.

"探索" 基金(DISCOVERY FOUNDATION)

探索基金乃卑斯省科學與科技計劃中的一個先導部門。作爲一個獨立及非牟利組織，基金的工作乃致力達成工業、政府與高等學府間的互相合作。基金早在一九七九年獲得省府撥款資助，目的爲使卑斯省一向倚靠天然資源的經濟可轉向高科技發展。基金屬下有三個行動單位：

一) "探索"公園機構(Discovery Parks Incorporated)

'探索'公園機構（DPI）是專責管理各高等學府鄰近的研究用地，以供科研機構所用。

為倡導基金的創新精神，所以DPI是一個運作靈活的部門。基金的研究設備可分別容納不同科研機構的要求。私人機構還可在研究用地裏自行興建研究設施，以樹立本身的形像。

DPI除在英屬哥倫比哥大學、維多利亞大學、西門富利沙大學及B.C理工學院隔鄰建立'探索'研究用地外，還在省內各在興建供特別研究用的設施。在溫哥華島上Nanaimo興建的水產研究中心便是其中一例。

二) "探索"企業有限公司(Discovery Enterprises Inc.)

'探索'企業（DEI）的成立是為資助有關機構作高科技產品後期研究之用。研究方案是根據商業上及技術上的風險、對就業的影響及還本期等因素作審核的標準。DEI所資助的方案的般都是本身沒有自費的條件的。而受資助的研究包括電子及應用於生物工程和機械操作的電腦軟件等。而受資助的機構則有成立的，在發展中的及重組的。

三) 卑斯創新辦事處(B.C. Innovation Office)

卑斯創新辦事處（BCIO）主要是一個諮詢和加強創新者互相聯絡的單位。BCIO利用其與政府及私人機構的廣泛接觸，藉以衡量新品在商業上和技術上的可行性。當BCIO搜集齊有關技術上的評估、市場及具體的商業計劃書、專利權及資金等資料後，便會為創新者提供意見。

DPI,DEI及BCIO三者的功能皆是促進政府、大學和工商業間的合作和溝通。這樣，新科技的發展和推廣便可加速進行。

卑斯省的理想工商氣候、有利的地理環境及美好的生活方式，實是孕育尖端科技的好地方。為表示對科研的支持，聯邦政府及省府皆設有贈研究用的款項和多項有關器材、員工支助及商業發展的貸款等。

在金融方面，溫哥華現已逐漸成為國際銀行業中心。而溫哥華的股票市場乃是北美洲最大的投機資金市場，再加上教育水平高、適應力強的勞工、表現良好的加元匯率和自給自足的能源，這一切均為卑斯省理想營商環境的一部份。

卑斯省的生活方式吸引了世界各地無數有天份的專才。他們在卑斯定居是因為我們具有綺麗的環境。溫哥華便是卑斯省生活方式的最佳寫照，因其既有新城市的繁榮，亦有古舊城市的風貌。

'探索'基金現全力建立一個有利尖端科技的環境。我們會為你提供研究用地、資金援助、人才發掘及市場拓展等援助。

我們可為你提供有關投資尖端科技的資料及援助。

SURREY
BRITISH COLUMBIA

On the move and growing fast

- 30 minutes from Vancouver
- 2nd largest municipality in B.C.
- Fastest population growth in the area
- Main gateway to the U.S.
- Flourishing industry
- Relaxed lifestyle

Come grow with us

FOR INVESTMENT OR
BUSINESS OPPORTUNITY
INFORMATION
CONTACT:

MR. FRANKLIN A. WILES
DISTRICT OF SURREY
ECONOMIC DEVELOPMENT DEPARTMENT
14245 - 56th Ave., Surrey, British Columbia
Canada V3W 1J2 Telephone 604/591-4128

Surrey: Fastest growing town in the West

Located in Western Canada, with suburban living costs but big city amenities, a municipality with the highest rate of population growth of any in its area, a burgeoning economy and closer to the world's richest market than the City of Vancouver — welcome to Surrey, British Columbia.

Surrey is the second largest major municipality in the province of British Columbia in both area and population encompassing nearly 130 square miles with five town centres and more than 180,000 citizens.

Over the past decade the population has increased by approximately 40 per cent — over 5 per cent in 1987 alone! By the year 2001 more than 300,000 people are expected to call Surrey home.

Half-a-million people live in the adjacent municipalities which make up its immediate trade area and triple that number in Greater Vancouver as a whole.

Surrey is British Columbia's main gateway to the United States and has the largest truck customs office and the busiest car crossing in Western Canada.

The fast growing municipality entered the 1980s with an impressive range of commercial and industrial development as well as an ample supply of residential and recreational land.

Surrey used to be largely agricultural and large areas are still devoted to farming to the extent that 60 per cent of British Columbia's greenhouses are located in the municipality. Agriculture and related food production for domestic and export markets are important contributors to local employment and prosperity.

A unique combination of moderate climate, prime agricultural land, modern transportation facilities, excellent retail hubs, extensive parks and sophisticated cultural centres — plus proximity to major markets has established Surrey as a major contender as a base for international trade and commerce.

At the same time, these factors have ensured Surrey's position as one of the most sought after communities in which to live in all Canada.

Today, Surrey is a choice destination for local, national and international corporations seeking a healthy economic environment for medium/light industry, high tech manufacturing, fabricating and processing endeavors.

Home of some of the most modern industrial plants and the source of many of the most innovative new products in North America, Surrey is making its mark on the international trade scene.

The late 1980s are turning out to be banner years for Surrey's economic growth as people from around the world are attracted to its opportunities and lifestyle.

This is reflected in the volume of municipal land sales and the issuance of building permits and business licences.

Growth of the magnitude and diversity that Surrey has experienced in recent years has created the need for careful community planning to guide future development and effectively meet the needs of all citizens — corporate and public, long term and prospective.

The implementation of a broadly based Community Plan has led to the development of four distinct, well defined industrial areas within the municipality. Each is appropriately serviced, designed to accommodate all sizes and types of industry and is accessible by road, rail and / or water transportation systems.

The largest, Port Kells, extends along the north-east Fraser River waterfront. Others are located along the Port Mann and Alex Fraser Bridges and in the Newton and Cloverdale areas.

These parks have already attracted a variety of manufacturing, metal fabricating and food processing companies.

Modern transportation facilities provide more than adequate means of moving goods — major arterial highways, air transport, rail and a major ocean-shipping port (Fraser-Surrey Docks).

While industry flourishes so, too, do the residential communities. The many people who have chosen to make their home in Surrey enjoy a variety of lifestyles.

Medium to high density housing developments bordered by gardens, public buildings and major retail centres, a community atmosphere and bustling town centres allow for both convenience and good living, while the many parks and farms in the district serve to enhance the natural beauty of the environment.

A relaxed pace and unlimited recreational pursuits appeal to sports and outdoor enthusiasts.

Activities such as golfing, boating, fishing, wind surfing, beach combing, jogging and gardening are enjoyed by many Surrey residents throughout the year. In addition the municipality operates six community centres where swimming, exercise classes, dancing and other organized events keep local residents busy on a regular basis.

With growth has come variety in the many special events staged in the municipality. From the Surrey Centennial Arts Centre to the renowned Cloverdale Rodeo and horse racing, there's something for everyone.

Approximately 80 schools serve an increasing number of primary and secondary students each year while the two campuses of Kwantien College give post-secondary and adult students expert instruction in university level, technical and vocational courses.

All facets of family and community life are represented here through planned amenities such as well planned neighbourhoods served by community centres, schools, colleges, sports complexes, hospitals, clinics, doctors, libraries, churches, retail outlets and art and cultural venues — all of which add up to a well balanced way of life that's hard to beat.

Ideally located just 30 minutes from downtown Vancouver, Surrey's boundaries include the Fraser River to the North, the U.S. state of Washington to the south and the Pacific Ocean to the West.

Proximity to the Port of Vancouver, as well as access to the North American continent as a whole and to Pacific Rim countries make Surrey the ideal location for both up-and-coming industrial ventures and well established corporations.

Surrey is on the move and growing fast. Come grow with us.

薩里市：一個發展迅速的西部城市

薩里市位於加拿大西部的卑斯省。薩市人口增長迅速，商業發達，所以市內既有大城市的方便，又有小鎮般的生活水平—薩里市歡迎您。

薩市乃卑斯省的第二大城市，面積一百三十平方哩，人口十八萬。

在過往十年，人口增長達百分之四十。單是一九八七年人口的增長就達百分之五！預料在二〇〇一年，人口將達三十萬的水平。

薩里市乃由卑斯省往美國途中的主要市集，所以交通十分繁忙，而加加拿大西部的最大貨運關卡也設於此。

踏進八十年代後，薩里市的工商業異常發達，土地發展及供應亦同時增加。

薩里市曾經一度以農業為主，至今市內的溫室種植場每年的出產佔全省的百分之六十，透過出口或內銷，為卑斯省帶來不少就業機會。

天氣溫和、土地肥沃、交通先進、銷售網廣、公園及文娛場所林立，這一切使薩里市在國際貿易上也佔一席位，同時也使該市成為一個宜居的地方。

今日的薩里市乃很多大小型企業所選擇設廠的地方，所以在薩市製造的新產品不計其數。現在仍不斷有新的機構來薩市發展。

以上的發展，可從薩里市的土地成交，建屋准許証數目及商業執照的增加盡見一斑。與此同時、城市規劃也顯得更為重要。現在，薩里市分別規劃出四個不同的工業區以容立大小工業，而所有工業地點皆有極方便的水陸交通設備。

至於住宅方便，新建的樓房四周環境優美，購物方便，加上公園林立，使市民可有憩息及戶外活動的機會。

市內亦不乏文娛的好去處，如薩里百年藝術中心、Cloverdale Rodeo及賽馬場等。

薩里市設有中小學八十間，大專院校如 Kwantien College 可為市民提供多項的專上課程。

薩里市離溫哥華祗有半小時路程，北有菲沙河，南是華盛頓市，西則是太平洋。其與溫哥華之接近，正好是閣下投資的好地方。

請與我們共同地長。

CHAPTER 13

Taxation in Canada

By William C. Chan,
Partner,
Price Waterhouse,
Toronto.

The principal government taxes in Canada include the following:

Federal:
Personal income taxes —
Individuals who are resident in Canada are subject to Canadian income taxes on their world-wide income, subject to credits or deductions for foreign taxes paid on income derived from non-Canadian sources. An individual resident in Canada for only part of the tax year is generally taxable in Canada on his world-wide income only for the period during which he was resident.

Federal income tax is determined by applying a graduated rate schedule to the taxable income of the taxpayer, subject to various adjustments and credits. In 1988, the rates rise from 17% on taxable income of up to $27,500 to 29% on taxable income in excess of $55,000.* In addition, there is a 3% surtax on the above federal income tax.

Corporate income taxes —
Generally, a company resident in Canada is liable to income tax on its world income. Corporations, including branch operations of foreign corporations, are taxed at the following federal rates effective July 1, 1988*:

	Basic Rate %	Provincial Abatement	Net Federal Rate
Basic federal rate	38%	(10)	28%
On Canadian manufacturing	36%	(10)	26%

*Tax reform proposals.

There is a 3% surtax on the above federal tax. Canadian-controlled private companies qualify for a reduction of up to 16% in federal rates on the first $200,000 of annual business income.

Sales taxes —
Federal sales tax is a single-stage commodity tax applicable only once, generally at the time the goods are sold by the manufacturer or when foreign-made goods are imported. The tax, generally 12%, is imposed on the manufacturer's selling price of Canadian manufactured goods and on the duty-paid value of imported goods. Most construction materials and equipment for buildings, are subject to an 8% rate of tax. Federal sales tax is a significant cost to most manufacturers. A manufacturer's annual federal sales tax liability frequently exceeds his liability for federal and provincial income taxes.

Customs and excise duties —
Excise taxes at various rates are levied under the Excise Tax Act at the manufacturer's level on specified luxury goods whether manufacturer or produced in Canada or imported into Canada. The list of such items includes jewellery, wines, lighters, cigarettes, tobacco, etc. In addition, excise duties are levied under the Excise Act at various rates on alcohol, alcoholic beverages other than wines, and tobacco products manufactured in Canada. In lieu of excise duties, imports are subject to equivalent customs duties.

Provincial and territorial governments:
Personal income taxes —
Income taxes for all provinces and territories except Quebec are calculated as a fixed percentage of basic federal tax (e.g., 50% in Ontario and 51.5% in British Columbia). From time to time, a province may impose a surtax. Quebec levies its own income tax, and individuals residing in that province or carrying on business there must file a separate Quebec income tax return.

Corporate income taxes —
In general, the taxable income of a corporation is allocated to those provinces and territories of Canada and to foreign jurisdictions in which the corporation maintains a permanent establishment (e.g., an office) based on the average of the ratios of gross revenue and salaries and wages attributable to a particular jurisdiction to total gross revenue and salaries and wages.

Provincial and territorial income tax is then calculated on the portion of the corporation's taxable income allocated to each province or territory. Provincial and territorial rates range from 10% to 17% of taxable income, with reduced rates on the first $200,000 of annual business income of Canadian-controlled private companies.

Retail sales tax —
All provinces except Alberta levy a retail sales tax on the ultimate consumer or user of tangible personal property and, in some cases, services for consumption or use in the province and on the purchaser of

selected services. The tax generally is based on the sales price or fair value of the goods or services. The rates range from 5% to 12% among the provinces.

Capital taxes —
The provinces of British Columbia, Newfoundland and Nova Scotia (bank and loan and trust companies only), Saskatchewan, Manitoba, Ontario and Quebec impose a tax on the taxable capital of corporations carrying on business in the respective provinces. Taxable capital generally includes capital stock, retained earnings, reserve funds, bonds, debentures, mortgages, notes, loans, advances, less allowances for investments and goodwill.

Taxable capital is allocated to permanent establishments (e.g., offices) of the corporation in the province based on the average of the ratios of gross revenues and salaries and wages in the province to total gross revenues and salaries and wages respectively. The rates range from 2/10 of 1% to 45/100 of 1% of taxable capital, with higher rates for banks, trust and loan corporations. Some provinces have a flat capital tax if taxable capital is below a certain amount.

Death taxes —
Although Canada does not have gift and succession duties, generally an individual who dies is considered to have sold each capital property owned by him immediately before his death. Any resulting capital gain may be subject to tax except where he leaves his estate to his spouse or the gains are exempt from tax.

Municipal taxes:
Real property taxes —
Municipalities impose real property taxes on all real property in the municipality unless they are specifically exempted. Such real property taxes are often in the form of both a property tax on the owner of the real property and a business tax on the person who occupies or uses property for business purposes.

CHAPTER 14

Business immigration into Canada: The new program

By

FRED KAN

THOMAS S. BARRIE

INTRODUCTION

Throughout the 120 years of Canada's existence as an independent nation, government policies on immigration have reflected changing perceptions of the national interest. Early statutes (dating from the *1853 Emigrants and Quarantine Laws,* 16 Vict., c. 86 of the British Imperial Government) tended towards subtle discouragement of foreign settlement of Canada. As early as 1859, legislation concerned with immigration prescribed inadmissible classes of immigrant.

During the 19th century, and into the early years of this century, the Immigration Department and its officers had great latitude in regard to defining, and excluding, "undesirable" or "vicious" classes of immigrant. Such classes were frequently declared by proclamation. Additionally, legislation was often worded so as to contemplate only immigration from European ports. It is fair criticism that early Canadian immigration law was used to discriminate against non-European immigrants.

Although it can be explained with hindsight as having been drafted by a young nation unsure of its standing in the world community, and concerned to assert the interests of its small population throughout a vast territory, early discriminatory immigration legislation was strongly repudiated by Canada (and by the United States, where similar laws were passed at approximately the same time) beginning in the decade of the

1940's. By the 1970's, racist laws and regulations of any kind were anathema to the Canadian government and people. Throughout Canada, civil liberties organizations maintain a constant vigil to protect the rights and equal treatment of all Canadians regardless of race or ethnic origin.

In the truest sense of the words, Canada in 1987 is a "cultural mosaic" comprised of peoples from all parts of the globe. Cultural pluralism is so basic and permanent a feature of the Canadian social fabric that the federal government appoints a senior portfolio minister to co-ordinate and assume responsibility for multiculturalism. The federal Minister of Multiculturalism is assisted, at the provincial level, by a counterpart official appointed in each of Canada's 10 provinces. The great majority of Canadians recognizes and applauds the enrichment of Canadian society made possible by immigration from Europe, Asia and other parts of the world.

Canadian government policy in 1987 is set out at s. 3 of the *Immigration Act, 1976*. This statute provides for the following general objectives:

"3. It is hereby declared that Canadian immigration policy and the rules and regulations made under this Act shall be designed and administered in such a manner as to promote the domestic and international interests of Canada, recognizing the need

(a) to support the attainment of such demographic goals as may be established by the government of Canada from time to time in respect of size, rate of growth, structure and demographic distribution of the Canadian population;

(b) to enrich and strengthen the cultural and social fabric of Canada, taking into account the federal and bilingual character of Canada;

(c) to facilitate the reunion in Canada of Canadian citizens and permanent residents with their close relatives from abroad;

(d) to encourage and facilitate the adoption of persons who have been granted admission as permanent residents to Canadian society by promoting co-operation between the government of Canada and other levels of government and non-governmental agencies in Canada with respect thereto;

(e) to facilitate the entry of visitors into Canada for the purpose of fostering trade and commerce, tourism, cultural and scientific activities and international understandings;

(f) to ensure that any person who seeks admission to Canada on either a permanent or temporary basis is subject to standards of admission that do not discriminate on grounds of race, national or ethnic origin, colour, religion or sex;

(g) to fulfill Canada's international legal obligations with respect to refugees and to uphold its humanitarian tradition with respect to the displaced and the persecuted;

(h) to foster the development of a strong and viable economy and the prosperity of all regions in Canada;

(i) to maintain and protect the health, safety and good order of Canadian society;

(j) to promote international order and justice by denying the use of Canadian territory to persons who are likely to engage in criminal activity."

In the exercise of its sovereignty, the Canadian federal government in 1987 continues to implement an immigration policy which it believes to be in the best interests of the country. The present *Immigration Act* provides for three broad classes of immigrant:

(a) Family Class;
(b) Humanitarian and Refugee Class; and
(c) Independent Class.

"Family Class" applicants are those individuals having close family already living in Canada as citizens or permanent residents. "Humanitarian and Refugee Class" applicants are those individuals, usually from war zones or areas of natural catastrophe, to whom Canada feels a moral responsibility to offer relocation. "Independent Class" applicants are individuals who, broadly, do not fit into either of these two general categories but wish to make independent application to immigrate to Canada. Historically, these individuals have been assessed against a "point system" which attempts to measure their desirability and allows a general prognosis of the likelihood of their successfully establishing themselves in the country.

On comparing year-by-year implementation of objectives set out at s. 3 of the **Immigration Act, 1976,** it is clear that there have been noticeable differences of emphasis in regard to admission of individuals from each of the three broad categories of applicant. While Family Class applications remain the cornerstone of Canada's immigration policy, the national interest has recently been somewhat differently defined in regard to the question of how many, and what type, of Independent Class applications should be accepted. In 1982, for example, a major economic recession in Canada resulted in a policy decision by the then-government to set lower overall annual immigration levels as well as lower levels, in particular, of Independent Class applicants. The political determination in 1982 was that individuals applying as Independent Class applicants (except for businessmen, entrepreneurs, and investors) could represent an unwelcome level of competition for Canadians already suffering the consequences of the economic recession. Accordingly, Embassy, Consulate and High Commission offices around the world were instructed to give priority to Family Class and Humanitarian and Refugee Class applicants and to relegate Independent Class individuals to a low tertiary level of importance.

In the last few years, however, the Canadian government has made a major commitment to increasing the attractiveness of Canada as a destination for international investment. The federal government, with the enthusiastic support of all the provinces, has decided to interpret s. 3 of the **Immigration Act, 1976** in such a way as to actively promote Canada to high net-worth individuals wishing to make their home here and hoping, through commitment of their expertise and experience, to invest in the country and its economy.

In this brief paper, we propose to highlight recent legislative enactments which, taken together, point to a considerable "window of opportunity" available to individuals wishing to invest in Canada or immigrate under the new Business Immigration Program.

THE INVESTMENT CANADA ACT

The **Investment Canada Act** (the "Act") represents a basic change in the political philosophy of the Canadian government. The Act replaces the **Foreign Investment Review Act** ("FIRA") promulgated during the mid-1970's with a new regime which does not so much "review" or "screen" investment applications as actively encourage and facilitate them. Implementation of the new policy has been mandated (under the **Financial Administration Act**) to a specialized agency known as "Investment Canada". This Agency reports directly to the Minister of Regional Industrial Expansion of the federal government in Ottawa. Through simplified procedural steps, and elimination of review where acquisitions are below stipulated ceilings, the Agency is charged with encouraging investment in Canada by both Canadians and non-Canadians. Many foreign investors have taken advantage of the Act since it was first proclaimed in force in 1985.

A. Acquisitions Not Subject to Review

Under the new regime, where investment by a non-Canadian is made in a "new Canadian business" (defined term), or where there is direct acquisition of a Canadian business with assets valued under C$5,000,000, or where there is indirect acquisition of a Canadian business with assets valued under C$50,000,000, the non-Canadian investor need only complete and forward to Investment Canada in Ottawa (within 30 days of implementation of his investment) a simple standard-form Notification (see Appendix 'A'). The Act defines "direct acquisition" as the acquisition of control of a Canadian business, either through acquisition of its holding interests or assets or through acquisition of control of its Canadian parent in Canada. "Indirect acquisition" is defined as the acquisition of control of a Canadian business through acquisition of control of the parent *outside* Canada.

B. Acquisitions Subject to Review

The Act provides that all direct acquisition of Canadian businesses with assets of C$5,000,000 or more, and all indirect acquisitions of Canadian businesses with assets of C$50,000,000 or more, as well as all indirect acquisitions of Canadian businesses having asset values of between C$5,000,000 and C$50,000,000 (and which represent more than 50% of the value of the total international transaction), shall be subject to review by Investment Canada. In addition, specific acquisitions or new business ventures in designated areas of activity (related to Canada's cultural heritage or national identity) are reviewable where the Governor in Council has reasonable grounds to believe that such review is in the public interest.

Regulations to the Act provide the form of document to be used in ap-

273

plying for review of a proposed investment (see Appendix 'B'). With certain exceptions, the investment may not be implemented until the review process has been completed. However, provision exists whereby the Minister may permit an investment o be implemented prior to completion of the review procedures where he is satisfied that delay would cause undue hardship to the acquiror or jeopardize operation of the Canadian business being acquired.

C. Review Procedure

In the normal course, Investment Canada submits the application to the Minister accompanied by whatever information or written undertaking may be given by the investor and any representation submitted by a province likely to be significantly affected by the investment. Where the Minister determines that the investment is likely to be of net benefit to Canada, it will be authorized. The factors of assessment prescribed in the Act, and to which the Minister must refer in making his decision, are as follows:

(a) the effect of the investment on the level and nature of economic activity in Canada, including the effect on employment, on resource processing, on utilization of parts, components and services produced in Canada, and on exports from Canada;

(b) the degree and significance of participation by Canadians in the Canadian business and in any industry in Canada of which it forms a part;

(c) the effect of the investment on productivity, industrial efficiency, technological development, product innovation and product variety in Canada;

(d) the effect of the investment on competition with any industry or industries in Canada;

(e) the compatability of the investment with national industrial, economic and cultural policies, taking into consideration industrial, economic and cultural policy objectives enunciated by the government or legislature of any province likely to be significantly affected by the investment; and

(f) the contribution of the investment to Canada's ability to compete in international markets.

D. Time Limits

Both Investment Canada and the Minister are subject to prescribed time limits within which review of the application and a decision in respect of its merits must be completed. The Minister must notify the investor within forty-five (45) days of receipt of a completed application whether:

(a) he is satisfied that the investment will be of net benefit to Canada; or

(b) he is unable to complete his review, in which case there will be a further thirty (30) day period (or longer with the written consent of the applicant) during which ministerial review can be completed; or

(c) he is *not* satisfied that the investment will be of any net benefit to Canada.

When forty-five (45) days from completion of the application have elapsed without any notice having been sent to the applicant, or the period of thirty (30) further days (or the agreed-upon number of days) has elapsed after notice that the Minister is unable to complete this review and no decision has been taken, then the Minister is *deemed* to be satisfied that the investment will be of net benefit to Canada. On receipt of any notice that the Minister believes the investment will be unlikely to be of net benefit to Canada, the applicant, as of right, may make representations and submit undertakings within thirty (30) days of the date of said notice.

The *Investment Canada Act* was passed both in the recognition that increased capital and technology would be a benefit to Canada and in order to encourage investment in Canada by Canadians and non-Canadians. The Act seeks to stimulate economic growth and employment opportunities within the country and is consistent with the policy decision of the Progressive Conservative government to expand Canadian involvement in international commerce. Accordingly, foreign investors may now be confident of a presumptively positive reception where review of their application to invest in Canada is necessary. The days of FIRA, of government-erected obstacles to foreign investors seeking to introduce capital and technology into Canada, are gone. The new Act's Notification and Review procedures have been considerably simplified as compared with those of the previous legislation. The Investment Canada Agency has served notice world-wide that Canada will actively welcome investment monies and facilitate their entry into the country.

BUSINESS IMMIGRATION PROGRAM

Another innovation of the present government was the expansion, effective January 1, 1986, of the Business Immigration Program to add a third category, that of "investor", to the already established categories of "entrepreneur" and "self-employed" acceptable Independent Class business immigrants. The prime objective of the Business Immigration Program is the promotion, encouragement and facilitation of immigration into Canada by experienced business persons able to make a positive contribution to the country's economic development. In particular, the high net-worth and skilled individuals whose immigration into the country is now to be encouraged will be applying their risk capital and know-how to Canadian business ventures which will create employment opportunities for Canadian residents.

Self-Employed

Self-employed immigrants are described in the Regulations as persons having the intention and ability to establish a business in Canada (which will employ *only* the applicant) and, at the same time, contribute to the economic, cultural, or artistic life of Canada. This category contemplates individuals who, although they may not actively and directly create jobs for Canadians, nevertheless make a significant contribution in economic and artistic terms. Examples of the type of individual who might be successfully received as a self-employed immigrant are farmers, sports personalities, artists, members of the performing arts, and other persons undertaking a business or economic activity which will result in betterment of the quality of life in a community. Self-employed applicants are assessed using the "point system" of suitability and receive 30 points as a bonus if it is determined that they fall within the regulatory definition of this category. In most cases, a minimum of 70 points is required to secure acceptance as an Independent Class applicant. Categories of assessment against which applications are reviewed include: education, specific vocational preparation, experience, pre-arranged employment, age, knowledge of one or both of Canada's official languages (English and French), and personal suitability.

Entrepreneurs

Entrepreneurs are described in the Regulations to the **Immigration Act** as persons having the intention and ability to establish, purchase, or make a substantial investment in a business venture in Canada which will be managed by the applicant on an active basis. The proposed venture must make a significant contribution to the economy and, at the same time, result in the creation or maintenance of employment opportunities for 1 or more Canadian citizens or permanent residents in addition to the entrepreneur and his dependents. This category has also been liberalized in that the number of Canadian residents (other than the Entrepreneur and his dependents) for whom an employment opportunity must be created has been reduced from the former minimum of 5 to the present minimum of 1. (NOTE: Despite this change in the Regulations, individual provinces can still set their own requirements as to the number of jobs required to be created/maintained by an Entrepreneur. Applicants should confirm this figure prior to preparation of their business plan.) This category contemplates applicants who have successful hands-on management experience of small to medium-size enterprises. While the amount of capital required to be made available for investment varies from province to province, at least C$100,000 is generally necessary if the application is to be seriously considered. Entrepreneurs are also assessed using the "point system" but need obtain only a minimum of 25 points (instead of the usual 70) if they fall within the regulatory definiton of the class.

Instituted in 1978, the Entrepreneur Immigrant Program has been highly successful and, in 1985 alone, attracted some 2,130 Entrepreneurs declaring estimated total net assets of C$1.2 billion. Enterprises founded by these Entrepreneurs, once fully operational, will create approximately 9,700 jobs for Canadians. Although government records indicate that Entrepreneurs now come to Canada from some 85 different countries, the three most significant points of origin are Hong Kong (which accounted for approximately 40% of the total in 1985), West Germany and the United States. Because the program is administered jointly by the federal and provincial governments, prospective immigrants must first have their applications assessed by the province of intended destination. However, the final decision as to acceptability remains exclusively within the jurisdiction of the federal power in Ottawa.

Although the provinces have established different priorities against

which applications under the Entrepreneur Immigrant Program are assessed, each of them welcomes applications which, if within the scope of the Program, will have the net effect of:
  (a) increasing exports;
  (b) replacing imports of foreign-made products; or
  (c) conferring an "economic benefit" on the host province.

Because of differences in regard to levels of economic/industrial activity, and types of industry located within their jurisdictions, the provincial governments have decided on different minimally-acceptable criteria in reviewing applications under the Entrepreneur program. For example, the number of jobs (exclusive of those for the applicant and his/her dependents) to be created — and the documentation to be submitted in support of the application — can vary from province to province. While many provinces comply strictly with the federal requirement that only one such job need be created, Ontario (Canada's richest, most populous and most industrialized province) requires creation of 5 permanent jobs.

For precise information about priority industrial sectors, minimum job creation requirements, and amount of investment funds required to be directed to the enterprise, interested persons should contact the office of the province of intended destination (see Appendix "C").

Suggested Procedure under the Entrepreneur Immigrant Category
Inasmuch as the initial contact will be to the province of intended destination, it is imperative that the Entrepreneur applicant understand clearly the minimum documentation which must accompany his application. In the case of Ontario, which receives over 50 percent of applications, and which is considered here as an example, this documentation consists of the following:
  (1) conclusive proof of his personal and direct experience in owning, managing and operating a financially successful business or commercial undertaking;
  (2) an Affidavit reciting his intention, and confirming his ability, to use his skills in providing active and ongoing management of the proposed business to be carried on in the province of destination;
  (3) a second Affidavit detailing, as precisely as possible, the business activity which it is proposed will be carried on in the province of destination;
  (4) confirmation by the Entrepreneur applicant that his investment will be by way of equity, or subordinated shareholder's loans; and
  (5) a formal business proposal or plan which, in as much detail as possible, should address all of the following concerns:
    (i) **Project Description**
        Project costs and proposed financing should be listed. Major categories of expenditures should be indicated. Manufacturing sources of any capital equipment that may be required should be noted.
    (ii) **Precise Location of Project**
        Municipal address, legal description of property, and any

277

available maps should be included.

(iii) **Management**

A summary of the relevant employment history and management experience for each member of the management team should be included.

(iv) **Immigrant's Function**

Details of the function(s) of the Entrepreneur(s) in management of the business should be included.

(v) **Employees**

The number of full-time employees, seasonal workers (and number of months seasonal employment per year) according to occupational categories should be indicated. Note that this figure should be exclusive of those relating directly to the Entrepreneur immigrant and his/her dependents. The number of jobs to be maintained and/or created should be indicated.

(vi) **Products**

The products to be created or manufactured should be described.

(vii) **Market**

A market summary providing the following should be included:

—supply and demand (suppliers, major customers and new business prospects); letters of confirmation if these are available;

—identification of existing competition;

—indication of effects of proposed project on existing businesses in the area;

—indication of effects of imports/exports.

(viii) **Contacts**

Names, addresses and telephone numbers of the following individuals should be included:

—authorized contact person(s);

—project legal advisor;

—project banker;

—project accountant;

—project insurance agent.

(ix) **Financial Information**

The following documentation should also be attached to the application:

—financial statements for the past three years, if the project is to be related to an existing business (submit an interim statement if the most recent statement is older than three months);

—documented proof of financial responsibility consisting of statements of personal net worth;

—forecast financial statements including pro forma balance sheet (showing proposed project), balance sheet at end of first full year of operation, and projected profit and loss statements for first three years of operation;

278

—source of funds to be used in the project where these are not 100% supplied by the applicant.

(x) **Corporate Structure**
This should be described in detail, explaining financing, shareholding arrangement and type of shares held. Citizenship of shareholders should be indicated.

Copies of all formal shareholder agreements should be included. In the event a shareholder agreement with a Canadian party has not yet been executed, an executed memorandum of agreement should be provided in lieu of the final document.

(xi) **Guarantees**
Where the proposal deals with the take-over of an existing business, the purchaser should ensure that the following guarantees are part of the purchase agreement:
—that all employment contracts and/or labour agreements in force immediately prior to assuming control of the business are to be honoured by the new owner or owners; and
—that employees on the payroll immediately prior to the purchaser/purchasers assuming control of the business will be retained by the new owners, subject to need, suitability, misdemeanour or other just cause.

(xii) **Government Grants, Loans and Subsidies**
Indication should be made of any government grants, loans and subsidies received or authorized during the past three years.

(xiii) **Litigation, Legal Proceedings**
Details of any pending litigation or legal proceedings should be provided.

(xix) **Application of Funds**
An explicit statement of the amount and timing of equity or shareholder's loans to be injected into the business by the immigrant should be provided. Indication should also be given as to the percentage of ownership.

(xx) **Economic Benefits**
Detailed description should be provided of the economic benefits to Ontario which are anticipated if the application is approved (i.e. jobs, new technology, impact on exports/imports).

Applicants under the Entrepreneur program should normally send one (1) copy of their proposal to the office of the province of intended destination at its address given in Appendix "C". Where the proposed business venture relates to tourism, however, two (2) copies of all documents should be forwarded.

Naturally, the information package outlined above may not be appropriate or sufficient in all cases. To obtain up-to-date advice as to what ought to be submitted in a particular circumstance, applicants should ar-

279

range to meet a Business Development Officer ("BDO") at the Canadian visa office in their home state. Such an interview will be especially helpful where the applicant knows that he wishes to emigrate to Canada, and establish a business or make an investment here, but does not believe himself ready to submit a detailed business plan in support of his application. The BDO will advise on the means by which the applicant can make an exploratory visit to Canada and, with support and assistance from the province of intended destination, assess the opportunities available to him. All the provinces (and even some municipalities) are equipped and willing to assist would-be Entrepreneur and Investor immigrants in preparation of a business plan which can later be submitted as part of a formal application. It is strongly recommended that prospective immigrants visit Canada and take advantage of this opportunity for consultation with provincial authorities prior to submitting a formal application.

In order to assist applicants under the Business Immigration Program, s. 15(1) of the *Immigration Act, 1976* is now being interpreted so as to provide for a conditional admission to Canada of up to two years in the case of Entrepreneur immigrants. During this initial two-year exploratory period, qualified Enrepreneurs will be able to undertake detailed evaluation of business opportunities and meet with provincial officials responsible for implementation of policy so as to ensure final government approval. During this time, the proposed business immigrant will have at his disposal a considerable range of counselling and advisory services upon which he can draw in determining which precise form of entrepreneural activity he wishes to carry on.

On the basis of information gathered during his period of conditional admission, the Entrepreneur can prepare a formal application (including business plan) which, in effect, will already have been designated as meeting the minimum criteria for "economic betterment" established by the particular province of intended destination. The net effect of using the conditional admission, therefore, will be a considerable expediting of provincial review of the application and an equally considerable heightening of the applicant's chances of final acceptance by Ottawa.

Investors

Investors are described in the Regulations as persons:
(a) having a proven business track record of owning, managing and operating a financially successful business or commercial undertaking;
(b) who have accumulated, by their own endeavours, a personal net worth of at least C$500,000; and
(c) who undertake to make an irrevocable investment, for a minimum period of three years, of C$250,000 (net of expenses, commissions and fees) in a business or commercial venture or investment syndicate designated by the province of intended destination.

In using the word "designated" to describe their active involvement in implementation of this program, provincial departments have deliberately chosen language which does not imply any element of government endorsement of the financial merits of the investment, or guarantee of financial return thereon. The successful Investor applicant will be an individual who makes a risk investment into a business or commercial venture or investment syndicate acceptable to the province of intended destination, and thereby causes it to "designate" the application (to the federal power in Ottawa) as being within the regulatory definition and as likely to bring "economic benefit" to the designating province. Provincial officials charged with implementation of the new program, and who were consulted in the course of preparing this material, were unanimous that the essential "economic benefit" looked for in assessing applications under the Investor program is job creation/maintenance.

Investor applicants can choose from among three investment options. They may choose to invest:

(a) in a business or commercial venture whose establishment, purchase, expansion or maintenance will be of significant economic benefit to the province in which it is located;

(b) in a privately-administered investment syndicate, designated by the province in which the syndicate will make investments, and which will have as its main purpose the provision of equity or loan capital to establish, purchase, expand or maintain business or commercial ventures which will be of significant economic benefit to the province in which the syndicate makes the investment; or

(c) in a government-administered venture capital fund, the main purpose of which is provision of equity or loan capital to establish, purchase, expand or maintain business or commercial ventures.

Provincial governments are free to elect from among these three options and can "designate" an immigration application in respect of any or all of them. As of the date of this writing, however, none of Canada's ten provinces is willing to make a designation in respect of an application in which the minimum C$250,000 is to be placed in a government-administered venture capital fund (option "C" above). With the notable exception of Ontario (and Prince Edward Island), however, all of the provinces will consider making a designation in respect of a proposal where the investment is made directly into a business or commercial venture, or into a privately-administered investment syndicate. Given the relative newness of this component of the Business Immigration Program, persons interested in coming to Canada as Investors are strongly urged to contact a Canadian visa office, or the province of intended destination, in order to ascertain the scope and availability of options at the time of application.

It is a precondition of issuing an Investor immigrant visa that all investments be confirmed in writing as meeting the regulatory requirements of the *Immigration Act*. In regard to the requirement that the investment be "irrevocable" for at least three years, Regulation 9(3) provides that documentation submitted in support of an Investor application may contain a condition that the minimum C$250,000 be refundable, at the instance of the Investor, if he/she is not granted an immigrant visa. In the case of investments into a privately-administered investment syndicate, for example, the Investor applicant should make certain that his/her agreement with the investment syndicate provides for retention of the investment monies in trust by a reputable financial institution until the application for permanent residence has been approved. The agreement should also provide that, where the application is refused, the investment monies are to be returned to the applicant with interest.

Suggested Procedure under the Investor Immigrant Category
As in the case of applications under the Entrepreneur program, only 25 points are required to be obtained by Investor business immigrants. Accordingly, Investor applicants should take care to file documentation sufficient to demonstrate that their application is within the special Regulations governing this category of Independent Class applicant. In this regard, reference should be made to the summary of documentation required for applications by Entrepreneurs. Generally, applications by Investors for a permanent residence visa should be submitted to a Canadian visa office in the applicant's country of residence. All applications must be accompanied by the following documentation:
(1) a curriculum vitae and a description of the applicant's business, industrial or managerial experience;
(2) a statement of resources, showing funds (denominated in Canadian dollars) already in Canada, funds available for immediate and later transfer, and proof of ownership;
(3) full and complete particulars of the business, venture, investment syndicate or fund in which it is proposed to invest (the covering letter attached to this information should indicate the province of intended destination, whether the applicant has visited the province of destination, and a summary account of the applicant's consultations with counselling and advisory personnel there);
(4) full and complete particulars of the jobs which, if the application is granted, it is proposed will be created or maintained for Canadian residents (where the Investor will be making a direct investment into a private business or commercial venture); and
(5) if applicable, a copy of the offering memorandum published by the privately-administered investment syndicate in which the Investor applicant has invested, or for which he/she has placed funds in escrow pending confirmation of the residency visa, as well as any agreement relating to units, shares or equity interests purchased by the proposed Investor.

Additionally, all submissions should include a formal Business Plan in the same format as suggested for Entrepreneur Immigrant applications.

Applicants under the Investor program should send four (4) copies of all proposals to the office of the province of intended destination at its address given at Appendix "C". With each copy of the proposal, there should be included a letter of transmittal which summarizes and outlines the proposal and its economic benefits, and indicates the action which the applicant wishes the province to take in respect of the application.

The Investor component of the new Business Immigration Program, like the Entrepreneur component described earlier, has been designed to

282

encourage settlement in Canada by individuals having proven competence in business and a sufficiently high personal net-worth that they can contribute to increased capital formation and creation/maintenance of employment opportunities for Canadians.

Methods of Admission

BDO's in the applicant's country of origin can grant either unconditional or conditional landing visas. An unconditional landing visa will be granted when the BDO is satisfied the Investor has met all regulatory criteria pertaining to qualifications and resources and when the province of intended destination has advised its satisfaction as to the economic benefits of the proposed investment. A conditional landing visa (valid for a period of up to three years in the case of Investors) may be issued in cases where the Investor has been able to satisfy the BDO that most but not all requirements under the Regulations have been met and that outstanding matters can be quickly and completely resolved once the applicant has been landed. This could occur, for example, in instances where only the final details of a business investment proposal remain to be ironed out and where the province of intended destination wishes to have the Investor enter its jurisdiction so that these might be dealt with more expeditiously. Where a conditional visa is granted, the Canada Employment & Immigration Commission will follow up to ensure that terms of the landing are complied with during the three-year period.

Investors wishing to immigrate into Canada from points in Asia can contact BDO's in any of the following Canadian visa offices:

Bangkok   New Delhi
Hong Kong   Seoul
Manila   Singapore

Residents Leaving Canada on a Temporary Basis

Individuals entering Canada as new immigrants may wish to leave Canada temporarily, and return to their country of origin, in order to look after some personal or business matter requiring their direct attention. Where the sojourn in the country of origin is brief, residents may leave and return without concern as to readmissibility. In the event of a protracted absence, however, it is often advisable to obtain a Returning Resident Permit prior to departure. This Permit can be obtained from any local Canada Immigration Centre and is especially important where the absence is for a period of 183 days. Where a resident is outside Canada for a period of 183 days, he or she is deemed to have lost entitlement to residency and must satisfy the Immigration Officer at the port of entry that there has been no abandonment of residency. Obtaining a Returning Resident Permit prior to leaving Canada is the most effective way of ensuring there will be no problems encountered on returning to Canada.

Level of Business Immigration in 1987

The *Annual Report to Parliament on Future Immigration Levels* was tabled in the House of Commons by the Honourable Gerry Weiner,

Minister of State (Immigration), on October 30th, 1986. The Report confirms the 1987 planning range for immigration to Canada as between 115,000 and 125,000 individuals. The Minister stressed in his report that the federal government is strongly committed to achieving the higher end of the 1987 planning range in terms of actual landings in the country. Additionally, and of the total number of individuals planned for, a projected level of 4,000 principal Business Immigrants, and a further 8,000 spouses and dependents of principal Business Immigrants, were announced in the Report.

CONCLUSION

As evidenced by the increase in levels of overall immigration during the past few years, and by the enthusiastic support of all ten provinces for the new Business Immigration Program, Canada'a perception of its national interest has changed dramatically since 1982. Business skills, entrepreneurship, and commitment of capital toward the creation of jobs are now recognized as indispensible for the country as it moves into the 21st century. The future is bright for Canada. And capable individuals willing to work and invest so as to help realize that future potential are most welcome here.

APPENDIX "C"
ADDRESSES OF PROVINCIAL DEPARTMENTS CONCERNED

NEWFOUNDLAND
Deputy Minister
Department of Labour and Manpower
Beothuck Building
Crosbie Place
St. John's, Newfoundland
A1C 6C9
Telex: 016-3325

NOVA SCOTIA
Chief, Recruitment & Selection
Can Plan Building
1888 Brunswick Street
P.O. Box 2463
Halifax, Nova Scotia
B3J 3E4
Tel: 426-2567

PRINCE EDWARD ISLAND
Chief of Research and Planning·
P.E.I. Department of Industry
P.O. Box 2000
Charlottetown, P.E.I.
C1A 7N8
Tel: (902) 892-5445

NEW BRUNSWICK
Labour Market Services Branch
Department of Labour and Manpower
P.O. Box 6000
Fredericton, New Brunswick
E3B 5H1
Tel: (506) 452-3711

QUEBEC
Ministère des Communautés culturelles
et de l'Immigration du Québec
Service aux entrepreneurs
355 McGill Street
Montreal, Quebec
H2Y 2E8

ONTARIO
Ministry of Industry, Trade and
  Technology
Immigrant Entrepreneur Section
Industrial Investment Branch
900 Bay Street
6th Floor, Hearst Block
Queen's Park
Toronto, Ontario M7A 2E1
Tel: (416) 965-5331
Attn: James C. Carrick

MANITOBA
Assistant Deputy Minister
Trade and Industry Division
Department of Industry, Trade
  & Technology
155 Carlton Street, 7th Floor
Winnipeg, Manitoba R3C 3H8
Tel: (204) 945-2435
Telex: 07 587-833 (MANITRADE WPG)

SASKATCHEWAN
International Operations Division
Sask. Economic Development and Trade
Bank of Montreal Bldg.
3rd Floor, 2103-11th Ave.
Regina, Saskatchewan S4P 3V7
Tel: (306) 787-9212
Telex: 071-2675
Attn: Peter Korol

**ALBERTA &
NORTHWEST TERRITORIES**
Manager, Alberta Services
Alberta Manpower
Parkside Office Building
10924 - 119 Street
Edmonton, Alberta T5H 3P5
Tel: (403) 427-8517
Telex: 037-3769 (ALTA MAN EDM)

**BRITISH COLUMBIA &
YUKON TERRITORY**
Ministry of International Trade
and Investment
800 Hornby Street
Suite 315, Robson Square
Vancouver, B.C. V6Z 2C5
Tel: (604) 660-4567
Telex: 04-55459 (BC RANDS)

285

簡家聰乃在港執業的加拿大律師

加拿大商業移民新計劃

　　加拿大自從成爲獨立國後，整整一百二十年來，政府的移民政策一直反映國家利益在改變中的觀念。較早的法規（從英國皇家政府域多利亞法規十六卷第八十六章即一八五三年移民與檢疫法律開始）是傾向阻止外國人在加定居的。早在一八五九年，已制訂了不得入境移民類的法律。

　　在十九世紀與本世紀初，移民局及它所屬官員對“不良”或“邪惡”移民曾下極廣泛之定義並拒絕此等移民入境。這類移民往往被正式宣佈後便不得入境。並且，立法時的用辭方面，也只是考慮從歐洲港口的移民。如果說早期的加拿大移民法律是歧視非歐洲地區移民的法律的話，這說法是公平的批評。

　　雖然，早期這歧視移民法律，在事後可解釋爲一個年青國家不明白自己在世界中的地位，又過份關心廣大本土上稀少人口之利益，因而擬出了上述的歧視政策。不過，早在一九四〇年代的十年間，加拿大（及在同時通過類似法律的美國），已強烈駁斥這種歧視的移民法律。到一九七零年，有關種族歧視的任何法律及條例，均被加拿大政府及人民所唾棄。全加各地不同的公民自由機構，都經常保持致力爲不同種族的所有加拿大人，爭取權利及平等待遇。

　　一九八七年的加拿大是名符其實的“文化多姿多彩”──它有來自世界上各國的人民。由於多元文化在加拿大社會組織上是最基本及最永久的一部份，聯邦政府聘任了一位高級部長來擔任聯繫及負責多元文化的事務，這位聯邦政府的“多元文化部長”在加拿大的十省內每省都聘有省級“多元文化官”來協助。大部份加拿大人承認及歡迎來自歐洲、亞洲及世界其它各地移民所帶給加拿大社會的新姿彩。

　　一九八七年的加拿大政府的移民政策，已在“一九七六年移民法案”第三節中列出，這法規規定了下列一般主旨：

　　第三節：加拿大移民政策及條例（在此法案下規定的）將爲推廣國內外利益而設計及執行，法律將考慮到下列的需要：

　　(A)支持及達到各地人口統計的目標；加拿大政府間或調查有關各地加拿大人口的密度，成長率，組織及人口分配的目標數字；

　　(B)根據聯邦組織及通用英、法兩種語言的特色，美化及鞏固加拿大文化及社會組合；

　　(C)給予加拿大公民及永久居民與國外近親團聚上之方便；

　　(D)鼓勵及便利加拿大社會接納已來加的永久居民，推廣加拿大政府及它各階層政府及非官方機構間在這方面的合作；

286

(E)方便那些來加有助於發展及推廣貿易、商業、旅遊、文化、科學活動及增進國際間之了解的各類旅客的訪問；

(F)保証任何申請來加人仕（永久或臨時居留者）皆適用同一審核標準，不得因種族、國籍或人種、膚色、宗教信仰或性別各異而歧視之；

(G)完成加拿大有關難民的國際法定義務及保持它在支持受迫害者及難民的人道立場；

(H)助長加拿大強大而活躍的經濟及各區的繁榮成長；

(I)維持及保護加拿大社會的健全、安全及安定；

(J)為維護國際間的安定與正義，拒絕有犯罪傾向的人利用加拿大領土從事不法行為。

為了運用國家主權，加拿大聯邦政府在一九八七年將繼續實施它確信為對本國最有利的移民政策，現行之"移民法案包括三大類移民即為：

(A)家屬類

(B)人道主義及難民類

(C)獨立類

"家屬類"的申請者包括那些已有近親現為居住加拿大的公民或永久居民。"人道主義及難民類"的申請人為居於戰爭或天災地區者，加拿大認為對這類人有給予道義上協助的責任，"獨立類"的申請者是非上述兩大類之人而意欲個別申請移民加拿大者。從前這類申請人均要通過"計分法"來估定是否適合，並斷定他們是否適宜安居加拿大。

在比較"一九七六年移民法案"第三節內目標之逐年實施情形，我們將很容易發現三大類中各分類申請批准的重點有顯著的改變。"家屬類"申請繼續是加拿大移民政策的基石，但"獨立類"申請—基於加拿大的國家利益近年來在需求上的改變—對於申請的人數量及類別已有不同的制定。例如，在一九八二年，由於經濟大衰退，加拿大當時執政府決定把每年移民總限額—特別是對"獨立類"申請限額—予以降低。當時的政治性決策是基於認為"獨立類"之申請人—（商人、企業家及投資者不在此例）可能不受歡迎，因為他們會與正在受害於經濟衰退之加拿大人競爭，於是，駐世界各地之加拿大公使館，領事館及公署都接到指示，優先處理"家屬類"及"人道主義及難民類"的申請，而把"獨立類"申請降為第三重要。

在最近幾年來，加拿大政府為了要增加加拿大作為國際投資地的吸引力而作出了重大的承諾，聯邦政府在各省的熱烈支持下，決定把"一九七六年移民法案"第三節的解釋譯，重點放在大力推廣吸引那些富商巨賈的個別申請者，希望他們來加安居，從而把他們的專長與經驗投資此地。

在這簡介中，我們希望把最近制定之法律簡單而扼要地列舉，總括來說：在新的商業移民計劃中，個別來加投資之移民，將發現很多"機會之窗"是為他們打開的。

投資加拿大法案

"投資加拿大法案"（簡稱"法案"）代表了加拿大政府政治哲學的基本改變，新"法案"取代了一九七零年代中期頒佈的"外國投資審核法案"(FIRA)，新的政府以主動鼓勵及方便代替了"審核"或"審查"投資計劃，新政策"財政管理法案"是委託一個特別機構名為"投資加拿大"機構去實施的，此機構直屬在渥太華之聯邦政府"屬區工業發展部"部長，通過簡化推行手續，廢除在投資金額低於法定最高額時的審核，該機構同時負責鼓勵加籍及非加籍人士之投資事宜。自從本法案在一九八五年實施以後，許多外國投資者已利用本法案進行投資。

287

(A)收購企業免經審核

在新政策下，如非加籍人士投資在"新加拿大企業"（已下定義），或直接收購資產低於加幣五百萬元，或間接收購資產低於五千萬之加拿大企業者，該投資者只需填寫指定通知表格（參閱附錄‘A’），送交渥太華之"投資加拿大"機構（在完成該投資卅天內）即可，法案中作出下列名詞的定義："直接收購企業"——即取得加拿大企業之控制權，包括收購該企業擁有的權益或資產，或收購該企業在加總公司之控制權。"間接收購企業"——即透過收購某公司在加境以外的總公司之控制權，從而控制該加拿大企業；

(B)收購企業需經審核

法案指定下列各情況下，必需先經由"投資加拿大機構"審核通過：

所有直接收購價值在加幣五百萬元或以上，間接收購在加幣五千萬元或以上之加拿大企業，及間接收購在加幣五百萬至五千萬元間之加拿大企業資產（而該金額超過該企業全部國際交易中之百份之五十者）。同時，在指定的交易範圍內（如有關加拿大之文化傳統或民族特色）新企業的特別收購，如總理有理由相信審核為合乎公眾利益者，則必須進行審核。

法案中之法律內有指定表格專為申請審核投資建議而設（參看附錄‘B’），除了某些例外情形，實際投資要在建議審核通過後才能進行，但在部長認為這項投資如因遲誤，將會使投資者遭遇嚴重的困難時或對被收購的加拿大企業的營業有妨礙時，則部長有權批准該項收購計劃審核程序完成前實施。

(C)審核程序

一般來說，"投資加拿大"機構將會把投資者的所有資料及書面保證，連同將受該投資顯著影響的省份之有關陳述書送交部長，如部長認為該投資對加可能有利的話，他將會批准該申請。法案中有左列評估因素的規定，部長必須以此為依歸作出決定：

(A)該投資對加經濟活動程度及本質之影响，包括對加就業，原料加工，零件及組件的運用，及服務增設，以及加拿大出口業務方面的影响；

(B)加拿大人士在該"加拿大企業"中及在任何該企業所屬行業中參與的程度及重要性；

(C)該投資對加拿大生產力、工業效率、技術發展、產品革新及產品種類的影响；

(D)該投資與在任何工業或各工業之間之競爭的影响；

(E)該投資與國家工業、經濟及文化、政策的可配合性，特別應注視有可能受該計劃顯著影响之政府及省立法機關所公佈之有關工業、經濟及文化政策目標；及

(F)該投資對增長加拿大在國際市場的競爭力之貢獻。

(C)時間的限制

"投資加拿大"機構及部長在審核申請書的程序中，均受到時限而必須在這指定時間內作出決定。部長必須在收到完整的申請書後的四十五天內，作出下述之一的決定及通知投資者：

(A)他認為該投資對加有純益；

(B)他認為無法在指定時間內完成審核工作，而再需要卅天（或在投資者書面同意下，更長的時間內），才能完成部長的審核工作；

(C)他認為該投資將不會帶給加拿大純益。

申請書投遞後，在下列情況下，則投資者有權認為部長已默認投資申請已合乎對加有純益之要求：

在四十五天內沒有收到部長的任何通知；

在接到部長通知再需要卅天的時間後，卅天（或申請者同意的時間）已過，部長仍未作出決定。

收到部長通知認爲投資將不會對加有純利時，申請人在卅天內依法可提出異議，並提交陳述書及保証書。

"投資加拿大法案"是爲了承認資金和科技的增加將會對加有利，及爲了鼓勵加拿大及非加拿大人在加投資而實施的。這法案的主旨在刺激加境內經濟的成長並製造就業的機會，而與進步保守政府之增進加拿大國際貿易的決策是一致的，所以，外來投資人士可以肯定，他們的投資申請—如必須經過審核的話—將會受到預期中的積極歡迎，"外國投資審核法案"時代的政府爲外來投資者在引進資金及科技來加時建立障礙的日子，已一去不復返了。新的法案內有關通知及審核程序，較以前法定的要求簡單得太多了。"投資加拿大"這機構的成立，向全世界宣佈了加拿大將主動歡迎投資資金及簡化引進手續。

"商業移民法案"

現在政府之另一革新爲在一九八六年元旦在新的"商業移民法案"內增設了新的"投資者"移民一分類，"獨立類"商業移民原已包括"企業家"及"自僱移民"的兩種分類，"投資者"即爲第三分類。"商業移民方案"的主要目的是：推廣、鼓勵、及方便能對加經濟發展有一定貢獻的資深商人移居加拿大—特別是那些既可引進資金，又可利用他們的經驗來增加加拿大居民就業機會者。

"商業移民計劃"的發展是配合前述的加拿大聯邦政府有關外國投資的廣大方針，"計劃"中的條例與指示都是以刺激經濟，鼓勵創造就業機會及減低國內失業水平爲依歸而草擬的，爲了保証新計劃推行的成功，政府已分配了雄厚的資金。各階層政府間更密切之合作，透過在世界各地的加拿大公使館、領事館及公署有力的推廣，加上新招募人員的主動力，改良訓練及輔導技術，使新的"商業移民計劃"與它的前身比較起來，已有可觀的改善。"計劃"中除了有很多要點放寬外，最大的更改毫無疑問是新的"投資者"分類之增設。下列是"商業移民計劃"內三大類的個別規定定義：

"自僱移民"

在法案中，"自僱移民"的定義爲，意欲及有能力在加建立企業（該企業將只僱用申請人自己），同時將會對加經濟、文化或藝術生活有貢獻。這類人雖不會活躍地或直接地增加加拿大人的就業機會，但在經濟上及藝術上將會有顯著的貢獻。及格的自僱移民例子包括：農民、運動家、藝術家、藝術團體之演員及任何可能令社會的商業或經濟活動更爲充實的從業員，自僱移民申請是用"計分法"來審核是否及格，如能合乎上述規定定義者，則另贈送卅分，在絕大部份的情形下，"獨立者"申請需最少取得七十分才能獲得成功，審核申請的其它項目包括：教育、特別職業訓練、經驗、已有現成僱主、年齡、對加拿大之一種或兩種法定語言（英文、法文）的知識及個人的適合程度。

"企業家"

在"移民法案"中，條例制定"企業家"即爲意欲及有能力在加創立，收購或大量投資在一個由申請人經營的企業上，計劃的投資必須對加在經濟方面有顯著的貢獻，並需同時增加或保持除申請人及其家屬以外的一個或多個加拿大公民或永久居民的就業者。這一類申請尺度的放寬是改變爲加拿大居民除申請人及其家屬以外）創造就業機會的數目—從以前之不少於五人到現在的最少一人。（註）這類申請人包括了那些曾在小型到中型企業間有實際管理經驗之人士，雖然，每省對投資資金上之限額的要求有異，一般投資者最少要擁有加幣十萬元才能接受，"企業家"如合乎上述規定的定義，也是採用"計分法"審核，但申請人只需獲得25分（通常是70分）。

（註）不管條例如此改變，個別省份仍可要求企業家所創造或所保持的就業機會數目。申請人在準備他們商業計劃以前必須先確定這個數目。

"企業家移民計劃"自一九七八年實施以來非常成功，單在一九八一年間，已吸納了二千一百三十個企業家，申報的淨值資產總值估計爲加幣十二億元（註）1 billion＝1,000,000,000。上述企業在全部實施開業後，估計將會增加約九千七百份的工作給加拿大人士。雖然，政府紀錄指出現行企業家來自八十五個不同的國家，但是主要的三個突出來源地爲：香港（約佔一九八五年總數百分之四十），西德及美國。因爲這"計劃"是由聯邦及省政府聯合管理，準移民的申請必須先經目的地省政府審核。不過，申請是否批准的最終決定，則是在渥太華的聯邦政府獨有的裁判權。

儘管各省對"企業家移民計劃"的審核先後有不同的優先權情形，但是各省均歡迎在"計劃"範圍內有對加有下列影响的申請者：

(A)增加出口；

(B)取代外國製成品的進口；或

(C)對投資省份的經濟有貢獻者。

在審核"企業家計劃"的申請中，由於各省的經濟工業活動水平及管轄區內工業種類各異，因此各省有不同的最低及格標準。例如：要僱用的人數（除申請人及家屬外）及申請書內提供的引証文件，每省的要求不一。很多省都嚴格遵守聯邦政府的規定：只需製造一人的工作機會，而安大略省（加拿大最富裕、人口最多及最工業化的省份），則需要製造五個永久性的工作機會。

有關某種工業有優先權的工業區，某省對創造就業機會的數目最低，及某種投資企業所需投資金額最低等之最正確資料，有關人士應直接與目的地的省政府辦事處聯繫（參看附錄'C'）。

企業家移民類申請的建議程序

不但"企業家"申請人應先向目的省聯繫，他們更須很清楚他們在申請時要呈上最起碼的文件。以在收到超過半數申請書的安大略省爲例，起碼文件包括：

(1)申請人的個人直接經驗、包括擁有、管理及經營一間經濟上成功的企業的決定性証據；

(2)申請人的信函：詳述他的意願—確認他的能力會用他的技能從事將在目的省建立之企業的管理；

(3)申請人的另一份信函：盡可能準確地說明他在目的地省份所要設立的事業；

(4)企業家申請人証明他的投資金是用本人淨資金或對附屬股東的借款；

(5)正式企業建議或計劃，並詳述下列各點：

(i)　　計劃的說明：

列述企業計劃的成本、如何集資、主要之支出項目、所需之資本裝備之製造來源。

(ii)　　開設企業的準確地點：

市區地址，財產的法定說明，如有地圖應附地圖。

(iii)　管理：

應附每一位管理團內成員的有關僱佣歷史及管理經驗摘要。

(iv)　移民申請人的功用：

應包括企業家在企業管理中的詳細功用。

(v)　僱員：

全時間僱員的人數，季節性的工人人數（及每年需用季節性僱工的月數），應照職業類別分列，請注意這不包括企業家移民及其家屬，該企業能保持或製造多少就業機會的數目要詳述。

(vi)　產品：

將製造之貨品應加以說明。

(vii)　市場：

市場摘要應包括下列各點：

—供應及需求（供應商、主要客戶及新企業的展望），如有能証實上述各點的書信亦應附上；

—現有的競爭者的証明；

—建議中企業對在該區內現有企業的影响；

—建議中企業對進、出口的影响；

(viii)　接洽人：

詳列下列諸人的姓名、地址及電話號碼：

—被受權之接洽人；

—企業計劃之法律顧問；

—企業計劃之銀行家；

—企業計劃之會計師；

—企業計劃之保險商；

—集資資料：

下列文件應連同申請書附上：

• 如屬現有之企業，過去三年來的財務報表（如最近的報表是超過三個月前的，請擬定中期報表）；

• 書面証明財務的責任，包括個人的淨值資產報表；

• 呈報財務報表包括形式上的資產負債表（說明建議中的企業計劃）包括第一年全年經營之資產負債表，及開業後前三年的損益預算表；

• 如企業計劃中的資金是非申請人全部自己所擁有的，應詳述其非申請人部份資金的來源。

(x)　公司組織：

公司的組織應詳列：集資、股權控制的安排及股票的種類、及股東所屬國籍等。

所有正式股東合約應呈遞副本，如與加拿大公民間存有尚未簽署之股東合約，均應呈遞該合約之已簽署之合約備忘錄；

(xi)　保証：

如果企業計劃是收購一間現有的企業，買家必須在購買合約內提供下列保証：

＊新買主承諾所有在買賣前所訂的員工或勞工之契約；

＊新買主承諾保持繼續僱用—除因需要、適合性、失職或其他合理由解僱外—原有僱員；

(xii)　政府補助，貸款及津貼：

在申請書上說明是否在過去三年內有接受或被授權接受政府任何補助、貸款及津貼。

(xiii) 訴訟或法律程序：

如有任何懸而未決的訴訟或法律程序，必須呈報詳情。

(xiv) 資金之運用：

應附詳細報表說明將投資於企業的移民申請人的淨資金或股東貸款的金額及擬投資於企業的時間，並應指出該兩種金額各佔總值的百分比。

(xv) 經濟利益：

詳述如果企業計劃被批准的話，對安省的經濟利益（即製造就業機會，引進新科技，對進出口的影响）的預估。

在"企業家計劃"下的申請人，一般要把計劃書一份寄至目的地省份之辦事處，地址參閱附錄'C'，如計劃有涉及旅遊事業者，則所有文件必須呈遞兩份。

不用說，上述的文件及資料並非一定都合乎或滿足申請的要求。所有申請，有關在某種情況下申請應附上何種文件，申請人應安排與當地加拿大簽証處會見一位"商業發展"官員(BDO)，聽取他最新的指示。這類商談特別對下述申請人更爲有助：申請人知道自己要移民加拿大及在加設立企業或投資，但同時相信自己還沒有辦法準備好遞一份詳細的企業計劃來支持自己的申請。"商業發展官員"將會協助申請人先到加拿大視察，及安排他與目的地省份之官員面談，隨而估計他在該地投資的機會，並協助及支持他的申請，所有的省份，（及有些市鎮）的官員是有能力而願意協助那些準"企業家"或"投資家"移民來擬定企業計劃，該計劃以後更可成爲正式申請移民時的一部份文件。我們建議準移民先來加考察及利用這機會與各省有關機構會商，然後才作出正式的移民申請。

爲了協助以"商業移民計劃"方式來申請的人士，"一九七六年移民法案"第十五條第一節現在將解釋爲："企業家"移民將可引用"有條件"居留長達兩年的方便，在這最初兩年的試驗期間，及格的"企業家"能對自己的"計劃"進行詳細的估價，更可與負責實施政策的官員會商，從而確保政府最終的批准，在這段期間內，該移民將能享有廣泛的協商及顧問性服務，來縮短他的投資活動確定形式的決定時間。

根據他在臨時居留期間搜集的資料，"企業家"能擬定正式申請書（包括企業計劃），而該計劃實際上已被"指定"爲合乎目的地省份的經濟利益的最低要求。引用"有條件"居留來引進移民的眞正效果就是促進了目的地省份對申請的審核及最終渥太華的批准。

"投資者"

"投資者"在條例中的定義特指下列人士：

(a)實際擁有，管理或經營一個經濟上成功的企業或商業機構；

(b)靠着投資者自己的嘗試個人擁有淨資金不少於加幣五十萬元；及

(c)保証在三年的最短期間內：以加幣廿五萬（不包括費用，佣金及薪金）不撤消地投資在一間目的地省份指定的企業或商務企業或商務企業組合。

在引用"指定"來引述它們在主動地推廣實行這"計劃"，省政府部門特別採用了那些字眼來說明這些"指定"投資，並非代表官方保証的有利投資，亦非保証這些投資會有利益的回收，個別的及格"投資者"申請人將是投資於一種有"冒險性"的企業，商務企業或商務企業組合，而這類"投資"是合乎目的地省份的要求者，因此，使該類"投資"成爲（渥太華聯邦政府）在該條例中"指定"爲對該目的地省份的經濟有利的"投資"，被委任爲新方案中實施者之省政府官員在該計劃的編寫有參與其事者，均一致指出：所謂"經濟有利"，在投資者計劃的審核過程中，最主要的是就業機會的製造及保留。

投資者申請人可在下列三種投資中，選擇一種投資方式：

(A)企業或商務企業━它的創立，收購或擴充及維持，對目的地省份的經濟有顯著利益者；

(B)在目的地省份的私人管理及被指定的投資組合，主旨是供應資金或貸款，用以設立，收購擴充或維持，對目的地省份的經濟有顯著利益的投資；

(C)政府管理下的資本基金企業，主旨在供應資金或貸款，用以設立，收購或擴充及維持企業或商務企業。

各省政府可自由選擇上述任何一種方式，並可對任何移民申請認可"指定"上述所有或任何一種方式。但直至本文編寫時，加拿大的十省中，沒有一個省份願意接受存放最低的加幣廿五萬元在政府管理下之資本基金企業之申請（上述'C'類），除了安大略省（及愛德華王子島）外，其它各省均接受考慮直接投資於企業，商務企業或投資於私人管理的投資組合的計劃。由於"商業移民計劃"內的"投資者"申請為較新的方式，意欲以"投資者"身份來加的人士，在申請時應先與當地加拿大簽証處或目的地省份聯繫，從而確定可選擇的範圍。

所有投資者必須取得已合乎"移民法案"規定要求的書面証明，這是簽發"投資者"移民簽証的先決條件。由於根據條例第九條（第三節），投資資金至少是在三年內"不可撤消"的，投資者的申請文件中可加如下條件：如果投資者被拒絕簽証時，所需的加幣廿五萬元應退還給投資者。例如，投資者如投資在私人管理的投資組合，則"投資者"申請人應在合約中規定，在取得永久居留申請批准前，把投資的資金存放在一家有信譽的財務機構。合約中也應該訂定在申請被拒絕時，資金及利息必須歸還給申請人。

"投資者移民申請的建議程序"

一如"企業家計劃"，投資者商業移民只要取得廿五分便可被接受，因此，投資者申請人只須填妥及呈遞合乎有關這類"獨立類申請者"的所需表格即可。關於這方面，請參閱有關企業家申請所需文件摘要，一般來說，投資者應在當地的加拿大簽証機構呈遞申請永久居留的簽証。所有申請必須呈交下列文件：

㈠申請人的履歷和其企業的說明、以及其工業或管理經驗；

㈡申請人投資資金來源的報表，詳列（用加幣算）已存放在加的資金，可立即或以後將轉滙至加拿大之資金，及擁有上述資金之証據；

㈢有關意欲投資之商業，企業，投資組合或將欲投資在上述諸企業之基金的完整資料（在呈交上述資料的隨函內應指出目的地省份、申請人曾否到達該地，及申請人在該省曾與該地的輔導及顧問團商討的摘要）；

㈣有關擬定投資計劃，如被批准的話，能製造或維持加拿大居民就業機會的完整資料（在申請人投資於私人企業或商務企業的情況下必須這樣呈報）；

㈤如投資者已投資，或已準備資金作為在申請批准時投資在私人管理的投資組合中，在可能範圍內呈遞一份該集團招股的備忘錄副本，及一份有關申請人預算投資的股票單位，股份及淨產資值的合約副本。

同時，所有申請均應呈遞一份與"企業家移民"申請格式相同的企業計劃書。

"投資者計劃"的申請人應將計劃書一式四份呈交目的地省份有關機構（地址請參閱附錄'C'），每份計劃書應附傳送信函一封扼要地說明該建議的大綱及該建議對加拿大之經濟利益，及表示申請人希望該省對他的申請書所應採取的行動。

正如前述之"企業家"類，新的加拿大"商業移民計劃"內的"投資者"類，是為鼓勵那些擁有可証實之商業經驗人士，以及擁有適當的個人淨資金人士來加以贊助資本的增加，並製造或維持加拿大就業機會。

引進方法

在申請人的原本寄居地，"商業發展官員"可簽發"無條件"或"有條件"的入口簽証。在"商業發展官員"滿意投資者已遵照資格及資金來源的規定標準又目的地省份已表示建議的投資對該目的地省份有經濟利益，即可簽發"無限制"簽証，商業發展官員在滿意"投資者"大致上已合乎條例的要求；但有局部條件有待申請人抵加後才能很快全部解決時，他可簽發，有條件簽証（在"投資者"之類的情況下，簽証的最長有效期間為三年）。這情況可用下述例子說明，例如，有些企業投資建議的最後細節有待解決，目的地省份希望申請人來加，以便上述細節可儘早解決。在簽發"有條件"簽証後，加拿大就業及移民委員會將在三年期間內隨時審核申請人是否履行移民的目標。

意欲移民加拿大之亞洲各地投資者，可向下列地點的"商務發展官員"諮詢：曼谷、香港、岷民拉、新德里、漢城及新加坡。

進入加拿大的新移民，為了個人或商業事務需要他們處理時，可能希望暫時離開加拿大回到他所來的國家。在原本寄居的國家逗留如係短暫可以自由往來，於再入境時不會遭遇困難。但如在外居留期間長久，則在離開加拿大以前，必須取得回加居民証，此証可在當地加拿大移民中心取得。如離加超過一百八十三日，則此証特別重要。如居民離加超出一百八十三日，他（或她）被認為已喪失居留權，回加時在入境口岸必須使移民官確信他（她）的居留權並沒有喪失。在離加之前取得回加居民証可確保回加時不會產生問題。

一九八七年商業移民的水平

一九八六年十月卅日，"韋納·諸里"─國家（移民）部長在下議院呈交了"未來移民水平呈國會年報"，該報告上証實了一九八七年計劃引進的移民數字在十一萬五千人至十二萬五千人之間，部長強調了聯邦政府已承諾了爭取在一九八七年計劃實際完成引進十二萬五千人的目標，同時，在上述的個人目標中，該報告書更預估其中有四千名主要商業移民及他們的八千名配偶及家屬。

結論

移民數字水平近年來不斷的增加，及所有十個省政府對新"商業移民計劃"的熱烈支持，証實了自一九八二年來，加拿大對國家利益的觀點已有戲劇性的改變。商業技能、企業家才能、及資金注入已被接受為進入廿一世紀時代增加加拿大就業機會的不可分割部份。加拿大的前景是光明的。所有有能力及意願為協助達成這未來目標而努力的人及投資者，將會是最受歡迎的。

About Gateway Books

Richard and Jenny Mann operate Canada's only Asian affairs publishing company, **Gateway Books** of Toronto.

Their initiative began in 1982 with the publication of Canada's first periodical dedicated to the country's developing investment and commercial relations with Asia — **TradeAsia** magazine. The magazine circulates to 13,000 companies across Canada.

They supported this annual publication with seminars and conferences and from 1983 onwards became commercial trade and investment mission organizers.

Between 1984 and 1986 they specialized in introducing Canadian computer software manufacturers to the markets of Asia attracting over 700 people to their computer software industry development and marketing conferences alone.

Mann was the first person to organize all-computer software export trade missions from Canada to markets in Hong Kong, The People's Republic of China, Singapore, Malaysia, Indonesia and Japan.

By 1988 the Manns had introduced over 80 companies to business and investment opportunities in Asia through participation in their missions.

Their 20 strong investment mission to Indonesia in 1987 assembled in collaboration with the Canadian International Development Agency (CIDA), the Indonesian Investment Co-ordinating Board (BKPM) and the United Nations Industrial Development Organization (UNIDO) was the largest foreign delegation to attend a special international investors forum in Jakarta.

Mission clients have nearly always been supported with funding from the Canadian federal government Department of External Affairs or by CIDA.

In 1986 the Manns were the first to organize a national import conference in Canada aimed at assisting Asian exporters achieve better penetration of the growing Canadian market.

In addition to seminars, conferences and missions Gateway Books specializes in the publication of titles about all aspects of the growing relations among the peoples of the Pacific Rim including immigration, investment and trade.

'You're Welcome - A guide to investment opportunities in Canada' is the second in what has become a five part series about Chinese emigration to Canada.

The first, **'Canada Our Land - The Chinese in Canada today'** is a rich and truthful account of Chinese life in Canada through the eyes of Canadian-Chinese themselves. It is currently on sale at all leading bookshops throughout southeast Asia.

Subsequent volumes deal with moving to Canada, studying in Canada and buying real estate in Canada.

Mann has also played a part in encouraging more Canadian investment in Asia, particularly among the six members of the Association of

Southeast Asian Nations (ASEAN).

In 1987 they published **'Canadians in Indonesia, a trade and investment primer'** and other similar studies have been undertaken in Malaysia and Thailand.

Gateway Books is pledged to expand its publishing activities throughout the southeast Asian region and currently releases about 10 new titles a year.

Mann is chairman of the Canadian-Indonesian Business Council and an executive committee member of the Canada-ASEAN Business Council. Jenny Mann is a director of the Hong Kong Canada Business Association and an active member of Dharma Wanita, the Indonesian women's association.

Richard Mann lived in Hong Kong from 1974 to 1981 working first for the **Hongkong Standard-Sing Tao Newspapers** and for five years for the **Hong Kong Government Information Services Department** where he was first a campaigns officer and latterly head of the Government Secretariat press office.

He became well known in Hong Kong for his work for government in promoting the Hong Kong Arts Festival for which a distinction was entered in his file and in 1976, during her visit to the territory to open the festival, Mann was presented to H.R.H. The Princess Alexandra.

He moved to Canada in 1980.

He has been a national editor of several leading Canadian computer publications and was the founding editor of Canada's national software newspaper for Maclean Hunter Limited.

He has contributed articles to many other national newspapers and magazines and speaks frequently to trade and professional organizations, federal and provincial government bodies, universities and polytechnics. He is quoted regularly in the media.

Born in Buckinghamshire, United Kingdom in 1942 Mann began his career in journalism and he has been a reporter, editor, special investigator, British Parliamentary Lobby COrrespondent (Education), industrial correspondent, war correspondent (Ulster), television presenter and print and electronic media campaigns manager.

His wife and business partner is Eurasian from Indonesia and he has two children, Ian aged 11 and Sarina, aged 9.

Opposite: Richard Mann